Library of
Davidson College

PRACTICAL ESSAYS.

BY

ALEXANDER BAIN

Essay Index Reprint Series

 BOOKS FOR LIBRARIES PRESS
FREEPORT, NEW YORK

First Published 1884
Reprinted 1972

081
B162p

Library of Congress Cataloging in Publication Data

Bain, Alexander, 1818-1903.
   Practical essays.

   (Essay index reprint series)
   Reprint of the 1884 ed.
   Includes bibliographical references.
   CONTENTS: Common errors on the mind.--Errors of
suppressed correlatives.--The civil service examinations.
[etc.]
    I. Title.
B1618.B23P7 1972   081   72-4533
ISBN 0-8369-2935-7

PRINTED IN THE UNITED STATES OF AMERICA

PREFACE.

The present volume is in great part a reprint of articles contributed to Reviews. The principal bond of union among them is their practical character. Beyond that, there is little to connect them apart from the individuality of the author and the range of his studies.

That there is a certain amount of novelty in the various suggestions here embodied, will be admitted on the most cursory perusal. The farther question of their worth is necessarily left open.

The first two essays are applications of the laws of mind to some prevailing Errors.

The next two have an educational bearing: the one is on the subjects proper for Competitive Examinations; the other, on the present position of the much vexed Classical controversy.

The fifth considers the range of Philosophical or Metaphysical Study, and the mode of conducting this study in Debating Societies.

The sixth contains a retrospect of the growth of the Universities, with more especial reference to those of Scotland; and also a discussion of the University Ideal, as something more than professional teaching.

The seventh is a chapter omitted from the author's "Science of Education"; it is mainly devoted to the methods of self-education by means of books. The situation thus assumed has peculiarities that admit of being handled apart from the general theory of Education.

The eighth contends for the extension of liberty of thought, as regards Sectarian Creeds and Subscription to Articles. The total emancipation of the clerical body from the thraldom of subscription, is here advocated without reservation.

The concluding essay discusses the Procedure of Deliberative Bodies. Its novelty lies chiefly in proposing to carry out, more thoroughly than has yet been done, a few devices already familiar. But for an extraordinary reluctance in all quarters to adapt simple and obvious remedies to a growing evil, the article need never have appeared. It so happens, that the case principally before the public mind at present, is the deadlock in the House of Commons; yet, had that stood alone, the author would not have ventured to meddle with the subject. The difficulty, however, is widely felt: and the principles here put forward are perfectly general; being applicable wherever deliberative bodies are numerously constituted and heavily laden with business.

ABERDEEN, *March*, 1884.

CONTENTS.

I.

COMMON ERRORS ON THE MIND.

	PAGE
Error regarding Mind as a whole—that Mind can be exerted without bodily expenditure,	3
Errors with regard to the FEELINGS,	4
I. Advice to take on cheerfulness,	*ib.*
Authorities for this prescription,	*ib.*
Presumptions against our ability to comply with it,	6
Concurrence of the cheerful temperament with youth and health,	*ib.*
With special corporeal vigour. With absence of care and anxiety,	7
Limitation of Force applies to the mind,	8
The only means of rescuing from dullness—to increase the supports and diminish the burdens of life,	10
Difficulties in the choice of amusements,	12
II. Prescribing certain tastes, or pursuits, to persons indiscriminately,	13
Tastes must repose as natural endowment, or else in prolonged education,	14
III. Inverted relationship of Feelings and Imagination,	15
Imagination does not determine Feeling, but the reverse,	
Examples :—Bacon, Shelley, Byron, Burke, Chalmers, the Orientals, the Chinese, the Celt, and the Saxon,	17
IV. Fallaciousness of the view, that happiness is best gained by not being aimed at,	19
Seemingly a self-contradiction,	20
Butler's view of the disinterestedness of Appetite,	21
Apart from pleasure and pain, Appetite would not move us,	23
Parallel from other ends of pursuit—Health,	24
Life has two aims—Happiness and Virtue—each to be sought directly on its own account,	25
Errors connected with the WILL,	26
I. Cost of energy of Will. Need of a suitable physical confirmation,	*ib.*
Courage, Prudence, Belief,	27
II. Free-will a centre of various fallacies,	29

CONTENTS.

	PAGE
Doctrines repudiated from the offence given to personal dignity. Operation of this on the history of Free-will,	29
III. Departing from the usual rendering of a fact, treated as denying the fact,	32
Metaphysical and Ethical examples,	33
Alliance of Mind and Matter,	ib.
Perception of a Material World,	34
IV. The terms Freedom and Necessity miss the real point of the human will,	36
V. Moral Ability and Inability.—Fallacy of seizing a question by the wrong end,	37
Proper signification of Moral Inability—insufficiency of the ordinary motives, but not of all motives,	39

II.

ERRORS OF SUPPRESSED CORRELATIVES.

Meanings of Relativity—intellectual and emotional,	43
All impressions greatest at first. Law of Accommodation and habit,	44
The pleasure of rest presupposes toil,	45
Knowledge has its charm from previous ignorance,	ib.
Silence is of value, after excess of speech,	46
Previous pain not, in all cases, necessary to pleasure,	ib.
Simplicity of Style praiseworthy only under prevailing artificiality,	47
To extol Knowledge is to reprobate Ignorance,	48
Authority appealed to, when in our favour, repudiated when against us,	49
Fallacy of declaring all labour honourable alike,	ib.
The happiness of Justice supposes reciprocity,	51
Love and Benevolence need to be reciprocated,	53
The *moral nature* of God—a fallacy of suppressed correlative,	54
A perpetual miracle—a self-contradiction,	ib.
Fallacy that, in the world, everything is mysterious,	55
Proper meaning of Mystery,	56
Locke and Newton on the true nature of Explanation,	57
The Understanding cannot transcend its own experience.—Time and Space, their Infinity,	58
We can assimilate facts, and generalise the many into one. This alone constitutes Explanation,	63
Example from Gravity: not now mysterious,	64
Body and Mind. In what ways the mysteriousness of their union might be done away with,	65

III.

THE CIVIL SERVICE EXAMINATIONS.

I. HISTORICAL SKETCH.

	PAGE
First official recommendation of Competitive Examinations,	71
Successive steps towards their adoption,	72
First absolutely open Competition—in the India Service,	73
Macaulay's Report on the subjects for examination and their values,	74
Table of Subjects. Innovations of Lord Salisbury,	76
An amended Table,	79

II. THE SCHEME CONSIDERED.

Doubts expressed as to the expediency of the competitive system,	80
Criticism of the present prescription for the higher Services,	81
The Commissioners' Scheme of Mathematics and Natural Science objectionable,	ib.
Classification of the Sciences into Abstract or fundamental, and Concrete or derivative,	82
Those of the first class have a fixed order, the order of dependence,	83
The other class is represented by the Natural History Sciences, which bring into play the Logic of Classification,	84
Each of these is allied to one or other members of the primary Sciences,	ib.
The Commissioners' Table misstates the relationships of the various Sciences,	86
The London University Scheme a better model,	87
The choice allowed by the Commissioners not founded on a proper principle,	88
The higher Mathematics encouraged to excess,	90
Amended scheme of comparative values,	91
Position of Languages in the examinations,	92
The place in education of Language generally,	ib.
Purposes of Language acquisition,	ib.
Altered position of the Classical languages,	93
Alleged benefits of these languages, after ceasing to be valuable in their original use,	94
The teaching of the languages does not correspond to these secondary values,	97
Languages are not a proper subject for competition with a view to appointments,	101
For foreign service, there should be a pass examination in the languages needful,	102

CONTENTS.

	PAGE
The training powers attributed to languages should be tested in its own character,	104
Instead of the Languages of Greece, Rome, &c., substitute the History and Literature,	105
Allocation of marks under this view,	107
Objections answered,	108
Certain subjects should be obligatory,	110

IV.

THE CLASSICAL CONTROVERSY.

ITS PRESENT ASPECT.

Attack on Classics by Combe, fifty years ago,	115
Alternative proposals at the present day:—	
1. The existing system,	116
Attempts at extending the Science course under this system,	117
2. Remitting Greek in favour of a modern language. A defective arrangement,	119
3. Remitting both Latin and Greek in favour of French and German,	121
4. Complete bifurcation of the Classical and the Modern sides,	122
The Universities must be prepared to admit a thorough modern alternative course,	ib.
Latin should not be compulsory in the modern side,	124
Defences of Classics,	126
The argument from the Greeks knowing only their own language—never answered,	ib.
Admission that the teaching of classics needs improvement,	127
Alleged results of contact with the great authors of Greece and Rome—unsupported by facts,	129
Amount of benefit attainable without knowledge of originals,	132
The element of training may be obtained from modern languages,	ib.
The classics said to keep the mind free from party bias,	133
Canon Liddon's argument in favour of Greek as a study,	134

V.

METAPHYSICS AND DEBATING SOCIETIES.

Metaphysics here taken as comprising Psychology, Logic, and their dependent sciences,	139
Importance of the two fundamental departments,	140
The great problems, such as Free-will and External Perception, should be run up into systematic Psychology,	141
Logic also requires to be followed out systematically,	142
Slender connection of Logic and Psychology,	144

CONTENTS.

	PAGE
Derivative Sciences:—Education,	145
Æsthetics—a corner of the larger field of Human Happiness,	148
The treatment of Happiness should be dissevered from Ethics,	150
Adam Smith's loose rendering of the conditions of happiness,	151
Sociology—treated, partly in its own field, and partly as a derivative of Psychology,	153
Through it lies the way to Ethics,	155
The sociological and the ethical ends compared,	157
Factitious applications of Metaphysical study,	158
Bearings on Theology, as regards both attack and defence,	159
Incapable of supplying the place of Theology,	165
Polemical handling of Metaphysics,	164
Methodised Debate in the Greek Schools,	ib.
Much must always be done by the solitary thinker,	165
Best openings for Polemic:—Settling the meanings of terms,	167
Discussing the broader generalities,	168
The Debate a fight for mastery, and ill-suited for nice adjustments,	169
The Essay should be a centre of amicable co-operation, which would have special advantages,	170
Avoidance of such debates as are from their very nature interminable,	172

VI.

THE UNIVERSITY IDEAL—PAST AND PRESENT.

The Higher Teaching in Greece,	176
The Middle Age and Boëthius,	177
Eve of the University,	178
Separation of Philosophy from Theology,	179
The Universities of Scotland founded—their history,	181
First Period.—The Teaching Body,	182
The Subjects taught and manner of teaching,	183
Second Period.—The Reformation,	186
Modified Curriculum—Andrew Melville,	187
Attempted reforms in teaching,	188
System of Disputation,	191
Improvements constituting the transition to the Third Period,	192
The Universities and the political revolutions,	193
How far the Universities are essential to professional teaching: perennial alternative of Apprenticeship,	194
The Ideal Graduate,	197

VII.

THE ART OF STUDY.

	PAGE
Study more immediately supposes learning from Books,	203
The Greeks did not found an Art of Study, but afforded examples:	
Demosthenes,	205
Quintilian's "Institutes" a landmark,	206
Bacon's Essay on Studies. Hobbes,	207
Milton's Tractate on Education,	208
Locke's "Conduct of the Understanding" very specific as to rules of Study,	209
Watts's work entitled "The Improvement of the Mind,"	210
What an Art of Study should attempt,	212
Mode of approaching it,	215
I. First Maxim—"Select a Text-book-in-chief,"	ib.
Violations of the maxim: Milton's system,	216
Form or Method to be looked to, in the chief text-book,	219
The Sciences. History,	ib.
Non-methodical subjects,	220
Repudiation of plans of study by some,	221
Merits to be sought in a principal Text-book,	222
Question as between old writers and new,	223
Paradoxical extreme—one book and no more,	224
Single all-sufficing books do not exist,	225
Illustration from Locke's treatment of the Bible,	226
II. "What constitutes the study of a book?"	228
1. Copying literally:—Defects of this plan,	ib.
2. Committing to memory word for word,	230
Profitable only for brief portions of a book,	ib.
Memory in extension and intension,	231
3. Making Abstract	232
Variety of modes of abstracting,	234
4. Locke's plan of reading,	236
A sense of Form must concur with abstracting,	237
Example from the Practice of Medicine,	238
Example from the Oratorical Art,	240
Choice of a series of Speeches to begin upon,	241
An oratorical scheme essential,	242
Exemplary Speeches,	243
Illustration from the oratorical quality of negative tact. Macaulay's Speeches on Reform,	245
Study for improvement in Style,	247
III. Distributing the Attention in Reading,	248

		PAGE
IV. Desultory Reading,		250
V. Proportion of book-reading to Observation at first hand,		251
VI. Adjuncts of Reading.—Conversation,		252
Original Composition,		253

VIII.

RELIGIOUS TESTS AND SUBSCRIPTIONS.

Pursuit of Truth has three departments :—order of nature, ends of practice, and the supernatural,	257
Growth of Intolerance. How innovations became possible,	261
In early society, religion a part of the civil government,	263
Beginnings of toleration—dissentients from the State Church,	264
Evils attendant on Subscription:—the practice inherently fallacious,	265
Enforcement of creeds nugatory for the end in view	268
Dogmatic uniformity only a part of the religious character: element of Feeling,	270
Recital of the general argument for religious liberty,	272
Beginnings of prosecution for heresy in Greece:—Anaxagoras, Socrates, Plato, Aristotle,	273
Forced reticence in recent times:—Carlyle, Macaulay, Lyell,	274
Evil of disfranchising the Clerical class,	275
Outspokenness a virtue to be encouraged,	276
Special necessities of the present time: conflict of advancing knowledge with the received orthodoxy,	277
Objections answered:—The Church has engaged itself to the State to teach given tenets,	281
Possible abuse of freedom by the clergy,	ib.
The history of the English Presbyterian Church exemplifies the absence of Subscription,	284
Various modes of transition from the prevailing practice,	287

IX.

PROCEDURE OF DELIBERATIVE BODIES.

Growing evil of the intolerable length of Debates,	291
Hurried decisions might be obviated by allowing an interval previous to the vote,	292
The oral debate reviewed.—Assumptions underlying it, fully examined,	294
Evidence that, in Parliament, it is not the main engine of persuasion,	295
Its real service is to supply the newspaper reports,	298
Printing, without speaking, would serve the end in view,	ib.

xvi   CONTENTS.

	PAGE
Proposal to print and distribute beforehand the reasons for each Motion,	298
Illustration from decisions on Reports of Committees,	299
Movers of Amendments to follow the same course,	300
Further proposal to give to each member the liberty of circulating a speech in print, instead of delivering it,	ib.
The dramatic element in legislation much thought of,	302
Comparison of the advantages of reading and of listening,	ib.
The numbers of backers to a motion should be proportioned to the size of the assembly,	303
Absurdity of giving so much power to individuals,	304
In the House of Commons twenty backers to each bill not too many,	305
The advantages of printed speeches. Objections,	307
Unworkability of the plan in Committees. How remedied,	308
In putting questions to Ministers, there should be at least ten backers,	310
How to compensate for the suppression of oratory in the House:—Sectional discussions,	311
The divisions occasioned at one sitting to be taken at the beginning of the next,	312
Every deliberative body must be free to determine what amount of speaking it requires,	313
The English Parliamentary system considered as a model,	314
Lord Derby and Lord Sherbrook on the extension of printing,	315
Defects of the present system becoming more apparent,	317

Notes and References in connection with Essay VIII. on Subscription.

First imposition of Tests after the English Reformation,	319
Dean Milman's speech in favour of total abolition of Tests,	321
Tests in Scotland: Mr. Taylor Innes on the "Law of Creeds,"	323
Resumption of Subscription in the English Presbyterian Church,	324
Other English Dissenting Churches,	ib.
Presbyterian Church in the United States,	ib.
French Protestant Church—its two divisions,	325
Switzerland:—Canton of Vaud,	328
Independent Evangelical Church of Neuchatel,	329
National Protestant Church of Geneva,	ib.
Free Church of Geneva. Germanic Switzerland,	332
Hungarian Reformed Church,	ib.
Germany:—Recent prosecutions for heresy,	333
Holland:—Calvinists and Modern School,	336

I.

COMMON ERRORS ON THE MIND.

COMMON ERRORS ON THE MIND.[1]

OF the prevailing errors on the mind, proposed to be considered in this paper, some relate to the Feelings, others to the Will.

In regard to Mind as a whole, there are still to be found among us some remnants of a mistake, once universally prevalent and deeply rooted, namely, the opinion that mind is not only a different fact from body—which is true, and a vital and fundamental truth —but is to a greater or less extent independent of the body. In former times, the remark seldom occurred to any one, unless obtruded by some extreme instance, that to work the mind is also to work a number of bodily organs; that not a feeling can arise, not a thought can pass, without a set of concurring bodily processes. At the present day, however, this doctrine is very generally preached by men of science. The improved treatment of the insane has been one consequence of its reception. The husbanding of mental power, through a bodily *régime*, is a no less important application. Instead of supposing that mind is something indefinite, elastic, inexhaustible,—a sort of perpetual motion, or magician's bottle, all expenditure,

[1] *Fortnightly Review*, August, 1868.

and no supply,—we now find that every single throb of pleasure, every smart of pain, every purpose, thought, argument, imagination, must have its fixed quota of oxygen, carbon, and other materials, combined and transformed in certain physical organs. And, as the possible extent of physical transformation in each person's framework is limited in amount, the forces resulting cannot be directed to one purpose without being lost for other purposes. If an extra share passes to the muscles, there is less for the nerves; if the cerebral functions are pushed to excess, other functions have to be correspondingly abated. In several of the prevailing opinions about to be criticised, failure to recognise this cardinal truth is the prime source of mistake.

To begin with the FEELINGS.

I. We shall first consider an advice or prescription repeatedly put forth, not merely by the unthinking mass, but by men of high repute: it is, that with a view to happiness, to virtue, and to the accomplishment of great designs, we should all be cheerful, light-hearted, gay.

I quote a passage from the writings of one of the Apostolic Fathers, the Pastor of Hermas, as given in Dr. Donaldson's abstract:—

"Command tenth affirms that sadness is the sister "of doubt, mistrust, and wrath; that it is worse than "all other spirits, and grieves the Holy Spirit. It is "therefore to be completely driven away, and, instead "of it, we are to put on cheerfulness, which is pleas-

"ing to God. 'Every cheerful man works well, and "always thinks those things which are good, and des- "pises sadness. The sad man, on the other hand, is "always bad.'"[1]

Dugald Stewart inculcates Good-humour as a means of happiness and virtue; his language implying that the quality is one within our power to appropriate.

In Mr. Smiles's work entitled "Self-Help," we find an analogous strain of remarks:—

"To wait patiently, however, man must work cheer- "fully. Cheerfulness is an excellent working quality, "imparting great elasticity to the character. As a "Bishop has said, 'Temper is nine-tenths of Christi- "anity,' so are cheerfulness and diligence [a consider- "able make-weight] nine-tenths of practical wisdom."

Sir Arthur Helps, in those essays of his, combining profound observation with strong genial sympathies and the highest charms of style, repeatedly adverts to the dulness, the want of sunny light-hearted enjoyment of the English temperament, and, on one occasion, piquantly quotes the remark of Froissart on our Saxon progenitors: "They took their pleasures sadly, as was their fashion; *ils se divertirent moult tristement à la mode de leur pays.*"

There is no dispute as to the value or the desirableness of this accomplishment. Hume, in his "Life," says of himself, "he was ever disposed to see the favourable more than the unfavourable side of things;

Donaldson's "History of Christian Literature and Doctrine," Vol. I., p. 277.

a turn of mind which it is more happy to possess than to be born to an estate of ten thousand a year ". This sanguine, happy temper, is merely another form of the cheerfulness recommended to general adoption.

I contend, nevertheless, that to bid a man be habitually cheerful, he not being so already, is like bidding him treble his fortune, or add a cubit to his stature. The quality of a cheerful, buoyant temperament partly belongs to the original cast of the constitution—like the bone, the muscle, the power of memory, the aptitude for science or for music; and is partly the outcome of the whole manner of life. In order to sustain the quality, the physical (as the support of the mental) forces of the system must run largely in one particular channel; and, of course, as the same forces are not available elsewhere, so notable a feature of strength will be accompanied with counterpart weaknesses or deficiencies. Let us briefly review the facts bearing upon the point.

The first presumption in favour of the position is grounded in the concomitance of the cheerful temperament with youth, health, abundant nourishment. It appears conspicuously along with whatever promotes physical vigour. The state is partially attained during holidays, in salubrious climates, and health-bringing avocations; it is lost in the midst of toils, in privation of comforts, and in physical prostration. The seeming exception of elated spirits in bodily decay, in fasting, and in ascetic practices, is no disproof of the general principle, but merely the introduction of another principle, namely, that we can feed one part of the system at the expense of degrading and prematurely wasting others.

A second presumption is furnished also from our familiar experience. The high-pitched, hilarious temperament and disposition commonly appear in company with some well-marked characteristics of corporeal vigour. Such persons are usually of a robust mould; often large and full in person, vigorous in circulation and in digestion; able for fatigue, endurance, and exhausting pleasures. An eminent example of this constitution was seen in Charles James Fox, whose sociability, cheerfulness, gaiety, and power of dissipation were the marvel of his age. Another example might be quoted in the admirable physical frame of Lord Palmerston. It is no more possible for an ordinarily constituted person to emulate the flow and the animation of these men, than it is to digest with another person's stomach, or to perform the twelve labours of Hercules.

A third fact, less on the surface, but no less certain, is, that the men of cheerful and buoyant temperament, as a rule, sit easy to the cares and obligations of life. They are not much given to care and anxiety as regards their own affairs, and it is not to be expected that they should be more anxious about other people's. In point of fact, this is the constitution of somewhat easy virtue: it is not distinguished by a severe, rigid attention to the obligations and the punctualities of life. We should not be justified in calling such persons selfish; still less should we call them cold-hearted : their exuberance overflows upon others in the form of heartiness, geniality, joviality, and even lavish generosity. Still, they can seldom be got to look far before them ; they do not often assume the painfully circumspect attitude required in the more arduous enterprises. They are not conscientious in trifles. They cast off readily the burdensome parts of life. All which is in keeping with our principle. To take on burdens and cares is to draw upon the vital forces—to leave so much the less to cheerfulness and buoyant spirits. The same corporeal framework cannot afford a lavish expenditure in several different ways at one time. Fox had no long-sightedness, no tendency to forecast evils, or to burden himself with possible misfortunes. It is very doubtful if Palmerston could have borne the part of Wellington in the Peninsula ; his easy-going temperament would not have submitted itself to all the anxieties and precautions of that vast enterprise. But Palmerston was hale and buoyant, and the Prime Minister of England at eighty : Wellington began to be infirm at sixty.

To these three experimental proofs we may add the confirmation derived from the grand doctrine named the Correlation, Conservation, Persistence, or Limitation of Force, as applied to the human body and the human mind. We cannot create force anywhere ; we merely appropriate existing force. The heat of our fires has been derived from the solar fire. We cannot lift a weight in the hand without the combustion of a certain amount of food ; we cannot think a thought without a similar demand; and the force that goes in one way is unavailable in any other way. While we are expending ourselves largely in any single function—in muscular exercise, in digestion, in thought and feeling, the remaining functions must continue for the time in comparative abeyance. Now, the maintenance of a high strain of elated feeling, unquestionably costs a great deal to the forces of the system. All the facts confirm this high estimate. An unusually copious supply of arterial blood to the brain is an indispensable requisite, even although other organs should be partially starved, and consequently be left in a weak condition, or else deteriorate before their time. To support the excessive demand of power for one object, less must be exacted from other functions. Hard bodily labour and severe mental application sap the very foundations of buoyancy; they may not entail much positive suffering, but they are scarcely compatible with exuberant spirits. There may be exceptional individuals whose *total* of power is a very large figure, who can bear more work, endure more privation, and yet display more buoyancy, without shortened life, than the average human being. Hardly any man can attain commanding greatness without being constituted larger than his fellows in the sum of human vitality. But until this is proved to be the fact in any given instance, we are safe in presuming that extraordinary endowment in one thing implies deficiency in other things. More especially must we conclude, provisionally at least, that a buoyant, hopeful, elated temperament lacks some other virtues, aptitudes, or powers, such as are seen flourishing in the men whose temperament is sombre, inclining to despondency. Most commonly the contradictory demand is reconciled by the proverbial "short life and merry".

Adverting now to the object that Helps had so earnestly at heart—namely, to rouse and rescue the English population from their comparative dulness to a more lively and cheerful flow of existence—let us reflect how, upon the foregoing principles, this is to be done. Not certainly by an eloquent appeal to the nation to get up and be amused. The process will turn out to be a more circuitous one.

The mental conformation of the English people, which we may admit to be less lively and less easily amused than the temperament of Irishmen, Frenchmen, Spaniards, Italians, or even the German branch of our own Teutonic race, is what it is from natural causes, whether remote descent, or that coupled with the operation of climate and other local peculiarities. How long would it take, and what would be the way to establish in us a second nature on the point of cheerfulness?

Again, with the national temperament such as it is, there may be great individual differences; and it may be possible by force of circumstances, to improve the hilarity and the buoyancy of any given person. Many of our countrymen are as joyous themselves, and as much the cause of joy in others, as the most light-hearted Irishman, or the gayest Frenchman or Italian.

How shall we increase the number of such, so as to make them the rule rather than the exception?

The only answer not at variance with the laws of the human constitution is—*Increase the supports and diminish the burdens of life.*

For example, if by any means you can raise the standard of health and longevity, you will at once effect a stride in the direction sought. But what an undertaking is this! It is not merely setting up what we call sanitary arrangements, to which, in our crowded populations, there must soon be a limit reached (for how can you secure to the mass of men even the one condition of sufficient breathing-space?); it is that health cannot be attained, in any high general standard, without worldly means far above the average at the disposal of the existing population; while the most abundant resources are often neutralised by ineradicable hereditary taint. To which it is to be added, that mankind can hardly as yet be said to be in earnest in the matter of health.

Farther: it is especially necessary to cheerfulness, that a man should not be overworked, as many of us are, whether from choice or from necessity. Much, I believe, turns upon this circumstance. Severe toil consumes the forces of the constitution, without leaving the remainder requisite for hilarity of tone. The Irishman fed upon three meals of potatoes a day, the lazy Highlander, the Lazaroni of Naples living upon sixpence a week, are very poorly supported; but then their vitality is so little drawn upon by work, that they may exceed in buoyancy of spirits the well-fed but hard-worked labourer. We, the English people, would not change places with them, notwithstanding: our *ideal* is industry with abundance; but then our industry sobers our temperament, and inclines us to the dulness that Helps regrets. Possibly, we may one day hit a happier mean; but to the human mind extremes have generally been found easiest.

Once more: the light-hearted races trouble themselves little about their political constitution, about despotism or liberty; they enjoy the passing moments of a despot's smiles, and if he turns round and crushes them, they quietly submit. We live in dread of tyranny. Our liberty is a serious object; it weighs upon our minds. Now any weight upon the mind is so much taken from our happiness; hilarity may attend on poverty, but not so well on a serious, forecasting disposition. Our regard to the future makes us both personally industrious and politically anxious; a temper not to be amused with the relaxations of the Parisian in his *café* on the boulevards, or with the Sunday merry-go-round of the light-hearted Dane. Our very pleasures have still a sadness in them.

Then, again, what are to be our amusements? By what recreative stimulants shall we irradiate the gloom of our idle hours and vacation periods? Doubtless there have been many amusements invented by the benefactors of our species—society, games, music, public entertainments, books; and in a well-chosen round of these, many contrive to pass their time in a tolerable flow of satisfaction. But they all cost something; they all cost money, either directly, to procure them, or indirectly, to be educated for them. There are few very cheap pleasures. Books are not so difficult to obtain, but the enjoying of them in any high degree implies an amount of cultivation that cannot be had cheaply.

Moreover, look at the difficulties that beset the pursuit of amusements. How fatiguing are they very often! How hard to distribute the time and the strength between them and our work or our duties! It needs some art to steer one's way in the midst of variety of pleasures. Hence there will always be, in a cautious-minded people, a disposition to remain satisfied with few and safe delights; to assume a sobriety of aims that Helps might call dulness, but that many of us call the middle path.

II. A second error against the limits of the human powers is the prescribing to persons indiscriminately, certain tastes, pursuits, and subjects of interest, on the ground that what is a spring of enjoyment to one or a few may be taken up, as a matter of course, by others with the same relish. It is, indeed, a part of happiness to have some taste, occupation, or pursuit, adequate to charm and engross us—a ruling passion, a favourite study. Accordingly, the victims of dulness and *ennui* are often advised to betake themselves to something of this potent character. Kingsley, in his little book on the "Wonders of the Shore," endeavoured to convert mankind at large into marine naturalists; and, some time ago, there appeared in the newspapers a letter from Carlyle, regretting that he himself had not been indoctrinated into the zoology of our waysides. I have heard a man out of health, hypochondriac, and idle, recommended to begin botany, geology, or chemistry, as a diversion of his misery. The idea is plausible and superficial. An overpowering taste for any subject—botany, zoology, antiquities, music—is properly affirmed to be born with a man. The forces of the brain must from the first incline largely to that one species of impressions, to which must be added years of engrossing pursuit. We may gaze with envy at the fervour of a botanist over his dried plants, and may wish to take up so fascinating a pursuit: we may just as easily wish to be Archimedes when he leaped out of the bath; a man cannot re-cast his brain nor re-live his life. A taste of a high order, founded on natural endowment, formed by education, and strengthened by active devotion, is also paid for by the atrophy of other tastes, pursuits, and powers. Carlyle might have contracted an interest in frogs, and spiders, and bees, and the other denizens of the wayside, but it would have been with the surrender of some other interest, the diversion of his genius out of its present channels. The strong emotions of the mind are not to be turned off and on, to this subject and to that. If you begin early with a human being, you may impress a particular direction upon the feelings, you may even cross a natural tendency, and work up a taste on a small basis of predisposition. Place any youth in the midst of artists, and you may induce a taste for art that shall at length be decided and strong. But if you were to take the same person in middle life and immure him in a laboratory, that he might become an enthusiastic chemist, the limits of human nature would probably forbid your success.

Such very strong tastes as impart a high and perennial zest to one's life are merely the special direction of a natural exuberance of feeling or emotion. A spare and thin emotional temperament will undoubtedly have preferences, likings and dislikings, but it can never supply the material for fervour or enthusiasm in anything.

The early determining of natural tastes is a subject of high practical interest. We shall only remark at present that a varied and broad groundwork of early education is the best known device for this end.

III. A third error, deserving of brief comment, is a singular inversion of the relationship of the Feelings to the Imagination. It is frequently affirmed, both in criticism and in philosophy, that the Feelings depend upon, or have their basis in, the Imagination.

An able and polished writer, discussing the character of Edmund Burke, remarks: "The passions of Burke were strong; this is attributable in great measure to the intensity of the imaginative faculty". Again, Dugald Stewart, observing upon the influence of the Imagination on Happiness, says: "All that part of our happiness or misery which arises from our *hopes* or our *fears* derives its existence entirely from the power of imagination". He even goes the length of affirming that "*cowardice* is entirely a disease of the imagination". Another writer accounts for the intensity of the amatory sentiments in Robert Burns by the strength of his imagination.

Now, I venture to affirm that this view very nearly reverses the fact. The Imagination is determined by the Feelings, and not the Feelings by the Imagination. Intensity of feeling, emotion, or passion, is the earlier fact: the intellect swayed and controlled by feeling, shaping forms to correspond with an existing emotional tone, is Imagination. It was not the imaginative faculty that gave Wordsworth, Byron, Shelley, and the poets generally, their great enjoyment of nature; but the love of nature, pre-existing, turned the attention and the thoughts upon nature, filling the mind as a consequence with the impressions, images, recollections of nature; out of which grew the poetic imaginings. Imagination is a compound of intellectual power and feeling. The intellectual power may be great, but if it is not accompanied with feeling, it will not minister to feeling; or it will minister to many feelings by turns, and to none in particular. As far as the intellectual power of a poet goes, few men have excelled Bacon. He had a mind stored with imagery, able to produce various and vivid illustrations of whatever thought came before him; but these illustrations touched no deep feeling; they were fresh, original, racy, fanciful, picturesque, a play of the head that never touched the heart. The man was by nature cold; he had not the emotional depth or compass of an average Englishman. Perhaps his strongest feeling of an enlarged or generous description was for human progress, but it did not rise to passion; there was no fervour, no fury in it. Compare him with Shelley on the same subject, and you will see the difference between meagreness and intensity of feeling. What intellect can be, without strong feeling, we have in Bacon; what intellect is, with strong feeling, we have in Shelley. The feeling gives the tone to the thoughts; sets the intellect at work to find language having its own intensity, to pile up lofty and impressive circumstances; and then we have the poet, the orator, the thoughts that breathe, and the words that burn. Bacon wrote on many impressive themes—on Truth, on Love, on Religion, on Death, and on the Virtues in detail; he was always original, illustrative, fanciful; if intellectual means and resources could make a man feel in these things, he would have felt deeply; yet he never did. The material of feeling is not contained in the intellect; it has a seat and a source apart. There was nothing in mere intellectual gifts to make Byron a misanthrope: but, given that state of the feelings, the intellect would be detained and engrossed by it; would minister to, expand, and illustrate it; and intellect so employed is Imagination.

Burke had indisputably a powerful imagination. He had both elements:—the intellectual power, or the richly stored and highly productive mind; and the emotional power, or the strength of passion that gives the lead to intellect. His intellectual strength was often put forth in the Baconian manner of illustration, in light and sportive fancies. There were many occasions where his feelings were not much roused. He had topics to urge, views to express, and he poured out arguments, and enlivened them with illustrations. He was, on those occasions, an able expounder, and no more. But when his passions were stirred to the depths by the French Revolution, his intellectual power, taking a new flight, supplied him with figures of extraordinary intensity; it was no longer the play of a cool man, but the thunders of an aroused man; we have then "the hoofs of the swinish multitude,"—"the ten thousand swords leaping from their scabbards". Such feelings were not produced by the speaker's imagination: they were produced by themselves; they had their independent source in the region of feeling: coupled with adequate powers of intellect, they burst out into strong imagery.

[1] Intensity of passion stands confessed in the self-delineations of men of imaginative genius. We forbear to quote the familiar instances of Wordsworth, Shelley, or Burns, but may refer to a remarkable chapter in the life of the famous Scotch preacher, Dr. Thomas Chalmers. The mere title of the chapter is enough for our purpose. It related to his early youth, and ran thus, in his own words:—"A year of mental elysium". It is while living at a white-heat that all the thoughts and conceptions take a lofty, hyperbolical character; and the outpouring of these at the time, or afterwards, is the imagination of the orator or the poet.

The spread of the misconception that we have been combating is perhaps accounted for by the circumstance that imagination in one man is the cause of feeling *in others*. Wordsworth, by his imaginative colouring, has excited a warmer sentiment for nature in many spectators of the lake country. That, however, is a different thing. We may also allow that the poet intensifies his own feelings by his creative embodiments of them.

The Orientals, as a rule, are distinguished for imaginative flights. This is apparent in their religion, their morality, their poetry, and their science. The explanation is to be sought in the strength of their feelings, coupled with a certain intellectual force. The same intellect, without the feelings, would have issued differently. The Chinese are the exception. They want the feelings, and they want the imagination. They are below Europeans in this respect. When we bring before them our own imaginative themes, our own cast of religion, accommodated as it is to our own peculiar temperament, we fail in the desired effect. Our august mysteries are responded to, not with reverential regard, but with cold analysis.

The Celt and the Saxon are often contrasted on the point of imagination; the prior fact is the comparative endowment for emotion.

IV. There is a fallacious mode of presenting the attainment of happiness; namely, that happiness is best secured by not being aimed at. We should be aiming always at something else.

When examined closely, the doctrine resolves itself into a kind of paradox. All sorts of puzzles come up when we attempt to follow it to its consequences.

We might ask, first, whether there is any other object of pursuit in the same predicament—wealth, health, knowledge, fame, power. These are, every one, a means or instrument of happiness, if not happiness itself. Must we, then, in the case of each, avoid aiming straight at the goal? must we look askance in some other direction?

Next, in the case of happiness proper, are we to aim at nothing at all, to drift at random; or may we aim at a definite object, provided it is not happiness; or, lastly, is there one side aim in' particular that we must take? The answer here would probably be—Aim at duty in general, and at the good of others in particular. These ends are not the same as happiness, yet by keeping them steadily in the view, and not thinking of self at all, we shall eventually realise our greatest happiness.

Without, at present, raising any question as to the fact alleged, we must again remark that the prescription seems to contradict itself. Moralists of the austere type will never allow us to pursue happiness at all; we must never mention the thing to ourselves: duty or virtue is the one single aim and end of being. Such teachers may be right or they may be wrong, but they do not contradict themselves. When, however, we are told that by aiming at virtue, we are on the best possible road to happiness, this is but another way of letting us into the secret of happiness, of putting us on the right, instead of on the wrong, track, to attain it. Our teacher assumes that we are in search of happiness, and he tells us how we are to proceed; not by keeping it straight in the view, but by keeping virtue straight in the view. Instead of pointing us to the vulgar happiness-seeker who would take the goal in a line, he corrects the course, and shows us the deviation that is necessary in order to arrive at it; like the sailor making allowance for the deviation of the magnetic pole, in steering. Happiness is not gained by a point-blank aim; we must take a boomerang flight in some other line, and come back upon the target by an oblique or reflected movement. It is the idea of Young on the Love of Praise (Satire I., 5.)—

> The love of Praise howe'er concealed by art,
> Reigns more or less and glows in every heart,
> The proud to gain it, toils on toils endure,
> *The modest shun it but to make it sure.*

Under this corrected method, we are happiness seekers all the same; only our aims are better directed, and our fruition more assured.

These remarks are intended to show that the doctrine of making men aim at virtue, in order to happiness, has no further effect than to teach us to include the interests of others with our own; by showing that our own interests do not thereby suffer, but the contrary. The doctrine does not substitute a virtuous motive for a selfish one; it is a refined artifice for squaring the two. The world is no doubt a gainer by the change of view, although the individual is not made really more meritorious.

We must next consider whether, in fact, the oblique aim at happiness is really the most effectual.

A few words, first, as to the original source of the doctrine of a devious course. Bishop Butler is renowned for his distinction between Self-Love and Appetite; he contends that in Appetite the object of pursuit is not the pleasure of eating, but the food:

consequently, eating is not properly a self-seeking act, it is an indifferent or disinterested act, to which there is an incidental accompaniment of pleasure. We should, under the stimulus of Hunger, seek the food, whether it gave us pleasure or not.

Now, any truth that there is in Butler's view amounts to this:—In our Appetites we are not thinking every instant of subduing pain and attaining pleasure; we are ultimately moved by these feelings; but, having once seen that the medium of their gratification is a certain material object (food), we direct our whole aim to procuring that. The hungry wolf ceases to think of his pains of hunger when he is in sight of a sheep; but for these pains he would have paid no heed to the sheep; yet when the sheep has to be caught, the hunger is submerged for the time; the only relevant course, even on its account, is to give the whole mind and body to the chase of the sheep. Butler calls this indifferent or disinterested pursuit; and as much as says, that the wolf is not self-seeking, but sheep-seeking, in its chase. Now, it is quite true that if the wolf could give no place in its mind for anything but its hungry pains, it would be in a bad way. It is wiser than that; it knows the remedy; it is prepared to dismiss the pains from its thoughts, in favour of a concentrated attention upon the distant flock. This proves nothing as to its unselfishness; nor does it prove that Appetite is a different thing from self-seeking or self-love.

There may be disinterested motives in our constitution; but Appetite is not in any sense one of these.

We may have instincts answering to the traditional phrase used in defining instinct, "a blind propensity" to act, without aiming at anything in particular, and without any expectation of pleasure or benefit. Such instincts would conform to Butler's notion of appetite: they would lie entirely out of the course of self-love or self-seeking of any sort. Whether the nest-building activity of birds, and the constructiveness of ants, bees, and beavers, comply with this condition, I do not undertake to say. There is one process better known to ourselves, not exactly an instinct, but probably a mixture of instinct and acquirement—I mean the process of Imitation—which works very much upon this model. Although coming under the control of the Will, yet in its own proper character it operates blindly, or without purpose; neither courting pleasure, nor chasing pain. In like manner, Sympathy, in its most characteristic form, proceeds without any distinct aim of pleasure to ourselves.

Nothing of this can be affirmed of the Appetites. In them, nature places us, as Bentham says, under the government of two sovereign masters, *pain* and *pleasure*. An appetite would cease to move us, if its painful and pleasurable accompaniments were done away with. It matters not that we remit our attention, at times, to the pain or the pleasure; these are always in the background; and the strength of the appetite is their strength.

So far as concerns Butler's example of the Appetites, there is no case for the view that to obtain happiness we must avoid aiming at it directly. If we do not aim at the pleasure in its own subjective character, we aim at the thing that immediately brings the pleasure; which is, for all practical purposes, to aim at the pleasure.

The prescription to look away from the final end, Happiness, in order to secure that end, may be tested on the example of one of our intermediate pursuits, as Health. It is not a good thing to be always dwelling on the state of our health: by doing so, we get into a morbid condition of self-consciousness, which is in itself pernicious. It does not follow that we are to live at random, without ever giving a thought to our health. There is a plain middle course. Guided by our own experience, and by the experience of those that have gone before us, we arrange our plan of life so as to preserve health; and our actions consist in adhering to that plan in the detail. So long as our scheme answers expectation, we think of nothing but of putting it in force, as occasion arises; we do not dwell upon our states of good health at all. It is some interruption that makes us self-conscious; and then it is that we have to exercise ourselves about a remedial course. This, when found, is likewise objectively pursued; our only subjectiveness lies in being aware of gradual recovery; and we are glad to get back to the state of paying no attention to the workings of our viscera. We do not, therefore, remit our pursuit; only, it is enough to observe the routine of outward actions, whose sole motive is to keep us in health.

The pursuit of the still wider end, Happiness, has

much in common with the narrower pursuit. When we have discovered what things promote, and what things impede our happiness, we transfer our attention to these, as the most direct mode of compassing the end. If we are satisfied that working for other people brings us happiness, we work accordingly; this is no side aim, it is as direct as any aim can be. It may involve immediate sacrifice, but that does not alter the case; we can get no considerable happiness from any source without temporary sacrifice.

If it be said that the best mode of attaining happiness is to put ourselves entirely out of account, and to work for others exclusively, this, as already noted, is a self-contradiction. It is to tell people not to think of their own happiness, and yet to know that they are securing that in the most effectual way. It is also very questionable, indeed absolutely erroneous, in fact. The most apparent way to secure happiness is to ply all the known means of happiness, just as far as, and no farther than, they are discovered to produce the effect. We must keep a check upon the methods that we employ, and abandon those that do not answer. So long as we find happiness in serving others, so long we continue in that course. And it is a melancholy fact that Pope's bold assertion—" Virtue alone is happiness below,"—cannot be upheld against the stern realities of life. Life needs to be made up of two aims—the one, Happiness, the other Virtue, each on its own account. There is a certain mutual connection of the two, but all attempts at making out their identity are failures.

It is of very great importance to teach men the bearings of virtue on happiness, so far as these are known. There will, however, always remain a portion of duty that detracts from happiness, and must be done as duty, nevertheless. Men are entitled to pursue happiness as directly as ever they please ; only, they must couple with the pursuit their round of duties to others ; in which they may or may not reap a share of the coveted good for self.

Let us, next, consider some of the difficulties and mistakes attaching to the WILL. Here there are the questions of world-renown, questions known even in Pandemonium—Free-will, Responsibility, Moral Ability, and Inability. It is now suspected, on good grounds, that, on these questions, we have somehow got into a wrong groove—that we are lost in a maze of our own constructing.

I. We shall first notice a misconception akin to some of the foregoing mistakes respecting the feelings. In addressing men with a view to spur their activity, there is usually a too low estimate of what is implied in great and energetic efforts of will. Here, exactly as in the cheerful temperament, we find a certain constitutional endowment, a certain natural force of character, having its physical supports of brain, muscle, and other tissue ; and neither persuasion, nor even education, can go very far to alter that character. If there be anything at all in the observations of phrenology, it is the connection of energetic determination with size of brain. Lay your hand first on the head of an energetic man, and then on the head of a feeble man, and you will find a difference that is not to be explained away. Now it passes all the powers of persuasion and education combined to make up for a great cranial inequality. Something always comes of assiduous discipline; but to set up a King Alfred, or a Luther, as a model to be imitated by an ordinary man, on the points of energy, perseverance, endurance, courage, is to pass the bounds of the human constitution. Persistent energy of a high order, like the temperament for happiness, costs a great deal to the human system. A large share of the total forces of the constitution go to support it; and the diversion of power often leaves great defects in other parts of the character, as for example, a low order of the sensibilities, and a narrow range of sympathies. The men of extraordinary vigour and activity—our Roman emperors and conquering heroes—are often brutal and coarse. Nature does not supply power profusely on all sides; and delicate sympathies, of themselves, use up a very large fraction of the forces of the organisation. Even intellectually estimated, the power of sympathising with many various minds and conditions would occupy as much room in the brain as a language, or an accomplishment. A man both energetic and sympathetic—a Pericles, a King Alfred, an Oliver Cromwell —is one of nature's giants, several men in one.

There is no more notable phase of our active nature than Courage. Great energy generally implies great courage, and courage—at least in nine-tenths of its amount—comes by nature. To exhort any one to be courageous is waste of words. We may animate, for the time, a naturally timid person, by explaining away the signs of danger, and by assuming a confident attitude ourselves; but the absolute force of courage is what neither we nor the man himself can add to. A long and careful education might effect a slight increase in this, as in other aspects of energy of character: we can hardly say how much, because it is a matter that is scarcely ever subjected to the trial; the very conditions of the experiment have not been thought of.

The moral qualities expressed by Prudence, Forethought, Circumspection, are talked of with a like insufficient estimate of what they cost. Great are the rewards of prudence, but great also is the expenditure of the prudent man. To retain an abiding sense of all the possible evils, risks and contingencies of an ordinary man's position—professional, family, and personal—is to go about under a constant burden; the difference between a thorough-going and an easy-going circumspection is a large additional demand upon the forces of the brain. The being on the alert to duck the head at every bullet is a charge to the vital powers; so much so, that there comes a point when it is better to run risks than to pile up costly precautions and bear worrying anxieties.

Lastly, the attribute of our active nature called Belief, Confidence, Conviction, is subject to the same line of remark. This great quality—the opposite of distrust and timidity, the ally of courage, the adjunct of a buoyant temperament—is not fed upon airy nothings. It is, indeed, a true mental quality, an offshoot of our mental nature ; yet, although not material, it is based upon certain forces of the physical constitution ; it grows when these grow, and is nourished when they are nourished. People possessed of great confidence have it as a gift all through life, like a broad chest or a good digestion. Preaching and education have their fractional efficacy, and deserve to be plied, provided the operator is aware of nature's impassable barriers, and does not suppose that he is working by charm. It is said of Hannibal that he dissolved obstructions in the Alps by vinegar; in the moral world, barriers are not to be removed either by acetic acid or by honey.

II. The question of Free-will might be a text for discoursing on some of the most inveterate erroneous tendencies of the mind.

For one thing, it gives occasion to remark on the influence exerted over our opinions by the feeling of Personal Dignity. Of sources of bias, prejudices, "Idola," "fallacies *à priori*," this may be allowed precedence. For example, the maxim has been enunciated by some philosophers, that, of two differing opinions, preference is to be given (not to what is true, but) to what ennobles and dignifies human nature. One of the objections seriously entertained against Darwin's theory is that it humbles our ancestral pride. So, to ascribe to our mental powers a material foundation is held to be degrading to our nobler part. Again, a philosopher of our own day—Sir W. Hamilton—has placed on the title-page of his principal work this piece of rhetoric: "On earth, there is nothing great but man; in man, there is nothing great but mind". Now one would suppose that there are on earth many things besides man deserving the appellation of "great"; and that the mechanism of the body is, in any view, quite as remarkable a piece of work as the mechanism of the mind. There was one step more that Hamilton, as an Aristotelian, should have made: "In mind, there is nothing great but intellect" Doubtless, we ought not to dissect an epigram; but epigrams brought into a perverting contact with science are not harmless. Such gross pandering to human vanity must be held as disfiguring a work on philosophy.

The sentiment of dignity has much to answer for in the doctrine of Free-will. In Aristotle, the question had not assumed its modern perplexity; but the vicious element of factitious personal importance had already peeped out, it being one of the few points wherein the bias of the feelings operated decidedly in his well-balanced mind. In maintaining the doctrine that vice is voluntary, he argues, that if virtue is voluntary, vice (its opposite) must also be voluntary; now to assert virtue not to be voluntary would be to cast an *indignity* upon it. This is the earliest association of the feeling of personal dignity with the exercise of the human will.

The Stoics are commonly said to have started the free-will difficulty. This needs an explanation. A leading tenet of theirs was the distinction between things in our power and things not in our power; and they greatly overstrained the limits of what is in our power. Looking at the sentiment about death, where the *idea* is everything, and at many of our desires and aversions, also purely sentimental, that is, made and unmade by our education (as, for example, pride of birth), they considered that pains in general, even physical pains and grief for the loss of friends, could be got over by a mental discipline, by intellectually holding them not to be pains. They extolled and magnified the power of the will that could command such a transcendent discipline, and infused an emotion of *pride* into the consciousness of this greatness of will. In subsequent ages, poets, moralists, and theologians followed up the theme; and the appeal to the pride of will may be said to be a standing engine of moral suasion. This originating of a point of honour or dignity in connection with our Will has been the main lure in bringing us into the jungle of Free-will and Necessity.

It is in the Alexandrian school that we find the next move in the question. In Philo Judæus, the good man is spoken of as free, the wicked man as a slave. Except as the medium of a compliment to virtue, the word "freedom" is not very apposite, seeing that, to the highest goodness, there attaches submission or restraint, rather than liberty.

The early Christian Fathers (notably Augustine) advanced the question to the Theological stage, by connecting it with the great doctrines of Original Sin and Predestination; in which stage it shared all the speculative difficulties attaching to these doctrines. The Theological world, however, has always been divided between Free-will and Necessity; and probably the weightiest names are to be found among the Necessitarians. No man ever brought greater acumen into theological controversy than did Jonathan Edwards; and he took the side of Necessity.

Latterly, however, since the question has become one of pure metaphysics, Free-will has been the favourite dogma, as being most consonant to the dignity of man, which appears to be its chief recommendation, and its only argument. The weight of reasoning is, I believe, in favour of necessity; but the word carries with it a seeming affront, and hardly any amount of argument will reconcile men to indignity.

III. Another weakness of the human mind receives illustration from the free-will controversy, and deserves to be noticed, as helping to account for the prolonged existence of the dispute: I mean the disposition to regard any departure from the accustomed rendering of a fact as denying the fact itself. The rose under another name is not merely less sweet, it is not a rose at all. Some of the greatest questions have suffered by this weakness.

The physical theory of matter that resolves it into *points of force* will seem to many as doing away with matter no less effectually than the Berkeleyan Idealism. A universe of inane mathematical points, attracting and repelling each other, must appear to the ordinary mind a sorry substitute for the firm-set earth, and the majestically-fretted vault of heaven, with its planets, stars, and galaxies. It takes a special education to reconcile any one to this theory. Even if it were everything that a scientific hypothesis should be, the previously established modes of speech would be a permanent obstruction to its being received as the popular doctrine.

But the best illustrations occur in the Ethical and Metaphysical departments. For example, some ethical theorists endeavour to show that Conscience is not a primitive and distinct power of the mind, like the sense of colour, or the feeling of resistance, but a growth and a compound, being made up of various primitive impulses, together with a process of education. Again and again has this view been represented as denying conscience altogether. Exactly parallel has been the handling of the sentiment of Benevolence. Some have attempted to resolve it into simpler elements of the mind, and have been attacked as denying the existence of the sentiment. Hobbes, in particular, has been subjected to this treatment. Because he held pity to be a form of self-love, his opponents charged him with declaring that there is no such thing as pity or sympathy in the human constitution.

A more notable example is the doctrine of the alliance of Mind with Matter. It is impossible that any mode of viewing this alliance can erase the distinction between the two modes of existence—the material and the mental; between extended inert bodies, on the one hand, and pleasures and pains, thoughts and volitions, on the other. Yet, after the world has been made familiar with the Cartesian doctrine of two distinct substances—the one for the inherence of material facts, and the other for mental facts—any thinker maintaining the separate mental substance to be unproved, and unnecessary, is denounced as trying to blot out our mental existence, and to resolve us into watches, steam-engines, or speaking and calculating machines. The upholder of the single substance has to spend himself in protestations that he is not denying the existence of the fact, or the phenomena called mind, but is merely challenging an arbitrary and unfounded hypothesis for representing that fact.

The still greater controversy—distinct from the foregoing, although often confounded with it—relating to the Perception of a Material World, is the crowning instance of the weakness we are considering. Berkeley has been unceasingly stigmatised as holding that there is no material world, merely because he exposed a self-contradiction in the mode of viewing it, common to the vulgar and to philosophers, and suggested a mode of escaping the contradiction by an altered rendering of the facts. The case is very peculiar. The received and self-contradictory view is exceedingly simple and intelligible in its statement; it is well adapted, not merely for all the commoner purposes of life, but even for most scientific purposes. The supposition of an independent material world, and an independent mental world, created apart, and coming into mutual contact—the one the objects perceived, and the other the mind perceiving—expresses (or over-expresses) the division of the sciences into sciences of matter and sciences of mind ; and the highest laws of the material world at least are in no respect falsified by it. On the other hand, any attempt to state the facts of the outer world on Berkeley's plan, or on any plan that avoids the self-contradiction, is most cumbrous and unmanageable. A smaller, but exactly parallel instance of the situation is familiar to us. The daily circuit of the sun around the earth, supposed to be fixed, so exactly answers all the common uses that, in spite of its being false, we adhere to it in the language of everyday life. It is a convenient misrepresentation, and deceives nobody. And such will, in all likelihood, be the usage regarding the external world, after the contradiction is admitted, and rectified by a metaphysical circumlocution. Speculators are still only trying their hand at an unobjectionable circumlocution ; but we may almost be sure that nothing will ever supersede, for practical uses, the notion of the distinct worlds of Mind and Matter. If, after the Copernican demonstration of the true position of the sun, we still find it requisite to keep up the fiction of his daily course ; much more, after the final accomplishment of the Berkeleyan revolution (to my mind inevitable), shall we retain the fiction of an independent external world : only, we shall then know how to fall back upon some mode of stating the case, without incurring the contradiction.

IV. To return to the Will. The fact that we have to save, and to represent in adequate language, is this:—A voluntary action is a sequence distinct and *sui generis*; a human being avoiding the cold, searching for food, and clinging to other beings, is not to be confounded with a pure material sequence, as the fall of rain, or the explosion of gunpowder. The phenomena, in both kinds, are phenomena of sequence, and of *regular* or *uniform* sequence; but the things that make up the sequence are widely different: in the one, a feeling of the mind, or a concurrence of feelings, is followed by a conscious muscular exertion; in the other, both steps are made up of purely material circumstances. It is the difference between a mental or psychological, and a material or physical sequence —in short, the difference between mind and matter; the greatest contrast within the whole compass of nature, within the universe of being. Now language must be found to give ample explicitness to this diametrical antithesis; still, I am satisfied that rarely in the usages of human speech has a more unfortunate choice been made than to employ, in the present instance, the antithetic couple—Freedom and Necessity. It misses the real point, and introduces meanings alien to the case. It converts the glory of the human character into a reproach (although its leading motive throughout has been to pay us a compliment). The *constancy* of man's emotional nature (but for which our life would be a chaos, an impossibility) has to be explained away, for no other reason than that, at one time, a blundering epithet was applied to designate the mental sequences. Great is the difference between Mind and Matter; but the terms Freedom and Necessity represent the point of agreement as the point of difference; and this being made familiar, through iteration, as the mode of expressing the contrast, the rectification is supposed to unsettle everything, and to obliterate the wide distinction of the two natures.

V. What is called Moral Ability and Inability is another artificial perplexity in regard to the will, and might also be the text for a sermon on prevailing errors. More especially, it exemplifies what may be termed *seizing a question by the wrong end.*

The votary, we shall say, of alcoholic liquor is found fault with, and makes the excuse, he cannot help it—he cannot resist the temptation. So far, the language may pass. But what shall we say to the not uncommon reply,—You could help it if you would. Surely there is some mystification here; it is not one of those plain statements that we desire in practical affairs. Whether we are dealing with matter or with mind, we ought to point out some clear and practicable method of attaining an end in view. To get a good crop, we till and enrich the soil; to make a youth knowing in mathematics, we send him to a good master, and stimulate his attention by combined reward and punishment. There are also intelligible courses of reforming the vicious: withdraw them from temptation till their habits are remodelled; entice them to other courses, by presenting objects of superior attraction; or, at lowest, keep the fact of punishment before their eyes. By these methods many are kept from vices, and not a few reclaimed after having fallen. But to say, "You can be virtuous if you will," is either unmeaning, or it disguises a real meaning. If it have any force at all—and it would not be used unless some efficacy had been found attaching to it,—the force must lie in the indirect circumstances or accompaniments. What, then, is the meaning that is so unhappily expressed? In the first place, it is a vehicle for conveying the strong wish and determination of the speaker; it is a clumsy substitute for—"I do wish you would amend your conduct"; an expression containing a real efficacy, greater or less according to the estimate formed of the speaker by the person spoken to. In the next place, it presents to the mind of the delinquent the *ideal* of improvement, which might also be done in unexceptionable phrase; as one might say—"Reflect upon your own state, and compare yourself with the correct and virtuous liver". Then, there is a touch of the stoical dignity and pride of will. Lastly, there may be a hint or suggestion to the mind of good and evil consequences, which is the most powerful motive of all. In giving rise to these various considerations, even the objectionable expression may have a genuine efficacy; but that does not justify the form itself, which by no interpretation can be construed into sense or intelligibility.

Moral Inability means that ordinary motives are insufficient, but not all motives. The confirmed drunkard or thief has got into the stage of moral inability; the common motives that keep mankind sober and honest have failed. Yet there are motives that would succeed, if we could command them. Men may be sometimes cured of intemperance when the constitution is so susceptible that pain follows at once on indulgence. And so long as pleasure and pain, in fact and in prospect, operate upon the will, so long as the individual is in a state wherein motives operate, there may be moral weakness, but there is nothing more. In such cases, punishment may be properly employed as a corrective, and is likely to answer its end. This is the state termed accountability, or, with more correctness, PUNISHABILITY, for being accountable is merely an incident bound up with liability to punishment. Moral weakness is a matter of a degree, and in its lowest grades shades into insanity, the state wherein motives have lost their usual power—when pleasure and pain cease to be apprehended by the mind in their proper character. At *this* point, punishment is unavailing; the moral inability has passed into something like physical inability; the loss of self-control is as complete as if the muscles were paralysed.

In the plea of insanity, entered on behalf of any one charged with crime, the business of the jury is to ascertain whether the accused is under the operation of the usual motives—whether pain in prospect has a deterring effect on the conduct. If a man is as ready to jump out of the window as to walk downstairs, of course he is not a moral agent; but so long as he observes, of his own accord, the usual precautions against harm to himself, he is to be punished for his misdeeds.

These various questions repecting the Will, if stripped of unsuitable phraseology, are not very difficult questions. They are about as easy to comprehend as the air-pump, the law of refraction of light, or the atomic theory of chemistry. Distort them by inapposite metaphors, view them in perplexing attitudes, and you may make them more abstruse than the hardest proposition of the "Principia". What is far worse, by involving a simple fact in inextricable contradictions, they have led people gravely to recognise self-contradiction as the natural and the proper condition of a certain class of questions. Consistency is very well so far, and for the humbler matters of every-day life, but there is a higher and a sacred region where it does not hold; where the principles are to be received all the more readily that they land us in contradictions. In ordinary matters, inconsistency is the test of falsehood; in transcendental subjects, it is accounted the badge of truth.

II.

ERRORS OF SUPPRESSED CORRELATIVES.

ERRORS OF SUPPRESSED COR-RELATIVES.[1]

By Relativity is here meant the all-pervading fact of our nature that we are not impressed, made conscious, or mentally alive, without some change of state or impression. An unvarying action on any of our senses is the same as no action at all. An even temperature, such as that enjoyed by the fishes in the tropical seas, leaves the mind an entire blank as regards heat and cold. We can neither feel nor know without recognising two distinct states. Hence all knowledge is double, or is the knowledge of contrasts or opposites: heavy is relative to light; up supposes down; being awake implies the state of sleep.

The applications of the law in the sphere of emotion are chiefly contemplated in what follows. Pleasure and pain are never absolute states; they have reference always to the previous condition. Until we know what that has been in any case, we cannot pronounce upon the efficacy of a present stimulation. We see a person reposing, apparently in luxurious ease; if the state has been immediately consequent upon a protracted and severe exertion, we are right in calling it highly pleasurable. Under other circumstances, it might be quite the reverse.

There is an offshoot or modification of the principle, arising out of the operation of habit. Impressions made upon us are greatest when they are absolutely new : after repetition they all lose something of their power ; although, by remission and alternative, the causes of pleasure and pain have still a very considerable efficacy. Many of the consequences of this great fact are sufficiently acknowledged, or, if they are not, it is from other causes than our ignorance. The weakness is moral, rather than intellectual, that makes us expect that the first flush of a great pleasure, a newly-attained joy or success, will continue unabated. The poor man, probably, does not overrate the gratification of newly-attained wealth ; what he fails to allow for is the deadening effect of an unbroken experience of ease and plenty. The author of " Romola " says of the hero and the heroine, in the early moments of their affection, that they could not look forward to a time when their kisses should be common things. So it is with the attainment of all great objects of pursuit : the first access of good fortune may not disappoint us ; but as we are more and more removed from the state of privation, as the memory of the prior experience fades away, so does the vividness of the present enjoyment. It is the same with changes for the worse : the agony of a great loss is at first overpowering ; gradually, however, the system accommodates itself to the new condition, and the severity dies away. What is called on these occasions the "force of custom" is the application of the law of Accommodation, or Relativity modified by habit.

It is a familiar experience of mankind, yet hard to realise upon mere testimony, that the pleasures of rest, repose, retirement, are wholly relative to foregone labour and toil; after the first shock of transition, they are less and less felt, and can be renewed only after a renewal of the contrasting experience. The description, in "Paradise Lost," of the delicious repose of Adam and Eve in Eden is fallacious; the poet credits them with an intensity of pleasure attainable only by the brow-sweating labourer under the curse.

The delights of Knowledge are relative to previous Ignorance; for, although the possession of knowledge is in many ways a lasting good, yet the full intensity of the charm is felt only at the moment of passing from mystery to explanation, from blankness of impression to intellectual attainment. This form of the pleasure is sustained only by new acquisitions and new discoveries. Moreover, in the minor forms of the gratification due to knowledge, we never escape the law of relativity; the "power" delights us by relation to our previous impotence. Plato supposed that, in knowledge, we have an example of a *pure* pleasure, meaning one that had no reference to foregone privation or pain; but such "purity" would be a barren fact, not unlike the pure air of a bladeless and waterless desert. A state of uninterrupted good health, although a prime condition of enjoyment, is of itself a state of neutrality or indifference. The man that has never been ill cannot sing the joys of health; the exultation of that strain is attainable only by the valetudinarian.

These examples have been remarked upon in every age. It is the moral weakness of being carried away by a present strong feeling, as if the state would last for ever, that blinds each of us in turn to the stern reality of the fact. There are, however, numerous instances, coming under Relativity, wherein the indispensable correlative is more or less dropped out of sight and disavowed. These are the proper errors or fallacies of Relativity, a branch of the comprehensive class termed "Fallacies of Confusion". The object of the present essay is to exhibit a few of these errors as they occur in questions of practical moment.

When it is said, as by Carlyle and others, "speech is silvern, silence is golden," there is implied a condition of things where speech has been in excess; and but for this excess, the assertion is untrue. One might as well talk of the delights of hunger, or of cold, or of solitary confinement, on the ground of there being times when food, warmth, or society may be in excess, and when the opposing states would be a joyful change.

The Relativity of Pleasures, although admitted in many individual cases, has often been misconceived. The view is sometimes expressed, that there can be no pleasure without a previous pain; but this goes beyond the exigencies of the principle. We cannot go on for ever with any delight; but mere remission, without any counterpart pain, is enough for our entering with zest on many of our pleasures. A healthy man enjoys his meals without any sensible previous pain of hunger. We do not need to have been miserable for some time as a preparation for the reading of a new poem. It is true that if the sense of privation has been acute, the pleasure is proportionally increased; and that few pleasures of any great intensity grow up from indifference: still, remission and alternation may give a zest for enjoyment without any consciousness of pain.

The principle of Comparison is capriciously made use of by Paley, in his account of the elements of Happiness. He applies it forcibly and felicitously to depreciate certain pleasures—as greatness, rank, and station—and withholds its application from the pleasures that he more particularly countenances,—namely, the social affections, the exercise of the faculties, and health.

The great praise often accorded to Simplicity of Style, in literature, is an example of the suppression of the correlative in a case of mutual relationship. Simplicity is not an absolute merit; it is frequently a merit by correlation. Thus, if a certain subject has never been treated except in abstruse and difficult terminology, a man of surpassing literary powers, setting it forth in homely and intelligible language, produces a work whose highest praise is expressed by

Simplicity. Again, after the last century period of artificial, complex, and highly-wrought composition, the reaction of Cowper and Wordsworth in favour of simplicity was an agreeable and refreshing change, and was in great part acceptable because of the change. It does not appear that Wordsworth comprehended this obvious fact ; to him, a simplicity that cost nothing to the composer, and brought no novelty to the reader, had still a transcendent merit.

It has been a frequent practice of late years to celebrate the praises of Knowledge. Many eloquent speakers have dilated on the happiness and the superiority of the enlightened and the cultivated man. Now, the correlative or obverse must be equally true : there must be a corresponding degradation and disqualification attaching to ignorance and the want of instruction. This correlative and equally cogent statement is suppressed on certain occasions, and by persons that would not demur to the praises of knowledge : as, when we are told of the native good sense, the untaught sagacity, the admirable instincts of the people,—that is, of the ignorant or the uneducated. Hence the great value of the expository device of following up every principle with its counter-statement, the matter denied when the principle is affirmed. If knowledge is a thing superlatively good, ignorance —the opposite of knowledge—is a thing superlatively bad. There is no middle standing ground.

In the way that people use the argument from

Authority, there is often an unfelt contradiction from not adverting to the correlative implication. If I lay stress upon some one's authority as lending weight to my opinion, I ought to be equally moved in the opposite direction when the same authority is against me. The common case, however, is to make a great flourish when the authority is one way, and to ignore it when it is the other way. This is especially the fashion in dealing with the ancient philosophers. Socrates, Plato, and Aristotle are quoted with much complacency when they chime in with a modern view; but, in points where they contradict our cherished sentiments, we treat them with a kind of pity as half-informed pagans. It is not seen that men liable to such gross errors as they are alleged to have committed—say on Ethics—are by that fact deprived of all weight in allied subjects, as, for example, Politics—in which Aristotle is still quoted as an authority.

Many of the sins against Relativity can be traced to rhetorical exaggeration. Some remarkable instances of this can be cited.

When a system of ranks and dignities has once been established, there are associations of dignity and of indignity with different conditions and occupations. It is more dignified to serve in the army than to engage in trade; to be a surgeon is more honourable than to be a watchmaker. In this state of things a fervid rhetorician, eager to redress the inequalities of mankind, starts forth to preach the dignity of *all* labour. The device is a self-contradiction. Make all labour alike dignified, and nothing is dignified; you simply abolish dignity by depriving it of the contrast that it subsists upon.

Pope's lines—

> Honour and shame from no condition rise;
> Act well your part; there all the honour lies—

cannot be exempted from the fallacy of self-contradiction. Differences of condition are made by differences in the degree of honour thereto attached. If every man that did his work well were put on a level, in point of honour, with every other man that did the same; if the gatekeeper of a mansion, by being unfailingly punctual in opening the gate, were to be equally honoured with a great leader of the House of Commons, then, indeed, equality of pay would be the only thing wanted to abolish all differences of condition. There is, no doubt, in society, a quantity of misplaced honour; but so long as there are employments exceptionally arduous, and virtues signally beneficent in their operation, honour is a legitimate spur and reward, and should be graduated according to the desert in each case.

In spurring the ardour of youth to studious exertion, it is common to repeat the Homeric maxim, "to supplant every one else, and stand out first". The stimulating effect is undoubted; it is strong rhetorical brandy. Yet only one man can be first, and the exhortation is given simultaneously to a thousand.[1]

---

[1] We may here recall an incident highly characteristic of the late Earl of Carlisle. Being elected on one occasion to the office of Lord

In the discussion and inculcation of the moral duties and virtues, there has been, in all ages, a tendency to suppress correlative facts, and to affirm unconditionally what is true only with a condition. Thus, the admirable nature of Justice, and the happiness of the Just man, are a proper theme to be extolled with all the power of eloquence. It has been so with every civilized people, pagan as well as Christian. In the dialogues of Plato, justice is a prominent subject, and is adorned with the full splendour of his genius. Aristotle, in one of the few moments when he rises to poetry, pronounces justice "greater than the evening-star or the morning-star". Now all this panegyric is admissible only on the supposition of *reciprocal* justice. Plato, indeed, had the hardihood to say that the just man is happy in himself, and by reason of his justice, even although others are unjust to him ; but the position is untenable. A man is happy in his justice if it procure for him justice in return ; as a citizen is happy in his civil obedience, if

Rector of Marischal College, Aberdeen, he had to deliver an address to the students on the usual topics of diligence and hopefulness in their studious career. Referring for a model to the addresses of former rectors, he found, in that of his immediate predecessor, Lord Eglinton, the Homeric sentiment above alluded to. It grated harshly on his mind, and he avowed the fact to the students. He could not reconcile himself to the elevating of one man upon the humiliation of all the rest. In a strain more befitting a civilized age, he urged upon his hearers the pursuit of excellence as such, without involving as a necessary accompaniment the supplanting or throwing down of other men. He probably did not sufficiently guard himself against a fallacy of Relativity ; for excellence is purely comparative ; it subsists upon inferior grades of attainment : still, there are many modes of it shared in by a great number, and not confined to one or a few.

it gain him protection in return. There are two parties in the case, and the moralist should obtain access to both; he should induce the one to fulfil his share before promising to the other the happiness of justice and obedience. It may be rhetorical, but it is not true, that justice will make a man happy in a society where it is not reciprocated. Justice, in these circumstances, is highly noble, praiseworthy, virtuous; but the applying of these lofty compliments is the proof that it does not bring happiness, and is an attempt to compensate the deficiency. There is a certain tendency, not very great as human nature is constituted, for justice to beget justice in return—for social virtue on one side to procure it on the other side. This is a certain encouragement to each man to perform his own part, in hope that the other party concerned may do the same. Still, the reciprocity occasionally fails, and with that the benefits to the just agent. It is necessary to urge strongly upon individuals, to impress upon the young, the necessity of performing their duty to society; it is equally implied, and equally indispensable, that society should perform its part to them. The suppressing of the correlative obligation of the State to the individual leaves a one-sided doctrine; the motive of the suppression, doubtless, is that society does not often fail of its duties to the individual, whereas individuals frequently fail of their duties to society. This may be the fact generally, but not always. It is not the fact where there are bad laws and corrupt administration. It is not the fact where the restraints on liberty are greater than the exigencies of the State demand. It is not the fact, so long as there is a single vestige of persecution for opinions. To be thoroughly veracious, for example, in a society that restrains the discussion and expression of opinions, is more than such a society is entitled to.

The same fallacy occurs in an allied theme,—the joys of Love and Benevolence. That love and benevolence are productive of great happiness is beyond question; but then the feeling must be mutual, it must be reciprocated. One-sided love or benevolence is a *virtue*, which is as much as to say it is *not* a pleasure. The delights of benevolence are the delights of reciprocated benevolence; until reciprocated, in some form, the benevolent man has, strictly speaking, the sacrifice and nothing more. There is a great reluctance to encounter this simple naked truth; to state it in theory, at least, for it is fully admitted in practice. We fence it off by the assumption that benevolence will always have its reward somehow; that if the objects of it are ungrateful, others will make good the defect at last. Now these qualifications are very pertinent, very suitable to be urged after allowing the plain truth, that benevolence is intrinsically a sacrifice, a painful act; and that this act is redeemed, and far more than redeemed, by a fair reciprocity of benevolence. Only such an admission can keep us out of a mesh of contradictions. Like justice in itself, Benevolence in itself is painful; any virtue is pain in the first instance, although, when equally responded to, it brings a surplus of pleasure. There may be acts of a beneficent tendency that cost the performer nothing, or that even may chance to be agreeable; but these examples must not be given as the rule, or the type. It is the essence of virtuous acts, the prevailing character of the class, to tax the agent, to deprive him of some satisfaction to himself; this is what we must start from; we are then in a position to explain how and when, and under what circumstances, and with what limitations, the virtuous man, whether his virtue be justice or benevolence, is from that cause a happy man.

It is a fallacy of the suppressed relative to describe virtue as determined by the *moral nature* of God, as opposed to his arbitrary will. The essence of Morality is obedience to a superior, to a Law; where there is no superior there is nothing either moral or immoral. The supreme power is incapable of an immoral act. Parliament may do what is injurious, it cannot do what is illegal. So the Deity may be beneficent or maleficent, he cannot be moral or immoral.

Among the various ways, proposed in the seventeenth century, of solving the difficulty of the mutual action of the heterogeneous agencies—matter and mind—one was a mode of Divine interference, called the "Theory of Occasional Causes". According to this view, the Deity exerted himself by a *perpetual miracle* to bring about the mental changes corresponding to the physical agents operating on our senses—light, sound, &c. Now in the mode of action suggested there is nothing self-contradictory; but in the use of the word "miracle" there is a mistake of relativity. The meaning of a miracle is an exceptional interference; it supposes an habitual state of things, from which it is a deviation. The very idea of miracle is abolished if every act is to be alike miraculous.

We shall devote the remainder of this exposition to a still more notable class of mistakes due to the suppression of a correlative member in a relative couple—those, namely, connected with the designation, "Mystery," a term greatly abused, in various ways, and especially by disregarding its relative character. Mystery supposes certain things that are plain, intelligible, knowable, revealed; and, by contrast to these, refers to certain other things that are obscure, unintelligible, unknowable, unrevealed. When a man's conduct is entirely plain, straightforward, or accounted for, we call that an intelligible case; when we are perplexed by the tortuosities of a crafty, double-dealing person, we say it is all very mysterious. So, in nature, we consider that we understand certain phenomena: such as gravity, and all its consequences, in the fall of bodies, the flow of rivers, the motions of the planets, the tides. On the other hand, earthquakes and volcanoes are very mysterious; we do not know what they depend upon, how or in what circumstances they are produced. Some of the operations of living bodies are understood,—as the heart's action in the mechanical propulsion of the blood; others, and the greater number, are mysterious, as the whole process of germination and growth. Now the existence of the contrast between things plainly understood, and things not understood, gives one distinct meaning to the term Mystery. In some cases, a mystery is formed by an apparent contradiction, as in the Theological mystery of Freewill and Divine Foreknowledge; here, too, there is a contrast with the great mass of consistent and reconcilable things. But now, when we are told by sensational writers, that *everything is mysterious;* that the simplest phenomenon in nature—the fall of a stone, the swing of a pendulum, the continuance of a ball shot in the air—are wonderful, marvellous, miraculous, our understanding is confounded; there being then nothing plain at all, there is nothing mysterious. The wonderful rises from the common; as the lofty is lofty by relation to something lower: if there is nothing common, then there is nothing wonderful; if all phenomena are mysterious, nothing is mysterious; if we are to stand aghast in amazement because three times four is twelve, what phenomenon can we take as the type of the plain and the intelligible? You must always keep up a standard of the common, the easy, the comprehensible, if you are to regard other things as wonderful, difficult, inexplicable.

The real character of a MYSTERY, and what constitutes the Explanation of a fact, have been greatly misconceived. The changes of view on these points make up a chapter in the history of the education of the human mind. Perhaps the most decisive turning point was the publication of Locke's "Essay concerning Human Understanding," the motive of which, as stated in the homely and forcible language of the preface, was to ascertain what our understandings can do, what subjects they are fit to deal with, and where they should stop. I quote a few sentences:—

"If by this inquiry into the nature of the Under-"standing, I can discover the powers thereof; how "far they reach; to what things they are in any "degree proportionate; and where they fail us: I "suppose it may be of use, to prevail with the busy "mind of man to be more cautious in meddling with "things exceeding its comprehension; to stop when "it is at the utmost extent of its tether; and to sit "down in a quiet ignorance of those things which, "upon examination, are proved to be beyond the "reach of our capacities." "The candle that is set "up in us, shines bright enough for all our purposes. "The discoveries we can make with this ought to "satisfy us. And we shall then use our Understand-"ings aright, when we entertain all objects in that "way and proportion that they are suited to our "faculties, and upon those grounds they are capable "of being proposed to us." "It is of great use for "the sailor to know the length of his line, though he "cannot fathom with it all the depths of the ocean."

The course of physical science was preparing the same salutary lesson. Locke's great contemporary and friend, Isaac Newton, was his fellow-worker in this tutorial undertaking; nor should Bacon be forgotten, although there is dispute as to the extent and character of his influence. The combined operation of these great leaders of thought was apparent in the altered views of scientific inquirers as to what is competent in research—what is the proper aim of inquiry. There arose a disposition to abandon the pursuit of mysterious essences and grand pervading unities, and ascertain with precision the facts and the laws of natural phenomena. The study of astronomy was inaugurated in Greenwich Observatory. The experiments of Priestley and of Franklin farther exemplified the eighteenth-century key to the secrets of the universe.

The lesson imparted by Newton and Locke and their successors still remains to be carried out and embodied in the subtler inquiries. The bearing upon what constitutes a Mystery, and what constitutes Explanation, or the accounting for appearances, may be expressed thus:—

In the first place, the Understanding can never pass out of its own experience—its acquired knowledge, whether of body or of mind. What we obtain by our various sensibilities to the world about us, and by our self-consciousness, are the foundation, the A B C of everything that we are capable of knowing. We know colours, and we know sound; we know pleasure and pain, and the various emotions of wonder, fear, love, anger. If there be any being endowed with senses different from ours, with that being we can have no communion. If there be any phenomena that escape our limited sensibilities, they transcend the possibility of our knowledge.

It is necessary, however, to take account of the combining or constructive aptitudes of the mind. We can go a certain length in putting together our alphabet of sensation and experience into many various compounds. We can imagine a paradise or a pandemonium ; but only as made up of our own knowledge of things good and evil. The limits of this constructive power are soon reached. We are baffled to enter into the feelings of our own kindred, when they are far removed in character and circumstances from ourselves. The youth at twenty cannot approximate to the feelings of men of middle age. The healthy are unable to comprehend the life of the invalid.

To come to the practical applications. The great leading notions called Time and Space are known to us only under the conditions of our own sensibility. Time is made known by all our actions, all our senses, all our feelings, and by the succession of our thoughts; it is experienced as a continuance and a repetition of movement, sight, sound, fear, or any other state of feeling, or of thinking. One motion or sensation is continued longer than another ; or it is more frequently repeated after intermission, giving the *numerical* estimate of time, as in the beats of the pendulum. In these ways we form estimates of seconds, minutes, hours, days. And our constructive faculty can be brought into play to conceive the larger tracts of duration—a century, or a hundred centuries. Nay, by our arithmetical powers we can put down in cipher, or conceive *symbolically* (which is the meagrest of all conceptions) millions of millions of centuries; these being after all but compounds of our alphabet of enduring or repeated sensations and thoughts. We can suppose this arithmetical process to operate upon past duration or upon future duration, and there is no limit to the numbers that we can write down. But there is one thing that we cannot do; we cannot fix upon a point when Time or succession began, or upon a point when it will cease. That is an operation not in keeping with our faculties; the very supposition is impracticable. We cannot entertain the notion of a state of things wherein the fact of continuance had no place; the effort belies itself. Time is inseparable from our mental nature; whatever we imagine, we must imagine as enduring. Some philosophers have supposed that we must be endowed by nature with the conception of Time, before we begin to exercise our senses; but the difficulty would be to deprive us of that adjunct without extinguishing our mental nature. Give us sensibility, and you cannot withhold the element of Time. The supposition of Kant and others, that it is implanted in us as an empty form, before we begin to employ our senses upon things, is needless; for as soon as we move, see, hear, think, are pleased or pained, we create time. And our notion of Time in general is exactly what these sensibilities make it, only enlarged by our constructive power already spoken of.

While all our senses and feelings give us time, it is

our experience of Motion and Resistance,—the energetic or active side of our nature alone,—that gives us Space. The simplest feature of Space is the alternation of Resistance and Non-Resistance, of obstructed motion and freedom to move. The hand presses dead upon an obstacle; the obstacle gives way and allows free motion; these two contrasting experiences are the elements of the two contrasting facts—Matter and Space. By none of the five senses, in their pure and proper character as senses, can we obtain these experiences; and hence at an earlier stage of inquiry into the mind, when our knowledge-giving sensibilities were referred to the five senses, there was no adequate account of the notion of Space or Extension. Space includes more than this simple contrast of the resisting and the non-resisting; it includes what we call the Co-existing or Contemporaneous, the great aggregate of the outspread world, as existing at any moment, a somewhat complicated attainment, which I am not now specially concerned with. It sufficiently illustrates the limitation of our knowledge by our sensibilities, from the nature of space, to fasten attention on the double and mutually supplementing experience of Matter and Void; the one resisting movement, and giving the consciousness of resistance, or dead strain, the other permitting movement, and giving the consciousness of the unobstructed sweep of the limbs or members. Whatever else may be in space, this freedom to move, to soar, to expatiate (in contrast to being hemmed in, obstructed, held fast), is an essential part of the conception, and is formed out of our active or moving sensibilities. Now, as far as movement is concerned, we must be in one of two states:—we must be putting forth energy without effecting movement, being met by obstacles called matter; or we must be putting forth energy unresisted and effecting movement, which is what we mean by empty space. There is no third position in the matter of putting forth our active energy. Where resistance ends and freedom begins, there is space; where freedom ends, and obstruction begins, there is matter. We find our sentient life to be made up, as regards movement, of a certain number and range of these two alternations; in other words, free spaces and resisting barriers. And we can, by the constructive power already mentioned, imagine other proportions of the two experiences; we can imagine the scope for movement, the absence of obstruction, to be enlarged more and more, to be counted by thousands and millions of miles; but the only terminus or boundary that we can imagine is resistance, a dead obstacle. We are able to conceive the starry spaces widened and prolonged from galaxy to galaxy through enormous strides of increasing amplitude, but when we try to think an end to this career, we can think only of a dead wall. There is no other end of space within the grasp of our faculties; and that termination is not an end of extension; for we know that solid matter, viewed in other ways than as obstructing movement, has the same property of the extended belonging to the empty void. The inference is, that the limitation of our means of knowledge renders altogether incompetent the imagination of an end to either Time or Space. The greatest efforts of our combining faculty cannot exceed the elements presented to it, and these elements contain nothing that would set forth the situation of space ending, and obstruction not beginning.

Under these circumstances, it is an irrevelant enquiry, to ask, Are Time and Space finite or infinite? Many philosophers have put the question, and even answered it. They say Time has no beginning and no end, and Space has no boundaries; or, as otherwise expressed,—Time and Space are Infinite: an answer of such vagueness as to mean anything, from a harmless and proper assertion of the limits of our faculties, up to the verge of extravagance and self-contradiction.

When, in fact, people talk of the Infinite in Time and Space, they can point to one intelligible signification; as to the rest, this word is not a subject for scientific propositions, and the attempt at such can lead only to contradictions. The Infinite is a phrase most various in its purport: it is for the most part an emotional word, expressing human desire and aspiration; a word of poetry, imagination, and preaching, not a word to be discussed under science; no intellectual definition would exhibit its emotional force.

The second property of our intelligence is, that we can generalise many facts into one. Tracing agreement among the multifarious appearances of things, we can comprehend in one statement a vast number of details. The single law of gravity expresses the fall of a stone, the flow of rivers, the retention of the moon in her circuit round the earth. Now, this generalising sweep is a real advance in our knowledge, an ascent in the matter of intelligence, a step towards centralising the empire of science. What is more, this is the only real meaning of EXPLANATION. A difficulty is solved, a mystery unriddled, when it can be shown to resemble something else; to be an example of a fact already known. Mystery is isolation, exception, or, it may be, apparent contradiction; the resolution of the mystery is found in assimilation, identity, fraternity. When all things are assimilated, so far as assimilation can go, so far as likeness holds, there is an end to explanation; there is an end to what the mind can do, or can intelligently desire.

Thus, when Gravity was generalised, by assimilating the terrestrial attraction seen in falling bodies with the celestial attraction of the sun and planets; and when, by fair presumption, the same power was extended to the remote stars; when, also, the *law* was ascertained, so that the movements of the various bodies could be computed and predicted, there was nothing further to be done; explanation was exhausted. Unless we can find some other force to fraternise with gravity, so that the two might become a still more comprehensive unity, we must rest in gravity as the ultimatum of our faculties. There is no conceivable modification, or substitute, that would better our position. Before Newton, it was a mystery what kept the moon and the planets in their places; the assimilation with falling bodies was the solution. But, say many persons, is not gravity itself a mystery? We say No; gravity has passed through all the stages of legitimate and possible explanation; it is the most highly generalised of all physical facts, and by no assignable transformation could it be made more intelligible than it is. It is singularly easy of comprehension; its law is exactly known; and, excepting the details of calculation, in its more complex workings, there is nothing to complain of, nothing to rectify, nothing to pretend ignorance about; it is the very pattern, the model, the consummation of knowledge. The path of science, as exhibited in modern times, is towards generality, wider and wider, until we reach the highest, the widest laws of every department of things; there explanation is finished, mystery ends, perfect vision is gained.

What is always reckoned the mystery by pre-eminence is the union of BODY and MIND. How, then, should we treat this Mystery according to the spirit of modern thought, according to the modern laws of explanation? The course is to *conceive* the elements according to the only possible plan, our own sensibility or consciousness; which gives us matter as one class of facts—extension, inertness, weight, and so on; and mind as another class of facts—pleasures, pains, volitions, ideas. The difference between these two is total, diametrical, complete; there is really nothing common to the experience of pleasure and the experience of a tree; difference has here reached its *acme;* agreement is eliminated; there is no higher genus to include these two in one; as the ultimate, the highest elements of knowledge, they admit of no fusion, no resolution, no unity. Our utmost flight of generality leaves us in possession of a double, a *couple* of absolutely heterogeneous elements. Matter cannot be resolved into mind; mind cannot be resolved into matter; each has its own definition; each negatives the other.

This being the fact, we accept it, and acquiesce. There is surely nothing to be dissatisfied with, to complain of, in the circumstance that the elements of our experience are, in the last resort, two, and not one. If we had been provided with fifty ultimate experiences, none of them having a single property in common with any other; and if we had only our present limited intellects, we might be entitled to complain of the world's mysteriousness in the one proper acceptation of mystery—namely, as overpowering our means of comprehension, as loading us with unassimilable facts. As it is, matter, in its commoner aspects and properties, is perfectly intelligible; in the great number and variety of its endowments or properties, it is revealed to us slowly and with much difficulty, and these subtle properties— the deep affinities and molecular arrangements—are the mysteries rightly so called. Mind in itself is also intelligible; a pleasure is as intelligible as would be any transmutation of it into the inscrutable essence that people often desiderate. It is one of the facts of our sensibility, and has a great many facts of its own kindred, which makes it all the more intelligible.

The varieties of pleasure, pain, and emotion are very numerous; and to know, remember, and classify them, is a work of labour, a *legitimate* mystery. The subtle links of thought are also very various, although probably all reducible to a small number; and the ascertaining and following out of these has been a work of labour and time; they have, therefore, been mysterious; mystery and intellectual toil being the real correlatives. The *complications* of matter and the *complications* of mind are genuine mysteries; the reducing or simplifying of these complications, by the exertions of thinking men, is the way, and the only way out of the darkness into light.

But what now of the mysterious *union* of the two great ultimate facts of human experience? What should the followers of Newton and Locke say to this crowning instance of deep and awful mystery? Only one answer can be given. Accept the union, and generalise it. Find out the fewest number of simple laws, such as will express all the phenomena of this conjoint life. Resolve into the highest possible generalities the connections of pleasure and pain, with all the physical stimulants of the senses—food, tastes, odours, sounds, lights—with all the play of feature and of gesture, and all the resulting movements and bodily changes; and when you have done that, you have so far truly, fully, finally explained the union of body and mind. Extend your generalities to the course of the thoughts; determine what physical changes accompany the memory, the reason, the imagination, and express those changes in the most general, comprehensive laws, and you have explained the how and the why brain causes thought, and thought works in brain. There is no other explanation needful, no other competent, no other that would be explanation. Instead of our being "unfortunate," as is sometimes said, in not being able to know the essence of either matter or mind—in not comprehending their union; our misfortune would be to have to know anything different from what we do or may know. If there be still much mystery attaching to this linking of the two extreme facts of our experience, it is simply this: that we have made so little way in ascertaining what in one goes with what in the other. We know a good deal about the feelings and their alliances, some of which are open and palpable to all mankind; and we have obtained some important generalities in these alliances. Of the connections of thought with physical changes we know very little: these connections, therefore, are truly and properly mysterious; but they are not intrinsically or hopelessly so. The advancing study of the physical organs, on the one hand, and of the mental functions, on the other, may gradually abate this mystery. And if a day arrive when the links that unite our intellectual workings with the workings of the nervous system and the other bodily organs shall be fully ascertained and adequately generalised, no one thoroughly educated in the scientific spirit of the last two centuries will call the union of mind and body any longer inscrutable or mysterious.

III.

THE CIVIL SERVICE EXAMINATIONS.

THE CIVIL SERVICE EXAMINATIONS.*

I. HISTORICAL SKETCH.

UP to the year 1853, the appointing of Civil Servants lay wholly in the hands of patrons. In 1853, patronage was severely condemned and competitive examination officially recommended, for the first time, in a Report by Sir Stafford Northcote and Sir Charles Trevelyan; but, while the recommendation was taken up in the following year and immediately acted upon in the Indian Civil Service, it was not till very much later that it was fully adopted in the Home Service. The history, indeed, of this last is somewhat peculiar. After the Report already referred to, came an Order of Council, of date May 21, 1855, in which we find it " ordered that all such young men as may be proposed to be appointed to any junior situation in any department of the Civil Service shall, before they are admitted to probation, be examined by or under the Directors of the said Commissioners, and shall receive from them a Certificate of Qualification for such situation". This order was rigorously carried out by

* *The Civil Service Examination Scheme, considered with reference* (1) *to Sciences, and* (2) *to Languages.* A paper read before the Educational Section of the Social Science Association, at the meeting in Aberdeen, 1877 : with additions relevant to Lord Salisbury's Scheme.

the Commissioners, and, although its absolute requirement was simply that the nominees should pass a certain examination, it, nevertheless, allowed the heads of departments to institute competition if they cared. Accordingly, we find that competition—*but limited*—was immediately set on foot in several of the offices, and the result led to the following remark in the Report of 1856:—

"We do not think it within our province to discuss the expediency of adopting the principle of open competition as contra-distinguished from examination; but we must remark that, both in the competitive examination for clerkships in our own and in other offices, those who have succeeded in attaining the appointments have appeared to us to possess considerably higher attainments than those who have come in upon simple nomination; and, we may add, that we cannot doubt that if it be adopted as a usual course to nominate several candidates to compete for each vacancy, the expectation of this ordeal will act most beneficially on the education and industry of those young persons who are looking forward to public employment."

In 1857, a near approach was made to open competition, in the case of four clerkships awarded by the competing examination in the Commissioners' own establishment. "The fact of the competition was not made public, but was communicated to one or two heads of schools and colleges, and mentioned casually to other persons at various times. The number of competitors who presented themselves was forty-six, of which number, forty-four were actually examined."

It was reserved for 1858 to see the first absolutely open competition, in the case of eight writerships in the Office of the Secretary of State for India; and in that year, too, a step in advance was made when the Commissioners in their Report "pointed out the advantage which would result from enlarging the field of competition by substituting, for the plan of nominating three persons only to compete for each vacant situation, the system of nominating a proportionate number of candidates to compete for several appointments at one examination".

The year 1860 sounded the death-knell of simple pass examination. It was then recommended by a Select Committee of the House of Commons, and the recommendation was adopted, that the competitive method, in its limited form, should be henceforth *universally* applied to junior situations. This recommendation was at once acted upon in the case of clerkships under the control of the Lords Commissioners of the Treasury, and others by and by followed; but, as matter of fact, it was never strictly carried out in all its scope and rigour; and as late as 1868 the Commissioners in their Report stated that "the number of situations filled on the competitive method has been comparatively small". Meanwhile, competitive examination was making way in other quarters.

From 1857, the Commissioners had been in the habit of examining competitively, at the request of the Lord Lieutenant of Ireland, such candidates as might be nominated for cadetships in the Royal Irish Constabulary; and, in 1861, the Lords Commissioners of the Admiralty "threw open to public competition" appointments as apprentices in Her Majesty's dockyards, and appointments as "engineer students" in the steam factories connected therewith.

In 1870, the end so long aimed at was attained, and by an Order in Council of June 4, open competition was made the only door of entry to the general Civil Service.

In entire contrast with this, as has been already said, was the action in the case of the Indian Civil Service. Here the principle of open competition was adopted from the first, and the examination took a very elevated start, comprising the highest branches of a learned education. These branches were duly specified in a Report drawn up in November, 1854, by a Committee, of which Lord Macaulay was chairman; and, with the exception of Sanskrit and Arabic, they included simply (as might have been expected) the literary and scientific subjects ordinarily taught at the principal seats of general education in the Kingdom. These were :—

English Language and Literature (Composition, History, and General Literature,—to each of which 500 marks were assigned, making a total of 1,500); Greek and Latin (each with 750 marks); French, German, and Italian (valued at 375 marks, respectively); Mathematics, pure and mixed (marks 1,000); Natural and Moral Sciences (each 500); Sanscrit and Arabic (375 each).

The principle of selection here is clear and obvious. It did not rest upon any doctrine regarding the utility or value of subjects for mental training, but simply upon this, that those subjects already in the field must be accepted, and that (as Mr. Jowett, in his letter to Sir Charles Trevelyan, of January, 1854, put it) "it will not do to frame our examination on any mere theory of education. We must test a young man's ability by what he knows, not by what we wish him to know." Indeed, this is explicitly avowed in the Report by the author of the Scheme himself. The Natural Sciences are included, because (it is confessed) "of late years they have been introduced as a part of general education into several of our universities and colleges": and, as for the Moral Sciences, "those Sciences are, it is well known, much studied both at Oxford and at the Scottish Universities".

Into the details of Macaulay's interesting Report, I need not here enter. Room, however, must be found for one quotation. It deals with the distribution of marks, and is both characteristic and puts the matter in small compass. "It will be necessary," says the writer, "that a certain number of marks should be assigned to each subject, and that the place of a candidate should be determined by the sum total of the marks which he has gained. The marks ought, we conceive, to be distributed among the subjects of examination in such a manner that no part of the kingdom, and no class of schools, shall exclusively furnish servants to the East India Company. It would be grossly unjust, for example, to the great academical institutions of England, not to allow skill in Greek and Latin versification to have a considerable share in determining the issue of the competition. Skill in Greek and Latin versification has, indeed, no direct tendency to form a judge, a financier, or a diplomatist. But the youth who does best what all the ablest and most ambitious youths about him are trying to do well will generally prove a superior man; nor can we doubt that an accomplishment by which Fox and Canning, Grenville and Wellesley, Mansfield and Tenterden first distinguished themselves above their fellows, indicates powers of mind, which, properly trained and directed, may do great service to the State. On the other hand, we must remember that in the north of this island the art of metrical composition in the ancient languages is very little cultivated, and that men so eminent as Dugald Stewart, Horner, Jeffrey, and Mackintosh, would probably have been quite unable to write a good copy of Latin alcaics, or to translate ten lines of Shakspeare into Greek iambics. We wish to see such a system of examination established as shall not exclude from the service of the East India Company either a Mackintosh or a Tenterden, either a Canning or a Horner."

Now, reverting to Macaulay's Table of Subjects as above exhibited, I may observe that, till quite recently, no very serious alterations were ever made upon it. The scale of marks, indeed, was altered more than once, and sometimes Sanskrit and Arabic were struck off, and Jurisprudence and Political Economy put in

ORIGINAL SCHEME FOR THE INDIA SERVICE.

their stead; but, if we except the exclusion of Political Philosophy in 1858, at the desire of the present Lord Derby, from the Moral Science branch, the list remained, till Lord Salisbury's late innovation, to all intents and purposes what it was at the beginning. Here, for instance, is the prescription for 1875:—

English Composition					500
History of England, including that of the laws and constitution.					500
English Language and Literature.					500
Language, literature, and history of Greece					750
,,	,,	,,	,,	Rome	750
,,	,,	,,	,,	France	375
,,	,,	,,	,,	Germany	375
,,	,,	,,	,,	Italy	375
Mathematics, pure and mixed					1,250
Natural Sciences, that is, (1) chemistry, including heat; (2) electricity and magnetism; (3) geology and mineralogy; (4) zoology; (5) botany					1,000

*** The total (1,000) marks may be obtained by adequate proficiency in any two or more of the five branches of science included under this head.

Moral Sciences, that is, logic, mental and moral philosophy	500
Sanskrit, language and literature.	500
Arabic, language and literature	500

But Lord Salisbury's changes have been great and sweeping. They are probably in keeping with the restriction of the competitor's age to " over 17 under

19"; but, if so, they serve only to shew all the more conclusively that the restriction is a mistake. A scheme that distributes marks on anything but a rational and intelligent system; a scheme that excludes the Natural History Sciences, Mineralogy and Geology, as well as Psychology and Moral Philosophy from its scope altogether; a scheme that prescribes only *Elements* and *Outlines* of such important subjects as Natural Science (Chemistry, Electricity and Magnetism, &c.) and Political Economy—stands self-condemned. But, to do it justice, let us produce the Table *in extenso* :—

	MARKS.
English Composition	300
History of England, including *a period selected by the candidate*	300
English Literature, including *books selected* by the candidate	300
Greek	600
Latin	800
French	500
German	500
Italian	400
Mathematics, pure and mixed	1,000
Natural Science, that is, the *Elements* of any two of the following Sciences viz. :—	
Chemistry, 500; Electricity and Magnetism, 300; Experimental Laws of Heat and Light, 300; Mechanical Philosophy, with *Outlines* of Astronomy, 300.	
Logic	300

Elements of Political Economy	300
Sanskrit	500
Arabic	500

Further remarks are reserved for the sequel. Meanwhile, I give the scheme advocated by myself in the present Essay:—

GENERAL SCIENCES:—

Mathematics	500
Natural Philosophy	500
Chemistry	500
Biology, as physiology	500
Mental Science	500

SPECIAL OR CONCRETE SCIENCES:—

Mineralogy	
Botany	each 250
Zoology	or 300
Geology	

As a substitute for language, literature, and philosophy of Greece, Rome, France, Germany, and Italy:—

Greece—Institutions and History	500
„ Literature	250
Rome—Institutions and History	500
„ Literature	250
France—Literature	250
Germany „	250
Italy „	250
Modern History	1,000

II. THE SCHEME CONSIDERED.

The system of competitive examinations for the

public service, of which I have laid before the Section a brief history compiled from the Reports, is one of those radical innovations that may ultimately lead to great consequences. For the present, however, it leads to many debates. Not merely does the working out of the scheme involve conflicting views, but there is still, in many quarters, great hesitation as to whether the innovation is to be productive of good or of evil. The Report of the Playfair Commission, and the more recent Report relative to the changes in the India Civil Service Regulations, indicate pretty broadly the doubts that still cleave to many minds on the whole question. It is enough to refer to the views of Sir Arthur Helps, W. R. Greg, and Dr. Farr, expressed to the Playfair Commission, as decidedly adverse to the competitive system. The authorities cited in the Report on the India Examinations scarcely go the length of total condemnation; but many acquiesce only because there is no hope of a reversal.

The question of the expediency of the system as a whole is not well suited to a sectional discussion. We shall be much better employed in adverting to some of those details in the conduct of the examinations that have a bearing on the general education of the country, as well as on the Civil Service itself. It was very well for the Commissioners, at first starting, to be guided, in their choice of subjects and in their assigning of values to those subjects, by the received branches of education in the schools and colleges. But, sooner or later, these subjects must be discussed on their intrinsic merits for the ends in view. Indeed, the scheme of Lord Salisbury has already made the venture that Macaulay declined to make; it has absolutely excluded some of the best recognised subjects of our school and college teaching, instead of leaving them to the option of the candidates.

I will occupy the present paper with the consideration of two departments in the examination programme—the one relating to the PHYSICAL or NATURAL SCIENCES, the other relating to LANGUAGES.

The Commissioners' scheme of Mathematics and Natural Science is not, in my opinion, accordant either with the best views of the relations of the sciences, or with the best teaching usages.

In the classification of the Sciences, the first and most important distinction is between the fundamental sciences, sometimes called the Abstract sciences, and the derivative or Concrete branches. My purpose does not require any nice clearing of the meanings of those technical terms. It is sufficient to say that the fundamental sciences are those that embrace distinct departments of the natural forces or phenomena; and the derivative or concrete departments assume all the laws laid down in the others, and apply them in certain spheres of natural objects. For example, Chemistry is a primary, fundamental, or abstract science; and Mineralogy is a derivative and concrete science. In Chemistry the stress lies in explaining a peculiar kind of force, called chemical force; in Mineralogy the stress is laid on the description and classification of a select group of natural objects.

The fundamental, or departmental sciences, as most commonly accepted, are these :—1. Mathematics; 2. Natural Philosophy, or Physics; 3. Chemistry; 4. Biology; 5. Psychology. They may be, therefore, expressed as Formal, Inanimate, Animate, and Mental. In these sciences, the idea is to view exhaustively some department of natural phenomena, and to assume the order best suited for the elucidation of the phenomena. Mathematics, the Formal Science, exhausts the relations of Quantity and Number; measure being a universal property of things. Natural Philosophy, in its two divisions (molar and molecular), deals with one kind of force; Chemistry with another: and the two together conspire to exhaust the phenomena of *inanimate* nature; being indispensably aided by the laws and formulæ of quantity, as given in Mathematics. Biology turns over a new leaf; it takes up the phenom no —Life, or the *animated* world. Finally, Psychology makes another stride, and embraces the sphere of *mind*.

Now, there is no fact or phenomenon of the world that is not comprised under the doctrines expounded in some one or other of these sciences. We may have fifty "ologies" besides, but they will merely repeat for special ends, or in special connections, the principles already comprised in these five fundamental subjects. The regular, systematic, exhaustive account of the laws of nature is to be found within their compass.

Again, these sciences have a fixed order or sequence, the order of dependence. Mathematics precedes them all, as being not dependent upon any, while all are more or less dependent upon it. The physical forces have to be viewed prior to the chemical; and both physical and chemical forces are preparatory to vital. So there are reasons for placing Mental Science last of all. Hence a student cannot comprehend chemistry without natural philosophy, nor biology without both. You cannot stand a thorough examination in chemistry without indirectly showing your knowledge of physics; and a testing examination in biology would guarantee, with some slight qualifications, both physics and chemistry.

Let us now turn to the other sciences—those that are not fundamental, but derivative. The chief examples are the three commonly called Natural History sciences—Mineralogy, Botany, Zoology. In these sciences no law or principle is at work that has not been already brought forward in the primary sciences. The properties of a Mineral are mathematical, physical, and chemical: the testing of minerals is by measurement, by physical tests, by chemical tests. The aim of this science is not to teach forces unknown to the student of physics and chemistry; it is to embrace, under the best classification, all the bodies called minerals, and to describe the species in detail under mathematical, physical, and chemical characters. It is the first in order of the *classificatory* sciences. Its purpose in the economy of education is distinct and peculiar; it imparts knowledge, not respecting laws, forces, or principles of operating, but respecting the concrete constituents of the world. It gives us a commanding view of one whole department of the material universe; supplying information useful in practice, and interesting to the feelings. It also brings into exercise the great logical process, wanted on many occasions, the process of CLASSIFICATION.

So much for an instance from the Inorganic world, as showing the distinction between the two kinds of sciences. Another example may be cited from the field of Biology; it is a little more perplexing. For "biology" is sometimes given as the name for the two concrete classificatory sciences—botany and zoology. In point of fact, however, there is a science that precedes those two branches, although blending with them; the science commonly expressed by the older term, 'Physiology, which is not a classificatory and a dependent science, but a mother science, like chemistry. It expounds the peculiarities of living bodies, as such, and the laws of living processes—such processes as assimilation, nutrition, respiration, innervation, reproduction, and so on. One division is Vegetable Physiology, which is generally fused with the classificatory science of botany. Animal Physiology is allied with zoology, but more commonly stands alone. Lastly, the Physiology of the Human animal has been from time immemorial a distinct branch of knowledge, and is, of course, the chief of them all. Man being the most complicated of all organised beings, not only are the laws of his vitality the most numerous, and the most practically interesting, but they go far to include all that is to be said of the workings of animal life in general. Thus, then, the mother science of Biology, as a general or fundamental science, comprises Vegetable, Animal, and Human physiology. The classificatory adjunct sciences are Botany and Zoology. It is in the various aspects of the mother science that we look for the account of all vital phenomena, and all practical applications to the preservation of life. Even if we stop at these, we shall have a full command of the laws of the animate world. But we may go farther, and embrace the sciences that arrange, classify, and describe the innumerable host of living beings. These have their own independent interest and value, but they are not the sciences that of themselves teach us the living processes.

Thus, then, a proper scheme of scientific instruction starts from the essential, fundamental, and law-giving sciences—Mathematics, Physics, Chemistry, Biology, and Mind. It then proceeds to the adjunct branches —such as Mineralogy, Botany, Zoology: and I might add others, as Geology, Meteorology, Geography, no one of which is primary; for they all repeat in new connections, and for special purposes, the laws systematically set forth in the primary sciences.

In the foregoing remarks, I do not advance any new or debatable views. I believe the scientific world to be substantially in accord upon all that I have here stated; any differences that there are in the manner of expressing the points do not affect my present purpose—namely, to discuss the scheme of the mathematical and physical sciences as set forth in the Civil Service Examinations.

Under Mathematics (pure and mixed) the Commissioners (in their Scheme of 1875), include mathematics, properly so called, and those departments of natural philosophy that are mathematically handled—statics, dynamics, and optics. But the next branch, entitled "Natural Science," is what I am chiefly to remark upon. Under it there is a fivefold enumeration: —(1) Chemistry, including Heat; (2) Electricity and Magnetism; (3) Geology and Mineralogy; (4) Zoology; (5) Botany. I cannot pretend to say where the Commissioners obtained this arrangement of natural knowledge. It is not supported by any authority that I am acquainted with. If the scheme just set forth is the correct one, it has *three* defects. First, it does not embrace in one group the remaining parts of natural philosophy, the *experimental* branches which, with the mathematical treatment, complete the department; one of these, Heat, is attached to chemistry, to which undoubtedly it has important relations, but not such as to withdraw it from physics and embody it in chemistry. Then, again, the physical branches, Electricity and Magnetism, are coupled in a department and made of co-equal value with chemistry together with heat. I need not say that the united couple—electricity and magnetism—is in point of extent of study not a half or a third of what is included in the other coupling. Lastly, the three remaining members of the enumeration are three natural history sciences; geology being coupled with mineralogy—which is a secondary consideration. Now I think it is quite right that these three sciences should have a place in the competition. What is objectionable is, that Biology is represented solely by its two classificatory components or adjuncts, botany and zoology; there is no mother science of Physiology: and consequently the knowledge of the vast region of the Laws of Life goes for nothing. Nor can it be said that physiology is given with the others. The subject of *vegetable* physiology could easily enough be taken with Botany: I would not make a quarrel upon this part. It is zoology and animal physiology that cannot be so coupled. If we look to the questions actually set under zoology, we shall see that there is no pretence to take in physiology. I contend, therefore, that there is a radical omission in the scheme of natural science; an omission that seems without any justification. I am not here to sing the praises of Physiology: its place is fixed and determined by the concurrence of all competent judges: I merely point out that Zoology does not include it, but presupposes it.

The Science scheme of the London University, to which the first Civil Service Commissioners, Sir Edward Ryan and Sir John Lefevre, were parties, is very nearly what I contend for. It gives the order—Mathematics, Natural Philosophy, Chemistry, Biology,

Mental Science (including Logic). In the working of that scheme, however, Biology is made to comprehend both the mother science, Physiology, and the two classificatory sciences, Botany and Zoology. Of course the presence of two such enormous adjuncts cramps and confines the purely physiological examination, which in my opinion should have full justice done to it in the first instance: still, the physiology is not suppressed nor reduced to a mere formality. Now, in any science scheme, I would provide for the general sciences first, and take the others, so far as expedient, in a new grouping, where those of a kind shall appear together, and stand in their proper character, not as law-giving, but as arranging and describing sciences. There is no more reason for coupling Zoology with Physiology, than for tacking on Mineralogy to Chemistry. In point of outward form, Mineralogy and Zoology are kindred subjects.

When the subjects are placed in the order that I have suggested, there is an end of that promiscuous and random choosing that the arrangement of the Commissioners suggests and encourages. To the specification of the five heads of natural science, it is added, that the whole of the 1,000 marks may be gained by high eminence in any two; as if the choice were a matter of indifference. Now, I cannot think that this suggestion is in conformity with a just view of the continuity of science. When the sciences are rightly arranged, there is but one order in the mother sciences; if we are to choose a single science, it must be (with some qualifications) the first; if two, the first and second, and so on. To choose one of the -higher sciences, Chemistry or Physiology, without the others that precede, is irrational. Indeed, it would scarcely ever be done, and for this reason. A man cannot have mastered Physiology without having gone through Physics and Chemistry ; and, although it is not necessary that he should retain a hold of everything in these previous sciences, yet he is sure to have done enough in both one and the other to make it worth his while to take these up in the examination. So a good chemist must have so much familiarity with Physics, as to make it bad economy on his part not to give in Physics as well. The only case where an earlier science might be dropped is Mathematics ; for although that finds its application extensively in Physics and indirectly in Chemistry, yet there is a very large body of physical and chemical doctrine that is not dependent upon any of the more difficult branches, so that these may admit of being partially neglected. But, as an examination in Physics ought to include (as in the London University) all the mathematical applications, short of the higher calculus, it is not likely that Mathematics would be often dropped. So that, as regards the *mother* sciences, the variation of choice would be reduced to the different lengths that the candidate would go in the order as laid down. As regards the other sciences—those of *classification* and *description* — the selection might certainly be arbitrary to this extent, that Mineralogy, Botany, and Zoology might each be prescribed alone. But then, whoever presented one of these would also present the related mother science. He that took up Mineralogy, would infallibly also take up the three first as far as Chemistry. He that gave in Botany would probably take up Physiology, although not so necessarily, because the area of plant Physiology is very limited, and has little bearing on descriptive Botany, so that anything like a familiarity with Physiology might be evaded. But he that took up Zoology, would to a certainty take up Physiology; and very probably also the antecedent members of the fundamental group. As to Geology, it is usually coupled with Mineralogy, although involving also a slight knowledge of Botany and Zoology. A competent mineralogist would be pretty sure to add Geology to his professional subjects.

Before considering the re-arrangement of marks entailed by the proposed distribution of the sciences, I must advert to the position of Mathematics in the Commissioners' scheme. This position was first assigned in the original draft of 1854, and on the motives therein set forth with such ostentatious candour; namely, the wish to reward the existing subjects of teaching, whatever they might be. Now, I contend that it is wholly beside the ends either of the Indian Civil Service, or of the Home Service, with known exceptions, to stimulate the very high mathematical knowledge that has hitherto entered into the examination scheme. A certain amount of Mathematics, the amount required in a pass examination in the London University, is essential as a basis of rational culture; but, for a good general education, all beyond that is misdirected energy. After receiving the modicum required, the student should pass on to the other sciences, and employ his strength in adding Experimental Physics and Chemistry to his stock. Whether a candidate succeeds or fails in the competitions, this is his best policy.

Without arguing the point farther, I will now come to the amended scheme of science markings. It would be over-refining, and would not bring conviction to the general public, to make out a case for inequality in the five fundamental branches. It may be said that Physiology is of more value than Chemistry, because it is farther on, and takes Chemistry with it; the answer is, let the Physiology candidate go in and take marks in Chemistry also, which he is sure to do. I have purposely avoided all discussion about Mental Science; I merely assume it as a branch co-ordinate with the prior sciences placed before it in the general list. I would then simply, in conclusion, give the *primary sciences*, Mathematics, Natural Philosophy, Chemistry, Biology (as explained), Mental Philosophy, each 500 marks. The other sciences, Mineralogy, Botany, Zoology, Geology, I would make equal as between themselves, but somewhat lower than the primaries. The reasons are already apparent: the candidate for them would always have some of the others to present; and their importance is, on the whole, less than the importance of the law-giving sciences. I should conceive that 250 or 300 marks apiece would be a proper amount of consideration shewn towards them. With that figure, I believe many science students could take up one or other in addition to the general sciences.

The other topic that I am to bring forward is one of very serious import. It concerns the Civil Service competitions only as a part of our whole scheme of Education. I mean the position of LANGUAGES in our examinations. While the vast field of Natural Science is comprised in one heading, with a total of 1,000 marks (raised finally to 1,400), our Civil Service scheme presents a row of five languages besides our own—two ancient, and three modern—with an aggregate value of 2,625 marks, or 2,800, as finally adjusted. The India scheme has, in addition, Sanskrit and Arabic, at 500 marks each; the reasons for this prescription being, however, not the same as for the foregoing.

The place of Language in education is not confined to the question as between the ancient and the modern languages. There is a wider enquiry as to the place of languages as a whole. In pursuing this enquiry, we may begin with certain things that are obvious and incontestable.

In the first place, it is apparent that if a man is sent to hold intercourse with the people of a foreign nation, he must be able to understand and to speak the language of that nation. Our India civil servants are on that ground required to master the Hindoo spoken dialects.

In the next place, if a certain range of information that you find indispensable is locked up in a foreign language, you are obliged to learn the language. If, in course of time, all this information is transferred to our native tongue, the necessity apparently ceases. These two extreme suppositions will be allowed at once. There may, however, be an indefinite number of intermediate stages. The information may be partially translated; and it will then be a question whether the trouble of learning the language should be incurred for the sake of the untranslated part. Or, it may be wholly translated: but, conscious of the necessary defects even of good translations, if the subject-matter be supremely important, some people will think it worth while to learn the language in order to obtain the knowledge in its greatest purity and precision. This is a situation that admits of no certain rule. Our clergy are expected to know the original languages of the Bible, notwithstanding the abundance of translations; many of which must be far superior in worth and authority to the judgment of a merely ordinary proficient in Hebrew and in Greek.

It is now generally conceded that the classical languages are no longer the exclusive depository of any kind of valuable information, as they were two or three centuries ago. Yet they are still continued in the schools as if they possessed their original function unabated. We do not speak in them, nor listen to them spoken, nor write in them, nor read in them, for obtaining information. Why then are they kept up? Many reasons are given, as we know. There is an endeavour to show that even in their original function, they are not quite effete. Certain professions are said to rely upon them for some points of information not fully communicated by the medium of English. Such is the rather indirect example of the clergy with Greek. So, it is said that Law is not thoroughly understood without Latin, because the great source of law, the Roman code, is written in Latin, and is in many points untranslatable. Further, it is contended that Greek philosophy cannot be fully mastered without a knowledge of the language of Plato and Aristotle. But an argument that is reduced to these examples must be near its vanishing point. Not one of the cases stands a rigorous scrutiny; and they are not relied upon as the main justification of the continuance of classics A new line of defence is opened up which was not at all present to the minds of sixteenth century scholars. We are told of numerous indirect and secondary advantages of cultivating language in general and the classic languages in particular, which make the acquisition a rewarding labour, even without one particle of the primary use. But for these secondary advantages, languages could have no claim to appear, with such enormous values, in the Civil Service scheme.

My purpose requires me to advert in these alleged secondary uses of language, not, however, for the view of counter-arguing them, but rather in order to indicate what seems to me the true mode of bringing them to the proof.

The most usual phraseology for describing the indirect benefit of languages is, that they supply a *training* to the powers of the mind; that, if not information, they are *culture*; that they re-act upon our mastery of our own language, and so on. It is quite necessary, however, to find phrases more definite and tangible than the slippery words "culture" and "training": we must know precisely what particular powers or aptitudes are increased by the study of a foreign language. Nevertheless, the conclusions set forth in this paper do not require me to work out an exhaustive review of these advantages. It is enough to give as many as will serve for examples.

Now, it must be freely admitted as a possible case, that a practice introduced in the first instance for a particular purpose, may be found applicable to many other purposes; so much so, that, ceasing to be employed for the original use, the practice may be kept up for the sake of the after uses. For example, clothing was no doubt primarily contrived for warmth; but it is not now confined to that: decoration or ornament, distinction of sexes, ranks and offices, modesty—are also attained by means of clothes. This example is a suggestive one. We have only to suppose ourselves migrating to some African climate, where clothing for warmth is absolutely dispensed with. We should not on that account adopt literal nudity — we should still desire to maintain those other advantages. The artistic decoration of the person would continue to be thought of; and, as no amount of painting and tattooing, with strings of beads superadded, would answer to our ideal of personal elegance, we should have recourse to some light filmy textures, such as would allow the varieties of drapery, colours, and design, and show off the poetry of motion ; we should also indicate the personal differences that we were accustomed to show by vesture. But now comes the point of the moral; we should not maintain our close heavy fabrics, our great-coats, shawls and cloaks. These would cease with the need for them. Perhaps the first emigrants would keep up the prejudice for their warm things, but not so their successors.

Well, then, suppose the extreme case of a foreign language that is entirely and avowedly superseded as regards communication and interpretation of thoughts, but still furnishing so many valuable aids to mental improvement, that we keep it up for the sake of these. As we are not to hear, speak, or read the language, we do not need absolutely to know the meaning of every word : we may, perhaps, dispense with much of the technicality of its grammar. The vocables and the grammar would be kept up exactly so far as to serve the other purposes, and no farther. The teacher would have in view the secondary uses alone. Supposing the language related to our own by derivation of words, and that this was what we put stress upon ; then the derivation would always be uppermost in the teacher's thoughts. If it were to illustrate Universal Grammar and Philology, this would be brought out to the neglect of translation.

I have made an imaginary supposition to prepare the way for the real case. The classical or language teacher, is assumed to be fully conscious of the fact that the primary use of the languages is as good as defunct; and that he is continued in office because of certain clearly assigned secondary uses, but for which he would be superseded entirely. Some of the secondary uses present to his mind, at all events one of those that are put forward in argument, is that a foreign language, and especially Latin, conduces to good composition in our own language. And as we do compose in our own language, and never compose in Latin, the teacher is bound to think mainly of the English part of the task—to see that the pupils succeed in the English translation, whether they succeed in the other or not. They may be left in a state of considerable ignorance of good Latin forms (ignorance will never expose them); but any defects in their English expression will be sure to be disclosed. Again, it is said that Universal Grammar or Philology is taught upon the basis of a foreign language. Is this object, in point of fact, present to the mind of every teacher, and brought forward, even to the sacrifice of the power of reading and writing, which, by the supposition, is never to be wanted? Further, the Latin Grammar is said to be a logical discipline. Is this, too, kept in view as a predominating end? Once more, it is declared that, through the classics, we attain the highest cultivation of Taste, by seeing models of unparalleled literary form. Be it so: is this habitually attended to in the teaching of these languages?

I believe I am safe in saying that, whilst these various secondary advantages are put forward in the polemic as to the value of languages, the teaching practice is by no means in harmony therewith.

Even when in word the supporters of classics put forward the secondary uses, in deed they belie themselves. Excellence in teaching is held by them to consist, in the first instance, in the power of accurate interpretation,—as if that obsolete use were still *the* use. If a teacher does this well, he is reckoned a good teacher, although he does little or nothing for the other ends, which in argument are treated as the reason of his existence. Indeed, this is the kind of teaching that is alone to be expected from the ordinary teacher; all the other ends are more difficult than simple word teaching. Even when English Composition, Logic and Taste are taught in the most direct way, they are more abstruse than the simple teaching of a foreign language for purposes of interpretation; but when tacked on as accessories to instruction in a language, they are still more troublesome to impart. A teacher of rare excellence may help his pupils in English style, in philology, in logic, and in taste; but the mass of teachers can do very little in any of those directions. They are never found fault with merely because their teaching does not rise to the height of the great arguments that justify their vocation; they would be found fault with, if their pupils were supposed to have made little way in that first function of language which is never to be called into exercise.

I do not rest satisfied with quoting the palpable inconsistency between the practice of the teacher and the polemic of the defender of languages. I believe, further, that it is not expedient to carry on so many different acquisitions together. If you want to teach thorough English, you need to arrange a course of English, allot a definite time to it, and follow it with undivided attention during that time. If you wish to teach Philology you must provide a systematic scheme, or else a text-book of Philology, and bring together all the most select illustrations from languages generally. So for Logic and for Taste. These subjects are far too serious to be imparted in passing allusions while the pupil is engaged in struggling with linguistic difficulties. They need a place in the programme to themselves; and, when so provided for, the small dropping contributions of the language teacher may easily be dispensed with.

The argument for Languages may, no doubt, take a bolder flight, and go so far as to maintain that the teacher does not need to turn aside from his plain path to secure these secondary ends—now the only valuable ends. The contention may be that in the close and rigorous attention to mere interpretation, just as if interpretation were still the living use, these other purposes are inevitably secured—good English, universal grammar, logic, taste, &c. I think, however, that this is too far from the fact to be very confidently maintained. Of course, were it correct, the teacher should never have departed from it, as the best teachers continually do, and glory in doing.

On the face of the thing, it must seem an unworkable position to surrender the value of a language, as a language, and keep it up for something else. The teaching must always be guided by the original, although defunct, use; this is the natural, the easy, course to follow; for the mass of teachers at all times it is the broad way. Whatever the necessities of argument may drive a man to say, yet in his teaching he cannot help postulating to himself, as an indispensable fiction, that his pupils are some day or other to hear, to read, to speak, or to write the language.

The intense conservatism in the matter of Languages—the alacrity to prescribe languages on all sides, without inquiring whether they are likely to be turned to account—may be referred to various causes. For one thing—although the remark may seem ungracious and invidious—many minds, not always of the highest force, are absorbed and intoxicated by languages. But apart from this, languages are, by comparison, easy to teach, and easy to examine upon. Now, if there is any motive in education more powerful than another, it is ease in the work itself. We are all, as teachers, copyists of that Irish celebrity who, when he came to a good bit of road, paced it to and fro a number of times before going forward to his destination on the rougher footing.

So far I may seem to be arguing against the teaching of language at all, or, at any rate, the languages expressively called dead. I am not, however, pressing this point farther than as an illustration. I do not ask anyone to give an opinion against Classics as a subject of instruction; although, undoubtedly, if this opinion were prevalent, my principal task would be very much lightened. I have merely analysed the utilities ascribed to the ancient and the modern languages, with a view to settling their place in competitive examinations.

My thesis, then, is, that languages are not a proper subject for competition with a view to professional appointments. The explanation falls under two heads.

In the first place, there are certain avocations where a foreign language must be known, because it has to be used in actual business. Such are the Indian spoken languages. Now, it is clear that in these cases the knowledge of the language, as being a *sine quâ non*, must be made imperative. This, however, as I think, is not a case for competition, but for a sufficient pass. There is a certain pitch of attainment that is desirable even at first entering the service, no one should fall below this, and to rise much above it cannot matter a great deal. At all events, I think the measure should be absolute and not relative. I would not give a man merit in a competition because another man happens to be worse than himself in a matter that all must know; both the men may be absolutely bad.

It may be the case that certain languages are so admirably constructed and so full of beauties that to study them is a liberal education in itself. But this does not necessarily hold of every language that an official of the British Empire may happen to need. It does not apply to the Indian tongues, nor to Chinese, nor, I should suppose, to the Fiji dialects. The only human faculty that is tested and brought into play in these acquisitions is the commonest kind of memory exercised for a certain time. The value to the Service of the man that can excel in spoken languages does not lie in his superior administrative ability, but in his being sooner fitted for actual duty. Undoubtedly, if two men go out to Calcutta so unequal in their knowledge of native languages, or in the preparation for that knowledge, that one can begin work in six months, while the other takes nine, there is an important difference between them. But what is the obvious mode of rewarding the difference? Not, I should think, by pronouncing one a higher man in the scale of the competition, but by giving him some money prize in proportion to the redemption of his time for official work.

Now, as regards the second kind of languages— those that are supposed to carry with them all the valuable indirect consequences that we have just reviewed. There are in the Civil Service Scheme five such languages — two ancient, and three modern. They are kept there, not because they are ever to be read or spoken in the Service, but because they exercise some magical efficacy in elevating the whole tone of the human intellect.

If I were discussing the Indian Civil Service in its own specialities, I would deprecate the introduction of extraneous languages into the competition, for this reason, that the Service itself taxes the verbal powers more than any other service. I do not think that Lord Macaulay and his colleagues had this circumstance fully in view. Macaulay was himself a glutton for language ; and, while in India, read a great quantity of Latin and Greek. But he was exempted from the ordinary lot of the Indian civil servant; he had no native languages to acquire and to use. If a man both speaks and writes in good English, and converses familiarly in several Oriental dialects, his language memory is sufficiently well taxed, and if he carries with him one European language besides, it is as much as belongs to the fitness of things in that department.

My proposal, then, goes the length of excluding all these five cultivated languages from the competition, notwithstanding the influence that they may be supposed to have as general culture. In supporting it, I shall assume that everything that can be said in their favour is true to the letter : that they assist us in our own language, that they cultivate logic and taste, that they exemplify universal grammar, and so on. All that my purpose requires is to affirm that the same good ends may be attained in other ways : that Latin, Greek, &c., are but one of several instruments for instructing us in English composition, reasoning, or taste. My contention, then, is that the *ends* themselves are to be looked to, and not the means or instruments, since these are very various. English composition is, of course, a valuable end, whether got through the study of Latin, or through the study of English authors themselves, or through the inspiration of natural genius. Whatever amount of skill and attainment a candidate can show in this department should be valued *in the examination for*

English; and all the good that Latin has done for him would thus be entered to his credit. If, then, the study of Latin is found the best means of securing good marks in English, it will be pursued on that account; if the candidate is able to discover other less laborious ways of attaining the end, he will prefer these ways.

The same applies to all the other secondary ends of language. Let them be valued *in their own departments*. Let the improvement of the reasoning faculty be counted wherever that is shown in the examination. Good reasoning powers will evince themselves in many places, and will have their reward.

The principle is a plain and obvious one. It is that of payment for results, without inquiring into the means. There are certain extreme cases where the means are not improperly coupled with the results in the final examination; and these are illustrations of the principle. Thus, in passing a candidate for the medical profession, the final end is his or her knowledge of diseases and their remedies. As it is admitted, however, that there are certain indispensable preparatory studies—anatomy, physiology, and materia medica—such studies are made part of the examination, because they contribute to the testing for the final end

The argument is not complete until we survey another branch of the subject of examination in languages. It will be observed in the wording of the programme that each separate language is coupled with 'literature and history (or, as latterly expressed, 'literature—including books selected by the candidate')'. It is the Language, Literature, and History of Rome, Greece, &c. And the examination questions show the exact scope of these adjuncts, and also the values attached to them, as compared with the language by itself.

Let us consider this matter a little. Take History first, as being the least perplexed. Greece and Rome have both a certain lasting importance attaching to their history and institutions; and these accordingly are a useful study Of course, the extant writings are the chief groundwork of our knowledge of these, and must be read. But, at the present day, all that can be extracted from the originals is presented to the student in English books; and to these he is exclusively referred for this part of his knowledge. In the small portion of original texts that a pupil at school or college toils through, he necessarily gets a few of the historical facts at first hand; but he could much more easily get these few where he gets the rest—in the English compilations. Admitting, then, that the history and institutions of Greece and Rome constitute a valuable education, it is in our power to secure it independently of the original tongues.

The other branch—Literature—is not so easily disposed of. In fact, the separating of the literature from the language, you will say, is a self-evident absurdity. That, however, only shows that you have not looked carefully into examination papers. I am not concerned with what the *a priori* imagination may suppose to be Literature, but with the actual questions put by examiners under that name. I find that such questions are, generally speaking, very few, perhaps one or two in a long paper, and nearly all pertain to the outworks of literature, so to speak. Here is the Latin literature of one paper:—In what special branch of literature were the Romans independent of the Greeks? Mention the principal writers in it, with the peculiar characteristics of each. Who was the first to employ the hexameter in Latin poetry, and in what poem? To what language is Latin most nearly related; and what is the cause of their great resemblance? The Greek literature of the same examination involves these points:—The Aristophanic estimate of Euripides, with criticisms on its taste and justice (for which, however, a historical subject is given as an alternative); the Greek chorus, and choric metres. Now such an examination is, in the first place, a most meagre view of literature · it does not necessarily exercise the faculty of critical discernment. In the next place, it is chiefly a matter of compilation from English sources; the actual readings of the candidate in Greek and Latin would be of little account in the matter. Of course, the choric metres could not be described without some knowledge of Greek, but the matter is of very trifling importance in an educational point of view. Generally speaking, the questions in literature, which in number bear no proportion to historical questions, are such as might be included under history, as the department of the History of Literature.

The distribution of the 750 marks allotted respectively to Latin and to Greek, in the scheme of 1875, is this. There are three papers: two are occupied exclusively with translation. The third is language, literature, and history: the language means purely grammatical questions; so that possibly 583 marks are for the language proper. The remaining number, 167, should be allotted equally between literature and history, but history has always the lion's share, and is in fact the only part of the whole examination that has, to my mind, any real worth. It is generally a very searching view of important institutions and events, together with what may be called their philosophy. Now, the reform that seems to me to be wanted is to strike out everything else from the examination. At the same time, I should like to see the experiment of a *real* literary examination, such as did not necessarily imply a knowledge of the originals.

It is interesting to turn to the examination in modern languages, where the ancient scheme is copied, by appending literature and history. Here the Literature is decidedly more prominent and thorough. There is also a fair paper of History questions. What strikes us, however, in this, is a slavish adherence to the form, without the reality, of the ancient situation. We have independent histories of Greece and Rome, but scarcely of Germany, France, and Italy. Instead of partitioning Modern European history among the language-examiners for English, French, German, Italian, it would be better to relieve them of history altogether, and place the subject as a whole in the hands of a distinct examiner. I would still allow merit for a literary examination in French, German, and Italian, but would strike off the languages, and let the candidate get up the literature as he chose. The basis of a candidate's literary knowledge, and his first introduction to literature, ought to be his own language: but he may extend his discrimination and his power by other literatures, either in translations or in originals, as he pleases; still the examination, as before, should test the discrimination and the power, and not the vocabulary of the languages themselves.

In order to do full justice to classical antiquity, I would allow markings at the rate of 500 for Political Institutions and History, and 250 for Literature. Some day this will be thought too much; but political philosophy or sociology may become more systematic than at present, and history questions will then take a different form.

In like manner, I would abolish the language-examination in modern languages, and give 250 marks for the literature of each of the three modern languages—French, German, Italian. The history would be taken as Modern History, with an adequate total value.

The objections to this proposal will mainly resolve themselves into its revolutionary character. The remark will at once be made that the classical languages would cease to be taught, and even the modern languages discouraged. The meaning of this I take to be, that, if such teaching is judged solely by its fruits, it must necessarily be condemned.

The only way to fence this unpalatable conclusion, is to maintain that the results could not be fully tested in an examination as suggested. Some of these are so fine, impalpable, and spiritual in their texture, that they cannot be seized by any questions that can be put; and would be dropped out if the present system were changed. But results so untraceable cannot be proved to exist at all.

So far from the results being missed by disusing the exercises of translation, one might contend that they would only begin to be appreciated fairly when the whole stress of the examination is put upon them. If an examiner sets a paper in Roman Law, containing long Latin extracts to be translated, he is starving the examination in Law by substituting for it an examination in Latin. Whatever knowledge of Latin terminology is necessary to the knowledge of Law should be required, and no more. So, it is not an examination in Aristotle to require long translations from the Greek; only by dispensing with all this, does the main subject receive proper attention.

If the properly literary part of the present examinations were much of a reality, there would be a nice discussion as to the amount of literary tact that could be imparted in connection with a foreign language, as translated or translatable. But I have made an ample concession, when I propose that the trial should be made of examining in literature in this fashion, and I do not see any difficulty beyond the initial repugnance of the professors of languages to be employed in this task, and the fear, on the part of candidates, that undue stress might be placed on points that need a knowledge of originals.

I will conclude with a remark on the apparent tendency of the wide options in the Commissioners' scheme. No one subject is obligatory; and the choice is so wide that by a very narrow range of acquirements a man may sometimes succeed. No doubt, as a rule, it requires a considerable mixture of subjects : both sciences and literature have to be included. But I find the case of a man entering the Indian Service by force of Languages alone, which I cannot but think a miscarriage. Then the very high marks assigned to Mathematics allow a man to win with no other science, and no other culture, but a middling examination in English. To those that think so highly of foreign languages, this must seem a much greater anomaly than it does to me. I would prefer, however, that such a candidate had traversed a wider field of science, instead of excelling in high mathematics alone.

There are, I should say, *three* great regions of study that should be fairly represented by every successful candidate. The first is the Sciences as a whole, in the form and order that I have suggested. The second is English Composition, in which successful men in the Indian competition sometimes show a cipher. The third is what I may call loosely the Humanities, meaning the department of institutions and history, with perhaps literature : to be computed in any or all of the regions of ancient and modern history. In every one of these three departments, I would fix a minimum, below which the candidate must not fall.

IV.
THE CLASSICAL CONTROVERSY.
ITS PRESENT ASPECT.

THE CLASSICAL CONTROVERSY.

ITS PRESENT ASPECT.

IN the present state of the controversy on classical studies, the publication of George Combe's contributions to Education is highly opportune. Combe took the lead in the attack on these studies fifty years ago, and Mr. Jolly, the editor of the volume, gives a connected view of the struggle that followed. The results were, on the whole, not very great. A small portion of natural science was introduced into the secondary schools; but as the classical teaching was kept up as before, the pupils were simply subjected to a greater crush of subjects; they could derive very little benefit from science introduced on such terms. The effect on the Universities was *nil;* they were true to Dugald Stewart's celebrated deliverance on their conservatism.[2] The general public, however, were

[1] CONTEMPORARY REVIEW, August, 1879. A few months previously, there were printed, in the Review, papers on the Classical question, by Professors Blackie and Bonamy Price; both of which are here alluded to and quoted, so far as either is controverted or concurred with.

[2] "The academical establishments of some parts of Europe are not without their use to the historian of the human mind. Immovably moored to the same station by the strength of their cables and the weight of their anchors, they enable him to measure the rapidity of the current by which the rest of the world is borne along."

not unmoved; during a number of years there was a most material reduction in the numbers attending all the Scotch Universities, and the anti-classical agitation was reputed to be the cause.

The reasonings of Combe will still repay perusal. He puts with great felicity and clearness the standing objections to the classical system; while he is exceedingly liberal in his concessions, and moderate in his demands. "I do not denounce the ancient languages and classical literature on their own account, or desire to see them cast into utter oblivion. I admit them to be refined studies, and think that there are individuals who, having a natural turn for them, learn them easily and enjoy them much. They ought, therefore, to be cultivated by all such persons. My objection is solely to the practice of rendering them the main substance of the education bestowed on young men who have no taste or talent for them, and whose pursuits in life will not render them a valuable acquisition."

Before alluding to the more recent utterances in defence of classical teaching, I wish to lay out as distinctly as I can the various alternatives that are apparently now before us as respects the higher education—that is to say, the education begun in the secondary or grammar schools, and completed and stamped in the Universities.

1. The existing system of requiring proficiency in both classical languages. Except in the University of London, this requirement is still imperative. The other Universities agree in exacting Latin and Greek as the condition of an Arts' Degree, and in very little

else. The defenders of classics say with some truth that these languages are the principal basis of uniformity in our degrees; if they were struck out, the public would not know what a degree meant.

How exclusive was the study of Latin and Greek in the schools in England, until lately, is too well known to need any detailed statement. A recent utterance of Mr. Gladstone, however, has felicitously supplied the crowning illustration. At Eton, in his time, the engrossment with classics was such as to keep out religious instruction!

As not many contend that Latin and Greek make an education in themselves, we may not improperly call to mind what other things it has been found possible to include with them in the scope of the Arts' Degree. The Scotch Universities were always distinguished from the English in the breadth of their requirements: they have comprised, for many ages, three other subjects mathematics, natural philosophy, and mental philosophy (including logic and ethics). In exceptional instances, another science is added; in one case, natural history, in another, chemistry. According to the notions of scientific order and completeness in the present day, a full course of the primary sciences would comprise mathematics, natural philosophy, chemistry, physiology or biology, and mental philosophy. The natural history branches are not looked upon as primary sciences; they give no laws, but repeat the laws of the primary sciences while classifying the kingdoms of Nature. (See above, p. 81).

In John Stuart Mill's celebrated Address at St. Andrews, he stood up for the continuance of the Classics in all their integrity, and suddenly became a great authority with numbers of persons who probably had never treated him as an authority before. But his advocacy of the classics was coupled with an equally strenuous advocacy for the extension of the scientific course to the full circle of the primary sciences; that is to say, he urged the addition of chemistry and physiology to the received sciences. Those that have so industriously brandished his authority for retaining classics, are discreetly silent upon this other recommendation. He was too little conversant with the working of Universities to be aware that the addition of two sciences to the existing course was impracticable; and he was never asked which alternative he would prefer. I am inclined to believe that he would have sacrificed the classics to scientific completeness; he would have been satisfied with the quantum of these already gained at school. But while we have no positive assurance on this point, I consider that his opinion should be wholly discounted as not bearing on the actual case.

The founders of the University of London attempted to realise Mill's conception to the full. They retained Classics; they added English and a modern language, and completed the course of the primary sciences by including both Chemistry and Physiology. This was a noble experiment, and we can now report on its success. The classical languages, English and

French or German, mathematics and natural philosophy, and (after a time) logic and moral philosophy, were all kept at a good standard; thus exceeding the requirements of the Scotch Universities at the time by English and a modern language. The amount of attainment in chemistry was very small, and was disposed of in the Matriculation examination. Physiology was reserved for the final B.A. examination, and was the least satisfactory of all. Having myself sat at the Examining Board while Dr. Sharpey was Examiner in Physiology, I had occasion to know that he considered it prudent to be content with a mere show of studying the subject. Thus, though the experience of the University of London, as well as of the Scotch Universities, proves that the classical languages are compatible with a very tolerable scientific education, yet these will need to be curtailed if every one of the fundamental sciences, as Mill urged, is to be represented at a passable figure.

In the various new proposals for extending the sphere of scientific knowledge, a much smaller amount of classics is to be required, but neither of the two languages is wholly dispensed with. If not taught at college, they must be taken up at school as a preparation for entering on the Arts' curriculum in the University. This can hardly be a permanent state of things, but it is likely to be in operation for some time.

2. The remitting of Greek in favour of a modern language is the alternative most prominently before the public at present. It accepts the mixed form of

the old curriculum, and replaces one of the dead languages by one of the living. Resisted by nearly the whole might of the classical party, this proposal finds favour with the lay professions as giving one language that will actually be useful to the pupils as a language. It is the very smallest change that would be a real relief. That it will speedily be carried we do not doubt.

Except as a relaxation of the grip of classicism, this change is not altogether satisfactory. That there must be two languages (besides English) in order to an Arts' Degree is far from obvious. Moreover, although it is very desirable that every pupil should have facilities at school or at college for commencing modern languages, these do not rank as indispensable and universal culture, like the knowledge of sciences and of literature generally. They would have to be taught along with their respective literatures to correspond to the classics.

Another objection to replacing classics by modern languages is the necessity of importing foreigners as teachers. Now, although there are plenty of Frenchmen and Germans that can teach as well as any Englishman, it is a painful fact that foreigners do oftener miscarry, both in teaching and in discipline, with English pupils, than our own countrymen. Foreign masters are well enough for those that go to them voluntarily with the desire of being taught ; it is as teachers in a compulsory curriculum that their inferiority becomes apparent.

The retort is sometimes made to this proposal—

Why omit Greek rather than Latin? Should you not retain the greater of the two languages? This may be pronounced as mainly a piece of tactics; for every one must know that the order of teaching Latin and Greek at the schools will never be topsyturvied to suit the fancy of an individual here and there, even although John Stuart Mill himself was educated in that order. On the scheme of withdrawing all foreign languages from the imperative curriculum, and providing for them as voluntary adjuncts, such freedom of selection would be easy.[1]

3. Another alternative is to remit both Latin and Greek in favour of French and German. Strange to say, this advance upon the previous alternative was actually contained in Mr. Gladstone's ill-fated Irish University Bill. Had that Bill succeeded, the Irish would have been for fourteen years in the enjoyment of a full option for both the languages.[2] From a careful perusal of the debates, I could not discover that the opposition ever fastened upon this bold surrender of the classical exclusiveness.

The proposal was facilitated by the existence of professors of French and German in the Queen's

[1] If the two Literatures were studied, as they might be, by means of expositions and translations, the Greek would be first as a thing of course. Historians of the Latin authors are obliged to trace their subject, in every department, to the corresponding authors in Greece.

[2] No doubt the classical languages would have been required, to some extent, in matriculating to enter college. This arrangement, however, as regarded the students that chose the modern languages, would have been found too burdensome by our Irish friends, and, on their expressing themselves to that effect, would have been soon dispensed with.

Colleges. In the English and Scotch Colleges endowments are not as yet provided for these languages; although it would be easy enough to make provision for them in Oxford and Cambridge.

In favour of this alternative, it is urged that the classics, if entered on at all, should be entered on thoroughly and entirely. The two languages and literatures form a coherent whole, a homogeneous discipline; and those that do not mean to follow this out should not begin it. Some of the upholders of classics take this view.

4. More thorough-going still is the scheme of complete bifurcation of the classical and the modern sides. In our great schools there has been instituted what is called the *modern side*, made up of sciences and modern languages, together with Latin. The understanding hitherto has been, that the votaries of the ancient and classical side should alone proceed to the Universities; the modern side being the introduction to commercial life, and to professions that dispense with a University degree. Here, as far as the schools are concerned, a fair scope is given to modern studies.

As was to be expected, the modern side is now demanding admission to the Universities on its own terms; that is, to continue the same line of studies there, and to be crowned with the same distinctions as the classical side. This attempt to render school and college homogeneous throughout, to treat ancient studies and modern studies as of equal value in the eye of the law, will of course be resisted to the utmost.

Yet it seems the only solution likely to bring about a settlement that will last.

The defenders of the classical system in its extreme exclusiveness are fond of adducing examples of very illustrious men who at college showed an utter incapacity for science in its simplest elements. They say that, by classics alone, these men are what they are, and if their way had been stopped by serious scientific requirements, they would have never come before the world at all. The allegation is somewhat strongly put; yet we shall assume it to be correct, on condition of being allowed to draw an inference. If some minds are so constituted for languages, and for classics in particular, may not there be other minds equally constituted for science, and equally incapable of taking up two classical languages? Should this be granted, the next question is—Ought these two classes of minds to be treated as equal in rights and privileges? The upholders of the present system say, No. The Language mind is the true aristocrat; the Science mind is an inferior creation. Degrees and privileges are for the man that can score languages, with never so little science; outer darkness is assigned to the man whose *forte* is science alone. But a war of caste in education is an unseemly thing; and, after all the levelling operations that we have passed through, it is not likely that this distinction will be long preserved.

The modern side, as at present constituted, still retains Latin. There is a considerable strength of feeling in favour of that language for all kinds of people; it is thought to be a proper appendage of the lay professions; and there is a wide-spread opinion in favour of its utility for English. So much is this the case, that the modern-siders are at present quite willing to come under a pledge to keep up Latin, and to pass in it with a view to the University. In fact, the schools find this for the present the most convenient arrangement. It is easier to supply teaching in Latin than in a modern language, or in most other things; and while Latin continues to be held in respect, it will remain untouched. Yet the quantity of time occupied by it, with so little result, must ultimately force a departure from the present curriculum. The real destination of the modern side is to be modern throughout. It should not be rigorously tied down even to a certain number of modern languages. English and one other language ought to be quite enough; and the choice should be free. On this footing, the modern side ought to have its place in the schools as the co-equal of classics; it would be the natural precursor of the modernised alternatives in the Universities; those where knowledge subjects predominate.

The proposal to give an *inferior degree* to a curriculum that excludes Greek should, in my judgment, be simply declined. It is, however, a matter of opinion whether, in point of tactics, the modern party did not do well to accept this as an instalment in the meantime. The Oxford offer, as I understand it, was so far liberal, that the new degree was to rank equal in privileges with the old, although inferior in *prestige*.

In Scotland, the degree conceded by the classical party to a Greekless education was worthless, and was offered for that very reason.[1]

Among the adherents of classics, Professor Blackie is distinguished for surrendering the study of them in the case of those that cannot profit by them. He believes that with a free alternative, such as the thorough bifurcation into two sides would give, they would still hold their ground, and bear all their present fruits. His classical brethren, however, do not in general share this conviction. They seem to think that if they can no longer compel every University graduate to pass beneath the double yoke of Rome and Greece, these two illustrious nationalities will be in danger of passing out of the popular mind altogether. For my own part, I do not share their fears, nor do I think that, even on the voluntary footing, the study of the two languages will decline with any great rapidity. As I have said, the belief in Latin is wide and deep. Whatever may be urged as to the extraordinary stringency of the intellectual discipline now said to be given by means of Latin and Greek, I am satisfied that the feeling with both teachers and scholars is, that the process of acquisition is not toilsome to either party; less so perhaps than anything that would come in their place. Of the hundreds of hours spent over them, a very large number are associated with listless idleness. Carlyle describes

---

[1] One possible consequence of a Natural Science Degree might have been, that the public would have turned to it with favour, while the old one sank into discredit.

Scott's novels as a beatific lubber land"; with the exception of the "beatific," we might say nearly the same of classics. To all which must be added the immense endowments of classical teaching; not only of old date but of recent acquisition. It will be a very long time before these endowments can be diverted, even although the study decline steadily in estimation.

The thing that stands to reason is to place the modern and the ancient studies on exactly the same footing; to accord a fair field and no favour. The public will decide for themselves in the long run. If the classical advocates are afraid of this test, they have no faith in the merits of their own case.

The arguments *pro* and *con* on the question have been almost exhausted. Nothing is left except to vary the expression and illustration. Still, so long as the monopoly exists, it will be argued and counter-argued; and, if there are no new reasons, the old will have to be iterated.

Perhaps the most hackneyed of all the answers to the case for the classics is the one that has been most rarely replied to. I mean the fact that the Greeks were not acquainted with any language but their own. I have never known an attempt to parry this thrust. Yet, besides the fact itself, there are strong presumptions in favour of the position that to know a language well, you should devote your time and strength to it alone, and not attempt to learn three or four. Of course, the Greeks were in possession of the most perfect language, and were not likely to be gainers by studying the languages of their contemporaries. So, we too are in possession of a very admirable language, although put together in a nondescript fashion; and it is not impossible that if Plato had his Dialogues to compose among us, he would give his whole strength to working up our own resources, and not trouble himself with Greek. The popular dictum—*multum non multa*, doing one thing well—may be plausibly adduced in behalf of parsimony in the study of languages.

The recent agitation in Cambridge, in Oxford, and indeed, all over the country, for remitting the study of Greek as an essential of the Arts' Degree, has led to a reproduction of the usual defences of things as they are. The articles in the March number of the *Contemporary Review, 1879,* by Professors Blackie and Bonamy Price, may claim to be the *derniers mots.*

Professor Blackie's article is a warning to the teachers of classics, to the effect that they must change their front; that, whereas the value of the classics as a key to thought has diminished, and is diminishing, they must by all means in the first place improve their drill. In fact, unless something can be done to lessen the labour of the acquisition by better teaching, and to secure the much-vaunted intellectual discipline of the languages, the battle will soon be lost. Accordingly, the professor goes minutely into what he conceives the best methods of teaching. It is not my purpose to follow him in this sufficiently interesting discussion. I simply remark that he is staking the case, for the continuance of Latin and Greek in the schools, on the possibility of something like an entire revolution in the teaching art. Revolution is not too strong a word for what is proposed. The weak part of the new position is that the value of the languages *as languages* has declined, and has to be made up by the incident of their value as *drill*. This is, to say the least, a paradoxical position for a language teacher. If it is mere drill that is wanted, a very small corner of one language would suffice. The teacher and the pupil alike are placed between the two stools—interpretation and drill. A new generation of teachers must arise to attain the dexterity requisite for the task.

Professor Blackie's concession is of no small importance in the actual situation. "No one is to receive a full degree without showing a fair proficiency in two foreign languages, one ancient and one modern, with free option." This would almost satisfy the present demand everywhere, and for some time to come.

The article of Professor Bonamy Price is conceived in even a higher strain than the other. There is so far a method of argumentation in it that the case is laid out under four distinct heads, but there is no decisive separation of reasons; many of the things said under one head might easily be transferred without the sense of dislocation to any other head. The writer indulges in high-flown rhetorical assertions rather than in specific facts and arguments. The first merit of classics is that "they are languages; not particular sciences, nor definite branches of knowledge, but literatures". Under this head we have such glowing sentences as these: "Think of the many elements of thought a boy comes in contact with when he reads Cæsar and Tacitus in succession, Herodotus and Homer, Thucydides and Aristotle". "See what is implied in having read Homer intelligently through, or Thucydides or Demosthenes; what light will have been shed on the essence and laws of human existence, on political society, on the relations of man to man, on human nature itself." There are various conceivable ways of counter-arguing these assertions, but the shortest is to call for the facts— the results upon the many thousands that have passed through their ten years of classical drill. Professor Campbell of St. Andrews, once remarked, with reference to the value of Greek in particular, that the question would have to be ultimately decided by the inner consciousness of those that have undergone the study. To this we are entitled to add, their powers as manifested to the world, of which powers spectators can be the judges. When, with a few brilliant exceptions, we discover nothing at all remarkable in the men that have been subjected to the classical training, we may consider it as almost a waste of time to analyse the grandiloquent assertions of Mr. Bonamy Price. But if we were to analyse them, we should find that *boys* never read Cæsar and Tacitus through in succession; still less Thucydides Demosthenes, and Aristotle; that very few *men* read and understand these writers; that the shortest way to come into contact with Aristotle is to avoid his Greek altogether, and take his expositors and translators in the modern languages.

The professor is not insensible to the reproach that the vaunted classical education has been a failure, as compared with these splendid promises. He says, however, that though many have failed to become classical scholars in the full sense of the word, "it does not follow that they have gained nothing from their study of Greek and Latin; just the contrary is the truth". The "contrary" must mean that they have gained something; which something is stated to be "the extent to which the faculties of the boy have been developed, the quantity of impalpable but not less real attainments he has achieved, and his general readiness for life, and for action as a man' But it is becoming more and more difficult to induce people to spend a long course of youthful years upon a confessedly *impalpable* result. We might give up a few months to a speculative and doubtful good, but we need palpable consequences to show for our years spent on classics. Next comes the admission that the teaching is often bad. But why should the teaching be so bad, and what is the hope of making it better? Then we are told that science by itself leaves the largest and most important portion of the youths' nature absolutely undeveloped. But, in the first place, it is not proposed to reduce the school and college curriculum to science alone; and, in the next place, who can say what are the "impalpable" results of science?

The second branch of the argument relates to the greatness of the classical writers. Undoubtedly the Greek and Roman worlds produced some very great writers, and a good many not great. But the greatness of Herodotus, Thucydides, Demosthenes, Plato, and Aristotle can be exhibited in a modern rendering; while no small portion of the poetical excellence of Homer and the Dramatists can be made apparent without toiling at the original tongues. The value of the languages then resolves itself, as has been often remarked, into a *residuum*. Something also is to be said for the greatness of the writers that have written in modern times. Sir John Herschel remarked long ago that the human intellect cannot have degenerated, so long as we are able to quote Newton, Lagrange and Laplace, against Aristotle and Archimedes. I would not undertake to say that any modern mind has equalled Aristotle in the *range* of his intellectual powers; but in point of intensity of grasp in any one subject, he has many rivals; so that to obtain his equal, we have only to take two or three first-rate moderns.

If a few fanatics are to go on lauding to the skies the exclusive and transcendent greatness of the classical writers, we shall probably be tempted to scrutinize their merits more severely than is usual. Many things could be said against their sufficiency as instructors in matters of thought; and many more against the low and barbarous tone of their *morale*—the inhumanity and brutality of both their principles and their practice. All this might no doubt be very easily overdone, and would certainly be so, if undertaken in the style of Professor Price's panegyric.

The professor's third branch of the argument comes to the real point; namely, what is there in Greek and Latin that there is not in the modern tongues? For one thing, says the professor, they are dead; which of course we allow. Then, being dead, they must be learnt by book and by rule; they cannot be learnt by ear. Here, however, Professor Blackie would dissent, and would say that the great improvement of teaching, on which the salvation of classical study now hangs, is to make it a teaching by the ear. But, says Professor Price: "A Greek or Latin sentence is a nut with a strong shell concealing the kernel—a puzzle, demanding reflection, adaptation of means to end, and labour for its solution, and the educational value resides in the shell and in the puzzle" As this strain of remark is not new, there is nothing new to be said in answer to it. Such puzzling efforts are certainly not the rule in learning Latin and Greek. Moreover, the very same terms would describe what may happen equally often in reading difficult authors in French, German, or Italian. Would not the pupil find puzzles and difficulties in Dante, or in Goethe? And are there not many puzzling exercises in deciphering English authors? Besides, what is the great objection to science, but that it is too puzzling for minds that are quite competent for the puzzles of Greek and Latin? Once more, the *teaching* of any language must be very imperfect, if it brings about habitually such situations of difficulty as are here described.

The professor relapses into a cooler and correcter strain when he remarks that the pupil's mind is necessarily more delayed over the expression of a thought in a foreign language (whether dead or alive matters not), and therefore remembers the meaning better. Here, however, the desiderated reform of teaching might come into play. Granted that the boy left to himself would go more rapidly through Burke than through Thucydides, might not his pace be retarded by a well-directed cross-examination; with this advantage, that the length of attention might be graduated according to the importance of the subject, and not according to the accidental difficulty of the language?

The professor boldly grapples with the alleged waste of time in classics, and urges that "the gain may be measured by the time expended," which is very like begging the question.

One advantage adduced under this head deserves notice. The languages being dead, as well as all the societies and interests that they represent, they do not excite the prejudices and passions of modern life. This, however, may need some qualification. Grote wrote his history of Greece to counterwork the party bias of Mitford. The battles of despotism, oligarchy, and democracy are to this hour fought over the dead bodies of Greece and Rome. If the professor meant to insinuate, that those that have gone through the classical training are less violent as partisans, more dispassionate in political judgments, than the rest of mankind, we can only say that we should not have known this from our actual experience. The discovery of some sweet, oblivious, antidote to party feeling seems, as far as we can judge, to be still in the future. If we want studies that will, while they last, thoroughly divert the mind from the prejudices of party, science is even better than ancient history; there are no party cries connected with the Binomial Theorem.

The professor's last branch of argument, I am obliged, with all deference, to say, contains no argument at all. It is that, in classical education, a close contact is established between the mind of the boy and the mind of the master. He does not even attempt to show how the effect is peculiar to classical teaching. The whole of this part of the paper is, in fact, addressed, by way of remonstrance, to the writer's own friends, the classical teachers. He reproaches them for their inefficiency, for their not being Arnolds. It is not my business to interfere between him and them in this matter. So much stress does he lay upon the teacher's part in the work, that I almost expected the admission—that a good teacher in English, German, natural history, political economy, might even be preferable to a bad teacher of Latin and Greek.

The recent Oxford contest has brought out the eminent oratorical powers of Canon Liddon; and we have some curiosity in noting his contributions to the classical side. I refer to his letters in the *Times*. The gist of his advocacy of Greek is contained in the following allegations. First, the present system enables a man to recur with profit and advantage to Greek literature. To this, it has been often replied, that by far the greater number are too little familiarized with the classical languages, and especially Greek, to make the literature easy reading. But farther, the recurring to the study of ancient authors by busy professional men in the present day, is an event of such extreme rarity that it cannot be taken into account in any question of public policy. The second remark is, that the half-knowledge of the ordinary graduate is a link between the total blank of the outer world, and the thorough knowledge of the accomplished classic. I am not much struck by the force of this argument. I think that the classical scholar, might, by expositions, commentaries, and translations, address the outer world equally well, without the intervening mass of imperfect scholars. Lastly, the Canon puts in a claim for his own cloth. The knowledge of Greek paves the way for serious men to enter the ministry in middle life. Argument would be thrown away upon any one that could for a moment entertain this as a sufficient reason for compelling every graduate in Arts to study Greek. The observation that I would make upon it has a wider bearing. Middle life is not too late for learning any language that we suddenly discover to be a want; the stimulus of necessity or of strong interest, and the wider compass of general knowledge, compensate for the diminution of verbal memory.

V.

METAPHYSICS AND DEBATING SOCIETIES.

METAPHYSICS AND DEBATING SOCIETIES.[1]

By "Metaphysical Study," or "Metaphysics," I here mean—what seems intended by the designation in its current employment at present—the circle of the mental or subjective sciences. The central department of the field is PSYCHOLOGY, and the adjunct to psychology is LOGIC, which has its foundations partly in psychology, but still more in the sciences altogether, whose procedure it gathers up and formulates. The outlying and dependent branches are: the narrower metaphysics or Ontology, Ethics, Sociology, together with Art or Æsthetics. There are other applied sciences of the department, as Education and Philology.

The branches most usually looked upon as the cognate or allied studies of the subjective department of human knowledge are, Psychology, Logic, Ontology, Ethics. The debates in a society like the present will generally be found to revolve in the orbit thus chalked out. It is the sphere of the most animated controversies, and the widest discordance of

[1] An Address, delivered on the 28th of March, 1877, to the Edinburgh University Philosophical Society. CONTEMPORARY REVIEW, April, 1877.

view. The additional branch most nearly connected with the group is Sociology, which under that name, and under the older title, the Philosophy of History, has opened up a new series of problems, of the kind to divide opinions and provoke debate. A quieter interest attaches to Æsthetics, although the subject is a not unfruitful application and test of psychological laws.

My remarks will embrace, first, the aims, real and factitious, in the study of this group of sciences; and next, the polemic conduct of such study, or the utility and management of debating societies, instituted in connection therewith.

The two sciences — PSYCHOLOGY and LOGIC — I consider the fundamental and knowledge-giving departments. The others are the applications of these to the more stirring questions of human life. Now, the successful cultivation of the field requires you to give at least as much attention to the root sciences as you give to the branch sciences. That is to say, psychology, in its pure and proper character, and logic, in its systematic array, should be kept before the view, concurrently with ontology, ethics, and sociology. Essays and debates tending to clear up and expound systematic psychology and systematic logic should make a full half of the society's work.

Does any one feel a doubt upon the point, as so stated? If so, it will lie upon him to show that Psychology, in its methodical pursuit, is a needless and superfluous employment of strength; that the problems of ethics, ontology, &c., can be solved without it—a hard task indeed, so long as they are unsolved in any way. I have no space for indulging in a dissertation on the value of methodical study and arrangement in the extension of our knowledge, as opposed to the promiscuous mingling of different kinds of facts, which is often required in practice, but repugnant to the increase of knowledge. If you want to improve our acquaintance with the sense of touch, you accumulate and methodize all the experiences relating to touch, you compare them, see whether they are consistent or inconsistent, select the good, reject the bad, improve the statement of one by light borrowed from the others; you mark desiderata, experiments to be tried, or observations to be sought. All that time, you refrain from wandering into other spheres of mental phenomena. You make use of comparison with the rest of the senses, it may be, but you keep strictly to the points of analogy, where mutual lights are to be had. This is the culture of knowledge as such, and is the best, the essential, preparation for practical questions involving the particular subject along with others.

To take an example from the question of the Will. I do not object to the detaching and isolating of the problem of free-will, as a matter for discussion and debate; but I think that it can be handled to equal, if not greater advantage, in the systematic psychology of voluntary power. Those that have never tried it in this last form have not obtained the best vantage-ground for overcoming the inevitable subtleties that invest it.

The great problem of External Perception has a psychological place, where its difficulties are very much attenuated, to say the least of it; and, however convenient it may be to treat it as a detached problem, we should carry with us into the discussion all the lights that we obtain while regarding it as it stands among the intellectual powers.

It is in systematic Psychology that we are most free to attend to the defining of terms (without which a professed science is mere moonshine), to the formulating of axioms and generalities, to the concatenating and taking stock of all the existing knowledge, and to the appraising of it at its real value. If these things are neglected, there is nothing that I see to constitute a psychology at all.

As to the other fundamental science, LOGIC, the same remarks may be repeated. Of debated questions, a certain number pertain properly to logic; yet most of these relate to logic at its points of contact with psychology. Since we have got out of the narrow round of the Aristotelian syllogism, we have agreed to call logic *ars artium*, or, better still, *scientia scientiarum*, the science that deals with the sciences altogether—both object sciences and subject sciences. Now this I take to be a study quite apart from psychology in particular, although, as I have said, touching it at several points. It reviews all science and all knowledge, as to its structure, method, arrangement, classification, probation, enlargement. It deals in generalities the most general of any. By taking up what belongs to all knowledge, it seems to rise above the matter of knowledge to the region of pure form; it demands, therefore, a peculiar subtlety of handling, and may easily land us, as we are all aware, in knotty questions and quagmires.

Now what I have to repeat in this connection is, that you should, in your debates, overhaul portions or chapters of systematic logic, with a view to present the difficulties in their natural position in the subject. You might, for example, take up the question as to the Province of logic, with its divisions, parts, and order—all which admit of many various views—and bring forward the vexed controversies under lights favourable to their resolution. Regarding logic as an aid to the faculties in tackling whatever is abstruse, you should endeavour to cultivate and enhance its powers, in this particular, by detailed exposition and criticism of all its canons and prescriptions. The department of Classification is a good instance; a region full of delicate subtleties as well as "bread-and-butter" applications.

It is in this last view of logic that we can canvass philosophical systems upon the ground of their method or procedure alone. Looking at the absence, in any given system, of the arts and precautions that are indispensable to the establishment of truth in the special case, we may pronounce against it, *à priori*; we know that such a system can be true only by accident, or else by miracle. We may reasonably demand of a system-builder—Is he in the narrow way that leadeth to truth, or in the broad way that leadeth somewhere else?

I have said that I consider the connection between Logic and Psychology to be but slender, although not unimportant. The amount and nature of this connection would reward a careful consideration. There would be considerable difficulty in seeing any connection at all between the Aristotelian Syllogism and psychology, but for the high-sounding designations appended to the notion and the proposition—simple apprehension and judgment—of which I fail to discover the propriety or relevance. I know that Grote gave a very profound turn to the employment of the term "judgment" by Aristotle, as being a recognition of the relativity of knowledge to the affirming mind. I am not to say, absolutely, "Ice is cold"; I am to say that, to the best of my judgment or belief, or in so far as I am concerned, ice is cold. This, however, has little to do with the logic of the syllogism, and not much with any logic. So, when we speak of a "notion," we must understand it as apprehended by some mind; but for nearly all purposes, this is assumed tacitly; it need not appear in a formal designation, which, not being wanted, is calculated to mislead.

With these remarks on the two fundamental sciences of our group, I now turn to the *applied* or *derivative* sciences, wherein the great controversies stand out most conspicuous, which, in fact, exist for the purpose of contention—Ontology and Ethics. These branches were in request long before the mother sciences—psychology and logic—came into being at all. They had occupied their chief positions without consulting the others, partly because these were not there to consult, and partly because they were not inclined to consult any extraneous authority. By Ontology we may designate the standing controversies of the intellectual powers—perception, innate ideas, nominalism *versus* realism, and noumenon *versus* phenomenon. I am not going to pronounce upon these questions; I have already recommended the alternative mode of approaching them under systematic psychology and logic; and I will now regard them as constituents of the fourfold enumeration of the metaphysical sciences.

The Germans may be credited for teaching us, or trying to teach us, to distinguish "bread and butter" from what passes beyond, transcends bread and butter. With them the distinction is thoroughly ingrained, and comes to hand at a moment's notice. If I am to review in detail what may be considered the practical or applied departments of logic and psychology, I am in danger of trenching on their "bread-and-butter" region. Before descending, therefore, into the larder, let us first spend a few seconds in considering psychology as the pursuit of *truth* in all that relates to our mental constitution. If difficulty be a stimulus to the human exertions, it may be found here. To ascertain, fix, and embody the precise truth in regard to the facts of the mind is about as hard an undertaking as could be prescribed to a man. But this is another way of saying that psychology is not a very advanced science ; is not well stored with clear and certain doctrines ; and is unable, therefore, to confer any very great precision on its dependent branches, whether purely speculative or practical. In a word, the greatest modesty or humility is the deportment most becoming to all that engage in this field of labour, even when doing their best; while the same virtues in even greater measure are due from those engaging in it without doing their best.

It must be admitted, however, that the highest evidence and safeguard of truth is application. In every other science, the utility test is final. The great parent sciences—mathematics, physics, chemistry, physiology—have each a host of filial dependents, in close contact with the supply of human wants; and the success of the applications is the testimony to the truth of the sciences applied. Thus, although we may not narrow the sphere of truth to bread and butter, yet we have no surer test of the truth itself. Our trade requires navigation, and navigation verifies astronomy ; and, but for navigation, we may be pretty confident that astronomy would now have very little accuracy to boast of.

To come then to the practical bearings or outgoings of psychology, assisted by logic. My contention is that the parent sciences and the filial sciences should be carried on together ; that theses should be extracted by turns from all ; that the lights thus obtained would be mutual. I will support the position by a review of the subjects thus drawn into the metaphysical field.

Foremost among these applied sciences I would place EDUCATION, the subject of the day. The priority of mention is due not so much to its special or pre-eminent importance, as to its being the most feasible and hopeful of the practical applications of conjoined psychology and logic. I say this, however, with a more express eye to *intellectual* education. I deem it quite possible to frame a practical science applicable to the training of the intellect that shall be precise and definite in a very considerable measure. The elements that make up our intellectual furniture can be stated with clearness; the laws of intellectual growth or acquisition are almost the best ascertained generalities of the human mind; even the most complicated studies can be analyzed into their components, partly by psychology and partly by the higher logic. In a word, if we cannot make a science of education, as far as Intellect is concerned, we may abandon metaphysical study altogether.

I do not speak with the same confidence as to *moral* education. There has long been in existence a respectable rule-of-thumb practice in this region, the result of a sufficiently wide experience. There are certain psychological laws, especially those relating to the formation of moral habits, that have a considerable value; but to frame a theory of moral education, on a level in a point of definiteness with the possible theory of intellectual education, is a task that I should not like to have imposed upon me. In point of fact, two problems are joined in one, to the confusion of both. There is *first* the vast question of *moral control*, which stretches far and wide over many fields, and would have to be tracked with immense labour: it belongs to the arts of government; it comes under moral suasion, as exercised by the preacher and orator; it even implicates the tact of diplomacy. I do not regard this as a properly educational question (although it refers to an art that every teacher must try to master); that is to say, its solution is not connected with education processes strictly so called. The *second* problem of moral education is the one really within the scope of the subject—the problem of *fixing moral bents* or habits, when the right conduct is once initiated. On this head, some scientific insight is attainable; and suggestions of solid value may in time accrue, although there never can be the precision attainable in the intellectual region.

I will next advert to the applied science of Art or ÆSTHETICS, long a barren ground so far as scientific handling was concerned, but now a land of promise. The old thesis, "What is Beauty?" a good debating society topic, is, I hope, past contending about. The numerous influences that concur in works of art, or in natural beauty, present a fine opening for delicate analysis; at the same time, they implicate the vaguest and least advanced portion of psychology—the Emotions. The German philosophers have usually ranked æsthetics as one of the subjective sciences; but, it is only of late that the department has taken shape in their country. Lessing gave a great impulse to literary art, and originated a number of pregnant suggestions; and the German love of music has necessarily led to theories as well as to compositions. We are now in the way to that consummation of æsthetics which may be described as containing (1) a reference to psychology as the mother science, (2) a classification, comparison, and contrast of the fine arts themselves, and (3) an induction of the principles of art composition from the best examples. Anything like a thorough sifting of fine-art questions would strain psychology at every point—senses, emotions, intellect; and, if criticism is to go deep, it must ground upon psychological reasons. Now the mere artist can never be a psychologist; the art critic may, but seldom will; hence, as they will not come over to us, some of us must go over to them. The Art discussion of the greatest fountains of human feeling —love and anger—would react with advantage upon the very difficult psychology of these emotions, so long the sport of superficiality.

But I hold that æsthetics is but a corner of a larger field that is seldom even named among the sciences of mind; I mean human happiness as a whole, "eudæmonics," or "hedonics," or whatever you please to call it. That the subject is neglected, I do not affirm; but it is not cultivated in the proper place, or in the proper light-giving connection—that is to say, under the psychology of the human feelings. It should have at once a close reference to psychology, and an independent construction; while either in comprehending æsthetics, or in lying side by side with that, it would give and receive illumination. The researches now making into the laws and limits of human sensibility, if they have any value, ought to lead to the economy of pleasure and the abatement of pain. The analysis of sensation and of emotion points to this end. Whoever raises any question as to human happiness should refer it, in the first instance, to psychology; in the next, to some general scheme that would answer for a science of happiness; and, thirdly, to an induction of the facts of human experience; the three distinct appeals correcting one another. If psychology can contribute nothing to the point, it confesses to a desideratum for future inquirers.

I am not at all satisfied with the coupling of happiness with ethics, as is usually done. Ethics is the sphere of duty; happiness is mentioned only to be repressed and discouraged. This is not the situation for unfolding all the blossoms of human delight, nor for studying to allay every rising uneasiness. He would be a rare ethical philosopher that would permit full scope to such an operation within his grounds; neither Epicurus nor Bentham could come up to this mark. But even if the thing were permitted, the lights are not there; it is only by combining the parent psychology and the hedonic derivative, that the work can be done. It is neither disrespect nor disadvantage to duty, that it is not mentioned in the department until the very end. To cultivate happiness is not selfishness or vice, unless you confine it to self; and the mere act of inquiring does not so confine it. If you are in other respects a selfish man, you will apply your knowledge for your own sole behoof; if you are not selfish, you will apply it for the good of your fellows also, which is another name for virtue.

But the obstacles to a science of happiness are not solely due to the gaps and deficiencies in our psychological knowledge; they are equally owing to the prevailing terrorism in favour of self-denial at all hands. Many of the maxims as to happiness would not stand examination if people felt themselves free to discuss them. You must work yourselves into a fervour of revolt and defiance, before you call in question Paley's declaration that "happiness is equally distributed among all orders of the community". I do not know whether I should wonder most at the cheerful temperament or the complacent optimism of Adam Smith, when he asks, "What can be added to the happiness of the man who is in health, who is out of debt, and has a clear conscience?"[1] When the

---

[1] This very plausible utterance begs every question. There would be some difficulty in condensing an equal amount of fallacy, confusion of thought, in so few words.

In the first place, it assumes that the three requisites—health, freedom from debt, and a good conscience—are matters of easy and general attainment; that they are, in fact, the rule among human beings. Is this really so?

Take Health, a word of very wide import. There is a certain small amount, such as is marked by being out of the physician's hands, but implying very little of the energy needed for the labours and the enjoyment of life. There is a high and resplendent degree that renders toil easy,

greatest philosophers talk thus, what is to be expected from the unphilosophic mob? The dependence of health on activity is always kept very loose, it may be for the convenience of shutting our mouths against and responds to the commonest stimulants, so that enjoyment cannot be quashed without unusually unfavourable circumstances. The first kind is widely diffused; the second is very rare, except in the earlier portion of life. Most men and women, as they pass middle age, lose the elasticity required for easy and spontaneous enjoyment, and, even if they keep the appearance of health, have too little animal spirits for enjoyment under cheap and ordinary excitements.

But there is more to be said. In order to obtain, and to retain, health, freedom from debt, and a good conscience, there are pre-supposed very considerable advantages. We cannot continue healthy and out of debt, unless we have a fair start in life, that is, unless we have a tolerable provision to begin with; a circumstance that the maxim keeps out of sight.

Yet farther. The conditions named are of themselves mere negatives; they imply simply the absence of certain decided causes of unhappiness—ill-health, poverty, and bad conduct. There is a farther stealthy assumption, namely, that the individual is placed in a situation otherwise conducive to happiness. Health, absence of debt, and a good conscience will not make happiness, under severe or ungenial toil, irritation, ill-usage, affliction, sorrow,—even if they could be long maintained under such circumstances. Nor even, in the case of exemption from the worst ills of life, can we be happy without some positive agreeables—family, general society, amusements, and gratifications. There is a certain degree of loneliness, seclusion, dulness, that destroys happiness without sapping health, or running us into debt and vice.

The maxim, as expressed, professes to aim at happiness, but it more properly belongs to duty. If we fail in the conditions mentioned, we run the risk rather of neglecting our duties than of missing our pleasures. It is not every form of ill-health that makes us miserable; and we may become seared to debt and ill-conduct, so as to suffer only the incidental misery of being dunned, which many can take with great composure.

The definition of happiness by Paley is vague and incomplete; but it does not omit the positive conditions. After health, Paley enumer-

complaints of being overworked. To render this dependence precise is a matter of pure psychology.

Before coming to Ethics I must, as a preparation, view another derivative branch of psychology, the old subject of politics and society, under its new name, SOCIOLOGY. It is obvious that all terms used in describing social facts and their generalities are terms of mind: command and obedience, law and right, order and progress, are notions made up of human feelings, purposes, and thoughts.

Sociology is usually studied in its own special field, and nowhere else; that is to say, the sociologist employs himself in observing and comparing the operations of societies under all varieties of circumstances, and in all historic ages. The field is essentially human nature, and the laws arrived at are laws of human nature. A consummate sociologist is not often to be found; the really great theorists in society could be counted on one's fingers. Some of them have been psychologists as well; I need mention only Aristotle, Hobbes, Locke, Hume, the Mills. Others as Vico, Montesquieu, Millar, Condorcet, Auguste Comte, De Tocqueville, have not independently studied the mind on the broad psychological basis. Now the bearings on sociology of a pure psychological

---

ates the exercise of the affections and some engaging occupation or pursuit; both which are highly relevant to the attainment of happiness. Indeed, with an exemption from cares, and a considerable share of the positive gratifications, we can enjoy life on a very slender stock of health; otherwise, where should we be in the inevitable decline that age brings with it?

preparation can be convincingly shown. The laws of society, if not the merest empiricisms, are derivative laws of the mind; hence a theorist cannot be trusted with the handling of a derivative law, unless he knows, as well as can be known, the simple or constituent laws. All the elements of human character crop up in men's social relations; in the foreground are their self-interest or sense of self-preservation, together with their social and anti-social promptings; a little farther back are their active energy, their intelligence, their artistic feelings, and their religious susceptibilities. Now all these should be broadly examined as elements of the mind, without an immediate reference to the political machine. Of course, the social feelings need a social situation, and cannot be studied without that; but there are many social situations that give scope for examining them, besides what is contemplated in political society, and the psychologist proper ought to avail himself of all the opportunities of rendering the statement of these various elements precise. For this purpose, his chief aim is the ultimate analysis of the various faculties and feelings. This analysis nobody but himself cares to institute; and yet a knowledge of the ultimate constitution of an emotional tendency is one of the best aids in appreciating its mode of working. Without a good preliminary analysis of the social and anti-social emotions, for example, you are almost sure to be counting the same thing twice over, or else confounding two different facts under one designation. On the one hand, the precise relationship of the states named love, sympathy, disinterestedness; and, on the other hand, the common basis of domination, resentment, pride, egotism,—should be distinctly cleared up, as is possible only in psychological study strictly so called. The workings of the religious sentiment cannot be shown sociologically, without a previous analysis of the constituent emotions.

An allusion so very slender to so vast a subject as sociology would be a waste of words, but for the conviction, that through sociology is the way to the great field of Ethics. This is to reverse the traditional arrangement—ethics, politics, or government—followed even by Bentham. The lights of ethics are, in the first instance, psychological; its discussions presuppose a number of definitions and distinctions that are pure psychology. But before these have to be adduced, the subject has to be set forth as a problem of sociology. "How is the King's government to be carried on?" "How is society to be held together?" is the first consideration; and the sociologist—as constitution-builder, administrator, judge—is the person to grapple with the problem. It is with him that law, obligation, right, command, obedience, sanction, have their origin and their explanation. Ethics is an important supplement to social or political law. But it is still a department of law. In any other view it is a maze, a mystery, a hopeless embroilment.

That ethics is involved in society is of course admitted; what is not admitted is, that ethical terms should be settled under the social science in the first place. I may refer to the leading term "law," whose meaning in sociology is remarkably clear; in ethics remarkably the reverse. The confusion deepens when the moral faculty is brought forward. In the eye of the sociologist, nothing could be simpler than the conception of that part of our nature that is appealed to for securing obedience. He assumes a certain effort of the intelligence for understanding the signification of a command or a law; and, for the motive part, he counts upon nothing but volition in its most ordinary form—the avoidance of a pain. Intelligence and Will, in their usual and recognised workings, are all that are required for social obedience; law is conceived and framed exactly to suit the every-day and every-hour manifestations of these powers. The lawgiver does not speak of an obedience-faculty, nor even of a social-faculty. If there were in the mind a power unique and apart, having nothing in common with our usual intelligence, and nothing in common with our usual will or volition, that power ought to be expressed in terms that exclude the smallest participation of both knowledge and will; it ought to have a form special to itself, and not the form:—" Do this, and ye shall be made to suffer"

I am quite aware that there are elements in ethics not included in the problem of social obedience; what I contend for is, that the ground should be cleared by marking out the two provinces, as is actually done by a very small number of theorists, of whom John Austin is about the best example.

The ethical philosopher, from not building on a

foregone sociology, is obliged to extemporize, in a paragraph, the social system; just as the physical philosopher would, if he had no regularly constructed mathematics to fall back upon, but had to stop every now and then to enunciate a mathematical theorem.

The question of the ethical end should first appear as the question of the sociological end. For what purpose or purposes is society maintained? All the ethical difficulties are here met by anticipation, and in a form much better adapted to their solution. It is from the point of view of the social ruler, that you learn reserve, moderation, and sobriety in your aims; you learn to think that something much less than the Utopias—universal happiness and universal virtue— should be propounded; you find that a definite and limited province can be assigned, separating what the social power is able to do, must do, and can advantageously do, from what it is unable to do, need not do, and cannot with advantage do; and this or a similar demarcation is reproducible in ethics.

The precepts of ethics are mainly the precepts of social authority; at all events the social precepts and their sanctions have the priority in scientific method. Some of the highest virtues are sociological; patriotic self-sacrifice is one of the conditions of social preservation. The inculcation of this and of many other virtues would not appear in ethics at all, or only in a supplementary treatment, if social science took its proper sphere, and fully occupied that sphere.

Once more. The great problem of moral control, which I would remove entirely from a science of education, would be first dealt with in Sociology. It there appears in the form of the choice and gradation of punishments, in prison discipline, and in the reformation of criminals,—all which have been made the subject of enlightened, not to say scientific, treatment. It is in the best experience in those subjects that I would begin to seek for lights on the comprehensive question. I would next go to diplomacy for the arts of delicate address in reconciling opposing interests; after which I would look to the management of parties and conflicting interests in the State. I would farther inquire how armies are disciplined, and subordination combined with the enthusiasm that leads to noble deeds.

There is an abundant field for the application of pure psychology to ethics, when it takes its own proper ground. The exact psychological character of disinterested impulse needs to be assigned; and, if that impulse can be fully referred to the sympathetic or social instincts and habits, the supposed moral faculty is finally eviscerated of its contents for all ethical purposes.

So far I have exemplified what seems to me real or genuine aims and applications of metaphysical study. I now proceed to the objects that are more or less factitious. We are here on delicate ground, and run the risk of discrediting our pursuit, as regards the very things that in the eyes of many people make its value.

First, then, as psychology involves all our sensibilities, pleasures, affections, aspirations, capacities, it is thought on that ground to have a special nobility and greatness, and a special power of evoking in the student the feelings themselves. The mathematician, dealing with conic sections, spirals, and differential equations, is in danger of being ultimately resolved into a function or a co-efficient; the metaphysician, by investigating conscience, must become conscientious; driving fat oxen is the way to grow fat.

But to pass to a far graver application. It has usually been supposed that metaphysical theory is more especially akin to the speculation that mounts to the supernatural and the transcendental world. "Man's relations to the infinite" is a frequent phrase in the mouth of the metaphysician. Metaphysics is supposed to be "philosophy" by way of eminence; and philosophy in the large sense has not merely to satisfy the curiosity of the human mind, it has to provide scope for its emotions and aspirations; in fact, to play the part of theology. In times when the prevailing orthodox beliefs are shaken, some scheme of philosophy is brought forward to take their place. If I understand aright the drift of the German metaphysical systems for a century back, they all more or less propose to themselves to supply the same spiritual wants as religion supplies. In our own country, such of us as are not under German influence put the matter differently; but we still consider that we have something to say on the "highest questions". We are apt to believe that on us more than on any other class of thinkers, does it depend whether the prevailing theology shall be upheld, impugned, or transformed. The chief weapons of the defenders of the faith are forged in the schools of metaphysics. Locke and Butler, Reid, Stewart and Brown are theological authorities. And when theology is attacked, its metaphysical buttresses have to be assailed as the very first thing. If these are declared unsound, either it must fall, or it must change its front. It is Natural Theology, more particularly, that is thus allied to metaphysics; yet, not exclusively; for the defence of Revelation by miracles involves at the outset a point of logic.

Now I do not mean to say, that this is a purely factitious and ill-grounded employment of the metaphysical sciences. I fully admit that the later defences of theology, as well as the attacks, have been furnished from psychology, logic, ethics, and ontology. The earliest beliefs in religion, the greatest and strongest convictions, had little to do with any of these departments of speculation. But when simple traditionary faith gave place to the questionings of the reason, the basis of religion was transferred to the reason-built sciences; and metaphysics came in for a large share in the decision.

What I maintain is, that there is something factitious in the degree of prominence given to metaphysics in this great enterprise; that its pretentions are excessive, its importance over-stated; and when most employed for such a purpose, it is least to be trusted. Theological polemic is only in part conducted through science; and physical science shares equally with moral. The most serious shocks to the traditional orthodoxy have come from the physical sciences. The argument from Design has no doubt a metaphysical or logical element — the estimate of the degree of analogy between the universe and a piece of human workmanship; but the argument itself needs a scientific survey of the entire phenomena of nature, both matter and mind. Our Bridgewater Treatises proceeded upon this view; they embraced the consideration of the whole circle of the sciences, as bearing on the theological argument. The scheme was so far just and to the purpose; the obvious drawback to the value of the Treatises lay in their being special pleadings, backed by a fee of a thousand pounds to each writer for maintaining one side. If a similar fee had been given to nine equally able writers to represent the other side, the argument from design would have been far more satisfactorily sifted than by the exclusively metaphysical criticism of Kant.

When theology is supported exclusively by such doctrines as—an independent and immaterial soul, a special moral faculty, and what is called free-will,— the metaphysician is a person of importance in the contest; he is powerful either to uphold or to subvert the fabric. But, if these were ever to constitute the chief stronghold of the faith, its tenure would not be very secure. It is only a metaphysician, however, that believes or disbelieves in metaphysical grounds alone; such a man as Cousin, no doubt, rests his whole spiritual philosophy on this foundation. But the great mass will either adhere to religion in spite of metaphysical difficulties, or else abandon it notwithstanding its metaphysical evidences. An eminent man now departed said in my hearing, that he was a believer in Christianity until he became acquainted with geology, when, finding the first chapter of Genesis at variance with geological doctrines, he applied to the Bible the rule *falsus in uno, falsus in omnibus*, and thenceforth abandoned his old belief. I never heard of any one that was so worked upon by a purely metaphysical argument.

The aspect of theological doctrine that has come most to the front of late is the question of the Divine goodness, as shown in the plan of the universe. Speculations are divided between optimism and pessimism. How shall we decide between these extremes, or, if repudiating both, how shall we fix the mean? Is a metaphysician more especially qualified to find out the truth? I hardly think so. I believe he could contribute, with others, to such a solution as may be possible. He has, we shall suppose, surveyed closely the compass of the human sensibilities, and is able to assign, with more than common precision, what things operate on them favourably or unfavourably. So far good. Then, as a logician, he is more expert at detecting bad inferences in regard to the form of reasoning; but whether certain allegations of fact are well or ill founded, he may not be able to say, at least out of his own department. If a mixed commission of ten were nominated to adjudicate upon this vast problem, metaphysics might claim to be represented by two.

Least of all, do I understand the claims made in behalf of this department to supply the spiritual void in case the old theology is no longer accredited. When one looks closely at the stream and tendency of thought, one sees a growing alliance and kinship between religion and poetry or art. There is, as we know, a dogmatic, precise, severe, logical side of theology, by which creeds are constructed, religious tests imposed, and belief made a matter of legal compulsion. There is also a sentimental, ideal, imaginative side that resists definition, that refuses dogmatic prescription, and seeks only to satisfy spiritual needs and emotions. Metaphysics may no doubt take a part in the dogmatic or doctrinal treatment, but it must qualify itself by biblical study, and become altogether theology. In the other aspect, metaphysics, as I conceive it, is unavailing; the poet is the proper medium for keeping up the emotional side, under all transformations of doctrinal belief. But as conceived by others, metaphysics is philosophy and poetry in one, to which I can never agree. The combination of the two, as hitherto exhibited, has been made at the expense of both. The leading terms of philosophy—reason, spirit, soul, the ideal, the infinite, the absolute, phenomenal truth, being, consciousness—are lubricated with emotion, and thrown together in ways that defy the understanding. The unintelligible, which ought to be the shame of philosophy, is made its glory.

These remarks prepare for the conclusion that I arrive at as to the scope of metaphysics with reference to the higher questions. That it has bearings upon these questions I allow; and those bearings are legitimately within the range of metaphysical debates. But I make a wide distinction between metaphysical discussion and theological discussion; and do not consider that they can be combined to advantage. In the great latitude of free inquiry in the present day, theology is freely canvassed, and societies might be properly devoted to that express object; but I cannot see any benefit that would arise by a philosophical society undertaking, in addition to its own province, to raise the questions belonging to theology. I am well aware that there is one society of very distinguished persons in the metropolis, calling itself metaphysical, that freely ventures upon the perilous seas of theological debate.[1] No doubt good comes from any exercise of the liberty of discussion, so long restrained in this region; yet, I can hardly suppose that purely metaphysical studies can thrive in such a connection. Many of the members must think far more of the theological issues than of the cultivation of mental and logical science; and a purely metaphysical debate can seldom be pursued with profit under these conditions.

I now pass to the POLEMICAL handling of the metaphysical subjects. We owe to the Greeks the study of philosophy through methodised debate; and

[1] This Society has since been dissolved.

the state of scientific knowledge in the age of the early Athenian schools was favourable to that mode of treatment. The conversations of Socrates, the Dialogues of Plato, and the Topics of Aristotle, are the monuments of Greek contentiousness, turned to account as a great refinement in social intercourse, as a stimulus to individual thought, and a means of advancing at least the speculative departments of knowledge. Grote, both in his "Plato," and in his "Aristotle," while copiously illustrating all these consequences, has laid extraordinary stress on still another aspect of the polemic of Socrates and Plato, the aspect of *free-thought*, as against venerated tradition and the received commonplaces of society. The assertion of the right of private judgment in matters of doctrine and belief, was, according to Grote, the greatest of all the fruits of the systematised negation begun by Zeno, and carried out in the "Search Dialogues" of Plato. In the "Exposition Dialogues" it is wanting; and in the "Topica," where Eristic is reduced to method and system by one of Aristotle's greatest logical achievements, the freethinker's wings are very much clipt; the execution of Socrates probably had to answer for that. It is to the Platonic dialogues that we look for the full grandeur of Grecian debate in all its phases. The Plato of Grote is the apotheosis of Negation; it is not a philosophy so much as an epic; the theme— "The Noble Wrath of the Greek Dissenter".

At all times, there is much that has to be achieved by solitary thinking. Some definite shape must be given to our thoughts before we can submit them to the operation of other minds; the greater the originality, the longer must be the process of solitary elaboration. The "Principia" was composed from first to last by recluse meditation; probably the attempt to discuss or debate any parts of it would have only fretted and paralysed the author's invention. Indeed, after an enormous strain of the constructive intellect, a man may be in no humour to have his work carped at, even to improve it. In the region of fact, in observation and experiment, there must be a mass of individual and unassisted exertion. The use of allies in this region is to check and confirm the accuracy of the first observer.

Again, an inquirer, by dint of prolonged familiarity with a subject, may be his own best critic; he may be better able to detect flaws than any one he could call in. This is another way of stating the superiority of a particular individual over all others in the same walk. Such a monarchical position as removes a man alike from the rivalry and from the sympathy of his fellows, is the exception; mutual criticism and mutual encouragement are the rule. The social stimulants are of avail in knowledge and in truth as well as everything else.

A comparison of the state of speculation in the golden age of debate, with the state of the sciences in the present day, both metaphysical and physical, shows us clearly enough, what are the fields where polemic is most profitable. I set aside the struggles of politics and theology, and look to the scientific form of knowledge, which is, after all, the type of our highest certainty everywhere. Now, undoubtedly, it is in classifying, generalising, defining, and in the so-called logical processes—induction and deduction—that a man can be least left to himself. Until many men have gone over the same field of facts, a classification, a definition, or an induction, cannot be held as safe and sound. In modern science, there are numerous matters that have passed through the fiery furnace of iterated criticism, seven times purified; but there are, attaching to every science, a number of things still in the furnace. Most of all does this apply to the metaphysical or subject sciences, where, according to the popular belief, nothing has yet passed finally out of the fiery trial. In psychology, in logic, in eudæmonics, in sociology, in ethics, the facts are nearly all around our feet; the question is how to classify, define, generalise, express them. This was the situation of Zeno, Socrates, and Plato, for which they invoked the militant ardour of the mind. Man, they saw, is a fighting being; if fighting will do a thing, he will do it well.

In conformity with this view, the foremost class of debates, and certainly not the least profitable, are such as discuss the meanings of important terms. The genius of Socrates perceived that this was the beginning of all valid knowledge, and, in seeing this, laid the foundation of reasoned truth. I need not repeat the leading terms of metaphysical philosophy; but you can at once understand the form of proceeding by such an instance as "consciousness," debated so as to bring out the question whether, as Hamilton supposed, it is necessarily grounded on knowledge.

Next to the leading terms are the broader and more fundamental generalities: for example, the law of relativity; the laws of memory and its conditions, such as the intensity of the present consciousness; Hamilton's inverse relationship of sensation and perception. These are a few psychological instances. The value of a debate on any of these questions depends entirely upon its resolving itself into an inductive survey of the facts, and such surveys are never without fruit.

A debating society that includes logic in its sphere should cultivate the methods of debate; setting an example to other societies and to mankind in general. The "Topica" of Aristotle shows an immensity of power expended on this object, doubtless without corresponding results. Nevertheless the attempt, if resumed at the present day, with our clearer and wider views of logical method, would not be barren. This is too little thought of by us; and we may say that polemic, as an art, is still immature. The best examples of procedure are to be found in the Law Courts, some of whose methods might be borrowed in other debates. For one thing, I think that each of the two leaders should provide the members beforehand with a synopsis of the leading arguments or positions to be set forth in the debate. This, I believe, should be insisted on everywhere, not even excepting the debates of Parliament.

THE DEBATE A FIGHT FOR MASTERY.

It is the custom of debating societies to alternate the Debate and the Essay: a very important distinction, as it seems to me; and I will endeavour to indicate how it should be maintained. Frequently there is no substantial distinction observed; an essay is simply the opening of a debate, and a debate the criticism of an essay. I should like to see the two carried out each on its own principle, as I shall now endeavour to explain.

The Debate is *the fight for mastery* as between two sides. The combatants strain their powers to say everything that can be said so as to shake the case of their opponents. The debate is a field-day, a challenge to a trial of strength. Now, while I admit that the intellectual powers may be quickened to unusual perspicacity under the sound of the trumpet and the shock of arms, I also see in the operation many perils and shortcomings, when the subject of contest is truth. In a heated controversy, only the more glaring and prominent facts, considerations, doctrines, distinctions, can obtain a footing. Now truth is the still small voice; it subsists often upon delicate differences, unobtrusive instances, fine calculations. Whether or not man is a wholly selfish being, may be submitted to a contentious debate, because the facts and appearances on both sides are broad and palpable; but whether all our actions are, in the last resort or final analysis, self-regarding, is almost too delicate for debate. Chalmers upholds, as a thesis, the intrinsic misery of the vicious affections: there could not be a finer topic of pure debate.

My conception of the Essay, on the other hand, is that it should represent *amicable co-operation*, with an eye to the truth. By it you should rise from the lower or competitive, to the higher or communistic, attitude. There may be a loss of energy, but there is a gain in the manner of applying it. The essayist should set himself to ascertain the truth upon a subject; he should not be anxious to make a case. The listeners, in the same spirit, should welcome all his suggestions, help him out where he is in difficulties, be indulgent to his failings, endeavour to see good in everything. If there be a real occasion for debate, it should be purposely forborne and reserved. In propounding subjects, the respective fitness for the debate and for the essay might be taken into account.

When questions have been often debated without coming nearer to a conclusion, it should be regarded as a sign that they are too delicate and subtle for debate. A trial should then be made of the amicable or co-operative treatment represented by the Essay. The Freedom of the Will might, I think, be adjusted by friendly accommodation, but not by force of contention. External Perception is beyond the province of debate. It is fair and legitimate to try all problems by debate, in the first instance, because the excitement quickens the intelligence, and leads to new suggestions; but if the question involves an adjustment of various considerations and minute differences, the contending sides will be contentious still.

A society that really aims at the furtherance of

knowledge, might test its operations by now and then preparing a report of progress; setting forth what problems had been debated, what themes elucidated, and with what results. It would be very refreshing to see a candid avowal that after several attempts—both debate and essay—some leading topic of the department remained exactly where it stood at the outset. After such a confession, the Society might well resolve itself into a Committee of the Whole House, to consider its ways, and indeed its entire position, with a view to a new start on some more hopeful tack.

My closing remark is, as to avoiding debates that are in their very nature interminable. It is easy to fix upon a few salient features that make all the difference between a hopeful and a hopeless controversy. For one thing, there is a certain intensity of emotion, interest, bias, or prejudice if you will, that can neither reason nor be reasoned with. On the purely intellectual side, the disqualifying circumstances are complexity and vagueness. If a topic necessarily hauls in numerous other topics of difficulty, the essay may do something for it, but not the debate. Worst of all is the presence of several large, ill-defined, or unsettled terms, of which there are still plenty in our department. A not unfrequent case is a combination of the several defects each perhaps in a small degree. A tinge of predilection or party, a double or triple complication of doctrines, and one or two hazy terms, will make a debate that is pretty sure to end as it began. Thus it is that a question, plausible to appearance, may contain within it capacities of misunderstanding, cross-purposes, and pointless issues, sufficient to occupy the long night of Pandemonium, or beguile the journey to the nearest fixed star.

VI

THE UNIVERSITY IDEAL—PAST AND PRESENT.

THE UNIVERSITY IDEAL—PAST AND PRESENT.*

GENTLEMEN,

By your flattering estimate of my services, I have been unexpectedly summoned from retirement, to assume the honours and the duties of the purple, and to occupy the most historically important office in the Universities of Europe.

The present demands upon the Rectorship somewhat resemble what we are told of the Homeric chief, who, in company with his Council or Senate, the *Boulē*, and the Popular Assembly, or *Agora*, made up the political constitution of the tribe. The functions of the chief, it is said, were to supply wise counsel to the *Boulē* (as we might call our Court), and unctuous eloquence to the *Agora*. The second of these requirements is what weighs upon me at the present moment.

Whatever may have been the practice of my predecessors, generally strangers to you, it would be altogether unbecoming in me to travel out of our University life, for the materials of an Address. My remarks then will principally bear on the UNIVERSITY IDEAL.

* RECTORIAL ADDRESS, to the Students of Aberdeen University, 15*th* *November*, 1882.

THE HIGHER TEACHING IN GREECE.

To the Greeks we are indebted for the earliest germ of the University. It was with them chiefly that education took that great leap, the greatest ever made, from the traditional teaching of the home, the shop, the social surroundings, to schoolmaster teaching properly so called. Nowadays, we, schoolmasters, think so much of ourselves, that we do not make full allowance for that other teaching, which was, for unknown ages, the only teaching of mankind. The Greeks were the first to introduce, not perhaps the primary schoolmaster, for the R's, but certainly the secondary or higher schoolmaster, known as Rhetorician or Sophist, who taught the higher professions; while their Philosophers or wise men, introduced a kind of knowledge that gave scope to the intellectual faculties, with or without professional applications; the very idea of our Faculty of Arts.

So self-asserting were these new-born teachers of the Sophist class, that Plato thought it necessary to recall attention to the good old perennial source of instruction, the home, the trade, and the society. He pointed out that the pretenders to teach virtue by moral lecturing, were as yet completely outrivalled by the influence of the family and the social pressure of the community. In like manner, the arts of life were all originally handed down by apprenticeship and imitation. The greatest statesmen and generals of early times had simply the education of the actual work. Philip of Macedon could have had no other teaching; his greater son was the first of the line to receive what we may call a liberal, or a general education, under the educator of all Europe.

THE MIDDLE AGE AND BOËTHIUS.

I must skip eight centuries, to introduce the man that linked the ancient and the modern world, and was almost the sole luminary in the west during the dark ages, namely, Boëthius, minister of the Gothic Emperor Theodoric. As much of Aristotle as was known between the 6th and the 11th centuries was handed down by him. During that time, only the logical treatises existed among the Latins; and of these the best parts were neglected. Historical importance attaches to a small circle of them known as the Old Logic (*vetus logica*), which were the pabulum of abstract thought for five dreary centuries. These consisted of the two treatises or chapters of Aristotle called the "Categories," and the "De Interpretatione," or the Theory of Propositions; and of a book of Porphyry the Neo-Platonist, entitled 'Introduction' (*Isagoge*), and treating of the so-called Five Predicables. A hundred average pages would include them all; and three weeks would suffice to master them.

Boëthius, however, did much more than hand on these works to the mediaeval students; he translated the whole of Aristotle's logical writings (the Organon), but the others were seldom taken up. It was he too that handled the question of Universals in his first

Dialogue on Porphyry, and sowed the seed that was not to germinate till four centuries afterwards, but which, when the time came, was to bear fruit in no measured amount. And Boëthius is the name associated with the scheme of higher education that preceded the University teaching, called the *quadrivium*, or quadruple group of subjects, namely, Arithmetic, Geometry, Music and Astronomy This, together with the *trivium*, or preparatory group of three subjects—Grammar, Rhetoric, and Logic—constituted what was known as the *seven liberal arts ;* but, in the darkest ages, the quadrivium was almost lost sight of, and few went beyond the trivium.

EVE OF THE UNIVERSITY.

In the 7th century, the era of deepest intellectual gloom, philosophy was at an entire stand-still. Light arises with the 8th, when we are introduced to the Cathedral and Cloister Schools of Charlemagne ; and the 9th saw these schools fully established, and an educational reform completed that was to be productive of lasting good results. But the range of instruction was still narrow, scarcely proceeding beyond the Old Logic, and the teachers were, as formerly, the Monks. The 11th century is really the period of dawn. The East was now opened up through the Crusades, and there was frequent intercourse with the learned Saracens of Spain ; and thus there were brought into the West the whole of Aristotle's works, with Arabic commentaries, chiefly in Latin translations. The effervescence was prodigious and alarming. The schools were reinforced by a higher class of teachers, Lay as well as Clerical; a marked advance was made in Logic and Dialectic; and the great controversy of Realism *versus* Nominalism, which had found its birth in the previous century, raged with extraordinary vigour. We are now on the eve of the founding of the Universities; Boogna, indeed, being already in existence.

SEPARATION OF PHILOSOPHY FROM THEOLOGY.

The University proper, however, can hardly be dated earlier than the 12th century; and the important particulars in its first constitution are these:—

First, the separation of Philosophy from Theology. To expound this, would be to give a chapter of mediæval history. Suffice it to say that Aristotle and the awakening intellect of the 11th century were the main causes of it. Two classes of minds at this time divided the Church—the pious, devout believers (such as St. Bernard), who needed no reasons for their faith, and the polemic speculative divines (such as Abaelard), who wished to make Theology rational. It was an age, too, of stirring political events; the crusading spirit was abroad, and found a certain gratification even in the war of words. The nature of Universals was eagerly debated; but when this controversy came into collision with such leading theological doctrines as the Trinity and Predestination, it was no longer possible for Philosophy and Theology to remain conjoined.

A separation was effected, and determined the leading feature of the University system. The foundation was Philosophy, and the fundamental Faculty the Faculty of Arts. Bologna, indeed, was eminent for Law or Jurisprudence, and this celebrity it retained for ages; but the University of Paris, which is the prototype of our Scottish Universities, as of so many others, taught nothing but Philosophy—in other words, had no Faculty but Arts—for many years. Neither Theology, Medicine, nor Law had existence there till the 13th century.

Second, the system of conferring Degrees, after appropriate trials. These were at first simply a licence to teach. They acquired their commanding importance through the action of Pope Nicholas I., who gave to the graduates of the University of Paris, the power of teaching everywhere, a power that our own countrymen were the foremost to turn to account.

THE OFFICE OF RECTOR.

Third, the Organisation of the primitive University. Europe was unsettled; even in the capitals, the civil power was often unhinged. Wherever multitudes came together, there was manifested a spirit of turbulence. The Universities often exemplified this fact; and it was found necessary to establish a government within themselves. The basis was popular; but, while, in Paris, only the teaching body was incorporated, in Bologna, the students had a voice. They elected the Rector, and his jurisdiction was very great indeed, and much more important than speechifying to his constituents. His Court had the power of internal regulation, with both a civil and criminal jurisdiction. The Scotch Universities, on this point, followed Bologna; and that fact is the remote cause of this day's meeting.

THE UNIVERSITIES OF SCOTLAND FOUNDED.

So started the University. The idea took; and in three centuries, many of the leading towns in Italy, France, the German Empire, had their Universities; in England arose Oxford and Cambridge; the model was Paris or Bologna.

Scotland did not at first enter the race of University-founding, but worked on the plan of the cuckoo, by laying its eggs in the nests of others. For two centuries, Scotchmen were almost shut out of England; and so could not make for themselves a career in Oxford and Cambridge, as in later times. They had, however, at home, good grammar schools, where they were grounded in Latin. They perambulated Europe, and were familiar figures in the great University towns, and especially Paris. From their disputatious and metaphysical aptitude, they worked their upward way—

And gladly would they learn and gladly teach.

At length, the nation did take up the work in good earnest. In 1411, was founded the first of the St. Andrews' Colleges; 1451 is the date of Glasgow; 1494, King's College, Aberdeen. These are the pre-

Reformation colleges; but for the Reformation, we might not have had any other. Their founders were ecclesiastics; their constitution and ceremonial were ecclesiastical. They were intended, no doubt, to keep the Scotch students at home. They were also expected to serve as bulwarks to the Church against the rising heretics of the times. In this they were a disappointment; the first-begotten of them became the cradle of the Reformation.

In these our three eldest foundations, we are to seek the primitive constitution and the teaching system of our Universities. In essentials, they were the same; only between the dates of Glasgow and Old Aberdeen occurred two great events. One was the taking of Constantinople, which spread the Greek scholars with their treasures over Europe. The other was the progress of printing. In 1451, when Glasgow commenced, there was no printed text-book. In 1494, when King's College began, the ancient classics had been largely printed; the early editions of Aristotle in our Library, show the date of 1486.

FIRST PERIOD—THE TEACHING BODY.

Our Universities have three well-marked periods; the first anterior to the Reformation; the second from the Reformation to the beginning of last century; the third, the last and present centuries. Confining ourselves still to the Faculty of Arts, the features of the Pre-Reformation University were these :—

First, as regards the teaching Body. The quadriennial Arts' course was conducted by so-called

Regents, who each carried the same students through all the four years, thus taking upon himself the burden of all the sciences—a walking Encyclopædia. The system was in full force, in spite of attempts to change it, during both the first and the second periods. You, the students of Arts, at the present day, encountering in your four years, seven faces, seven voices, seven repositories of knowledge, need an effort to understand how your predecessors could be cheerful and happy, confined all through to one personality; sometimes juvenile, sometimes senile, often feeble at his best.

THE SUBJECTS TAUGHT.

Next, as regards the Subjects taught. To know these you have simply to know what are the writings of Aristotle. The little work on him by Sir Alexander Grant supplies the needful information. The records of the Glasgow University furnish the curriculum of Arts soon after its foundation. The subjects are laid out in two heads—Logic and Philosophy The Logic comprised first the three Treatises of the Old Logic; to these were now added the whole of the works making up Aristotle's Organon. This brought in the Syllógism, and allied matters. There was also a selection from the work known as the *Topics*, not now included in Logical teaching, yet one of the most remarkable and distinctive of Aristotle's writings. It is a highly laboured account of the whole art of Disputation, laid out under his scheme of the Predicables. The selection fell chiefly on two books

—the second, comprising what Aristotle had to say on Induction, and the sixth, on Definition; together with the "Logical Captions" or Fallacies. Disputation was one of the products of the Greek mind; and Aristotle was its prophet.

Now for Philosophy. This comprised nearly the whole of Aristotle's Physical treatises—his very worst side—together with his Metaphysics, some parts of which are hardly distinguishable from the Physics. Next was the very difficult treatise—*De Anima*, on the mind, or Soul—and some allied Psychological treatises, as that on Memory. Such was the ordinary and sufficing curriculum. It was allowed to be varied with a part of the Ethics; but in this age we do not find the Politics; and the Rhetoric is never mentioned. So also, the really valuable Biological works of Aristotle, including his book on Animals, appear to have been neglected.

Certain portions of Mathematics always found a place in the curriculum. Likewise, some work on Astronomy, which was one of the quadrivium subjects.

All this was given in Latin. Greek was not then known (it was introduced into Scotland, in 1534). No classical Latin author is given; the education in Latin was finished at the Grammar School.

MANNER OF TEACHING.

Such was the Arts' Faculty of the 15th century; a dreary, single-manned, Aristotelian quadriennium.

The position is not completely before us, till we understand farther the manner of working.

The pupils could not, as a rule, possess the text of Aristotle. The teacher read and expounded the text for them; but a very large portion of the time was always occupied in dictating, or "diting," notes, which the pupils were examined upon, *vivâ voce;* their best plan usually being to get them by heart, as any one might ask them to repeat passages literally; while perhaps few could examine well upon the meaning. The notes would be selections and abridgments from Aristotle, with the comments of modern writers. The "diting" system was often complained of as waste of time, but was not discontinued till the third, or present, University dynasty, and not entirely then, as many of us know.

The teaching was thus exclusively *Text* teaching. The teacher had little or nothing to say for himself (at least in the earliest period). He was even restricted in the remarks he might make by way of commentary. He was as nearly as possible a machine.

But lastly, to complete the view of the first period, we must add the practice of Disputation, of which we shall have a better idea from the records of the next period. This practice was co-eval with the Universities; it was the single mode of stimulating the thought of the individual student; the chief antidote to the mechanical teaching by Text-books and dictation.

The pre-Reformation period of Aberdeen University was little more than sixty years. For a portion of those years it attained celebrity. In 1541, the town was honoured by a visit from James V., and the University contributed to his entertainment. The somewhat penny-a-lining account is, that there were exercises and disputations in Greek, Latin, and other languages! The official records, however, show that the College at that very time had sunk into a convent and conventual school.

SECOND PERIOD—THE REFORMATION.

The Reformation introduced the second period, and made important changes. First of all, in the great convulsion of European thought, the ascendancy of Aristotle was shaken. It is enough to mention two incidents in the downfall of the mighty Stagyrite. One was the attack on him by the renowned Peter Ramus, in the University of Paris. Our countryman, Andrew Melville, attended Ramus's Lectures, and became the means of introducing his system into Scotland. The other incident is still more notable. The Reformers had to consider their attitude towards Aristotle. At first their opinion was condemnatory. Luther regarded him as a very devil; he was "a godless bulwark of the Papists". Melancthon was also hostile; but he soon perceived that Theology would crumble into fanatical dissolution without the co-operation of some philosophy. As yet there was nothing to fall back upon except the pagan systems. Of these, Melancthon was obliged to confess that Aristotle was the least objectionable, and was, moreover, in possession. The plan, therefore, was to accept him as a basis, and fence him round with orthodox emendations. This done, Aristotle, no longer despotic, but as a limited constitutional monarch, had his reign prolonged a century and a half.

THE MODIFIED CURRICULUM—ANDREW MELVILLE.

The first thing, after the Reformation in Scotland, was to purge the Universities of the inflexible adherents of the old faith. Then came the question of amending the Curriculum, not simply with a view to Protestantism, but for the sake of an enlightened teaching. The right man appeared at the right moment. In 1574, Andrew Melville, then in Geneva, received pressing invitations to come home and take part in the needed reforms. He was immediately made Principal of Glasgow University, at that time in a state of utter collapse and ruin. He had matured his plans, after consultation with George Buchanan, and they were worthy of a great reformer. He sketched a curriculum, substantially the curriculum of the second University period. The modifications upon the almost exclusive Aristotelianism of the first period, were significant. The Greek language was introduced, and Greek classical authors read. The reading in the Roman classics was extended. A text-book on Rhetoric accompanied the classical readings. The dialectics of Ramus made the prelude to Logic, instead of the three treatises of the old Logic. The Mathematics included Euclid. Geography and Cosmography were taken up. Then came a course of Moral Philosophy on an enlarged basis. With the Ethics and Politics of Aristotle, were combined Cicero's Ethical works and certain Dialogues of Plato. Finally, in the Physics, Melville still used Aristotle, but along with a more modern treatise. He also gave a view of Universal History and Chronology.

This curriculum, which Melville took upon himself to teach, in order to train future teachers, was the point of departure of the courses in all the Universities during the second period. With variations of time and place, the Arts' course may be described as made up of the Greek and Latin classics, with Rhetoric, Logic, and Dialectics, Moral Philosophy, or Ethics, Mathematics, Physics, and Astronomy. The little text-book of Rhetoric, by Talon or Talæus, was made up of notes from the Lectures of Peter Ramus, and used in all our Colleges till superseded by the better compilation of the Dutch scholar, Gerard John Voss.

Melville had to contend with many opponents, among them the sticklers for the infallibility of the Stagyrite. Like the German Reformers, he had accepted Aristotelianism as a basis, with a similar process of reconciliation. So it was that Aristotle and Calvin were brought to kiss each other.

ATTEMPT TO ABOLISH REGENTING.

Melville's next proposal was all too revolutionary. It consisted in restricting the Regents each to a special group of subjects; in fact, anticipating our modern professoriate. He actually set up this plan in Glasgow. one Regent took Greek and Latin; another, his nephew, James Melville, took Mathematics, Logic, and Moral Philosophy; a third, Physics and Astronomy. The system went on, in appearance at least, for fifty years; it is only in 1642, that we find the Regents given without a specific designation. Why it should have gone on so long, and been then dropt, we are not informed. Melville's influence started it in the other Universities, but it was defeated in every one from the very outset. After six years at Glasgow, he went to St. Andrew's as Principal and Professor of Divinity, and tried there the same reforms, but the resistance was too great. In spite of a public enactment, the division of labour among the Regents was never carried out. Yet such was Melville's authority, that the same enactment was extended to King's College, in a scheme having a remarkable history—the so-called New Foundation of Aberdeen University, promulgated in a Royal Charter of about the year 1581. The Earl Marischal was a chief promoter of the plan of reform comprised in this charter. The division of labour among the Regents was most expressly enjoined. The plan fell through; and there was a legal dispute fifty years afterwards as to whether it had ever any legal validity. Charles I. was made to express indignation at the idea of reducing the University to a school!

We now approach the foundation of Marischal College. The Earl Marischal may have been actuated by the failure of his attempt to reform King's

College. At all events, his mind was made up to follow Melville in assigning separate subjects to his Regents. The Charter is explicit on this head. Yet in spite of the Charter and in spite of his own presence, the intention was thwarted; the old Regenting lasted 160 years.

ARISTOTELIAN PHYSICS TOO LONG MAINTAINED.

Still the Curriculum reform was gained. There was, indeed, one great miss. The year before Marischal College was founded, Galileo had published his work on Mechanics, which, taken with what had been accomplished by Archimedes and others, laid the foundations of our modern Physics. Copernicus had already published his work on the Heavens. It was now time that the Aristotelian Physics should be clean swept away. In this whole department, Aristotle had made a reign of confusion; he had thrown the subject back, being himself off the rails from first to last. Had there been in Scotland an adviser in this department, like Melville in general literature, or like Napier of Merchiston in pure mathematics, one fourth of the college teaching might have been reclaimed from utter waste, and a healthy tone of thinking diffused through the remainder.

A curious fascination always attached to the study of Astronomy, even when there was not much to be said, apart from the unsatisfactory disquisitions of Aristotle. A little book, entitled "*Sacrobosco* on the Sphere," containing little more than what we should now teach to boys and girls, along with the Globes, was a University text-book throughout Europe for centuries. I was informed by a late King's College professor that the Use of the Globes was, within his memory, taught in the Magistrand Class. This would be simply what is termed a "survival".

SYSTEM OF DISPUTATION.

Now as to the mode of instruction. There were *vivâ voce* examinations upon the notes, such as we can imagine. But the stress was laid on Disputations and Declamations in various forms. Besides disputing and declaiming on the regular class work before the Regent, we find that, in Edinburgh, and I suppose elsewhere, the classes were divided into companies, who met apart, and conferred and debated among themselves daily. The students were occupied, altogether, six hours a day. Then the higher classes were frequently pitched against each other. This was a favourite occupation on Saturdays. The doctrines espoused by the leading students became their nicknames. The pass for Graduation consisted in the *propugning* or *impugning* of questions by each candidate in turn. An elaborate Thesis was drawn up by the Regent, giving the heads of his philosophy course; this was accepted by the candidates, signed by them, and printed at their expense. Then on the day of trial, at a long sitting, each candidate stood up and propunged or impunged a portion of the Thesis; all were heard in turn; and on the result the Degree was conferred. A good many of these Theses are preserved in our Library; some of them are very long—

a hundred pages of close type; they are our best clue to the teaching of the period. We can see how far Aristotle was qualified by modern views.

REGENTING DOOMED.

I said there might have been times when the students never had the relief of a second face all the four years. The exceptions are of importance. First, as regards Marischal College. Within a few years of the foundation, Dr. Duncan Liddell founded the Mathematical Chair, and thus withdrew from the Regents the subject that most of all needed a specialist; a succession of very able mathematicians sat in this chair. King's College had not the same good fortune. From its foundation it possessed a separate functionary, the Humanist or Grammarian; but he had also, till 1753, to act as Rector of the Grammar School. Edinburgh obtained from an early date a Mathematical chair, occupied by men of celebrity. There was no other innovation till near the end of the 17th century, when Greek was isolated both in Edinburgh and in Marischal College; but the end of Regenting was then near.

The old system, however, had some curious writhings. During the troubled 17th century, University reform could not command persistent attention. But after the 1688-Revolution, opinions were strongly expressed in favour of the Melville system. The obvious argument was urged, that, by division of labour each man would be able to master a special subject, and do it justice in teaching. Yet, it was replied, that, by the continued intercourse, the master knew better the humours, inclinations, and talents of their scholars. To which the answer was — the humours and inclinations of scholars are not so deeply hid but that in a few weeks they appear. Moreover, it was said, the students are more respectful to a Master while he is new to them.

The final division of subjects took place in Edinburgh, in 1708; in Glasgow, in 1727; in St. Andrews, in 1747. In Marischal College, the change was made by a minute of 11th Jan., 1753; but, whether from ignorance, or from want of grace, the Senatus did not record its satisfaction at having, after a lapse of five generations, fulfilled the wishes of the pious founder. In King's College, the old system lasted till 1798.

This closes the second age of the Universities, and introduces the third age, the age of the Professoriate, of Lecturing instead of Text-books, the end of Disputation, and the use of the English Language. It was now, and not till now, that the Scottish Universities stood forth, in several leading departments of knowledge, as the teachers of the world.

THE UNIVERSITIES AND THE POLITICAL REVOLUTIONS.

The second age of the Universities was Scotland's most trying time. In a hundred and thirty years, the country had passed through four revolutions and counter-revolutions; every one of which told upon the Universitites. The victorious party imposed its test upon the University teacher, and drove out recusants. You must all know something of the purging of the University and the Ministry of Aberdeen by the Covenanting General Assembly of 1640. These deposed Aberdeen doctors may have had too strong leanings to episcopacy in the Church and to absolutism in the State, but they were not Vicars of Bray. The first half of the century was adorned by a band of scholars, who have gained renown by their cultivation of Latin poetry; a little oasis in the desert of Aristotelian Dialectics. It would be needless and ungracious to enquire whether this was the best thing that could have been done for the generation of Bishop Patrick Forbes.

Your reading in the History of Scotland will thus bring you face to face with the great powers that contended for the mastery from 1560: the Monarchy, always striving to be absolute; the Church, whose position made it the advocate of popular freedom; the Universities, fluctuating as regards political liberty, but standing up for intellectual liberty. In the 17th century the Church ruled the Universities; in the 18th, it may be said, that the Universities returned the compliment.

UNIVERSITIES NOT ESSENTIAL FOR PROFESSIONS.

Enough for the past. A word or two on the present. What is now the need for a University system, and what must the system be to answer that need? Many things are altered since the 12th century.

First, then, Universities, as I understand them, are not absolutely essential to the teaching of professions. Let me make an extreme supposition. A great naval commander, like Nelson, is sent on board ship, at eleven or twelve; his previous knowledge, or general training, is what you may suppose for that age. It is in the course of actual service, and in no other way, that he acquires his professional fitness for commanding fleets. Is this right or is it wrong? Perhaps it is wrong, but it has gone on so for a long time. Well, why may not a preacher be formed on the same plan? John Wesley was not a greater man in preaching, than Nelson in seamanship. Take, then, a youth of thirteen from the school. Apprentice him to the minister of a parish. Let him make at once preparations for clerical work. Let him store his memory with sermons, let him make abstracts of Divinity systems; master the best exegetical commentators. Then, in a year or two, he would begin to catechise the young, to give addresses in the way of exposition, exhortation, encouragement, and rebuke. Practice would bring facility. Might not, I say, seven years of the actual work, in the susceptible period of life, make a preacher of no mean power, without the Grammar School, without the Arts' Classes, without the Divinity Hall?

What then do we gain by taking such a roundabout approach to our professional work? The answer is twofold.

First, as regards the profession itself. Nearly every skilled occupation, in our time, involves principles and facts that have been investigated, and are taught, outside the profession; to the medical man are given courses of Chemistry, Physiology, and so on. Hence to be completely equipped for your professional work, you must repair to the teachers of those tributary departments of knowledge. The requirement, however, is not absolute; it admits of being evaded. Your professional teachers ought to master these outside subjects, and give you just as much of them as you need, and no more; which would be an obvious economy of your valuable time.

Thus, I apprehend, the strictly professional uses of general knowledge fail to justify the Grammar School and the Arts' curriculum. Something, indeed, may still be said for the higher grades of professional excellence, and for introducing improved methods into the practice of the several crafts; for which wider outside studies lend their aid. This, however, is not enough; inventors are the exception. In fact, the ground must be widened, and include, secondly, *the life beyond the profession*. We are citizens of a self-governed country; members of various smaller societies; heads, or members of families. We have, moreover, to carve out recreation and enjoyment as the alternative and the reward of our professional toil. Now the entire tone and character of this life outside the profession, is profoundly dependent on the compass of our early studies. He that leaves the school for the shop at thirteen, is on one platform. He that spends the years from thirteen to twenty in acquiring general knowledge, is on a totally different platform;

he is, in the best sense, an aristocrat. Those that begin work at thirteen, and those that are born not to work at all, are alike his inferiors. He should be able to spread light all around. He it is that may stand forth before the world as the model man.

THE IDEAL GRADUATE.

All this supposes that you realise the position ; that you fill up the measure of the opportunities ; that you keep in view at once the Professional life, the Citizen life, and the life of Intellectual tastes. The mere professional man, however prosperous, cannot be a power in society, as the Arts' graduate may become. His leisure occupations are all of a lower stamp. He does not participate in the march of knowledge. He must be aware of his incompetence to judge for himself in the greater questions of our destiny ; his part is to be a follower, and not a leader.

It is not, then, the name of graduate that will do all this. It is not a scrape pass ; it is not decent mediocrity with a languid interest. It is a fair and even attention throughout, supplemented by auxiliaries to the class work. It is such a hold of the leading subjects, such a mastery of the various alphabets, as will make future references intelligible, and a continuation of the study possible.

Our curriculum is one of the completest in the country, or perhaps anywhere. By the happy thought of the Senatus of Marischal College, in 1753, you have a fundamental class (Natural History) not existing in the other colleges. You have a fair representation of the three great lines of science—the Abstract, the Experimental, and the Classifying. When it is a general education that you are thinking of, every scheme of option is imperfect that does not provide for such three-sided cultivation of our reasoning powers. A larger quantity of one will no more serve for the absence of the rest than a double covering of one part of the body, will enable another part to be left bare.

VOLUNTARY EXTENSION OF THE BASIS.

Your time in the Arts' curriculum is not entirely used up by the classes. You can make up for deficiencies in the course, when once you have formed your ideal of completeness. For a year or two after graduating, while still rejoicing in youthful freshness, you can be widening your foundations. The thing then is, to possess a good scheme and to abide by it. Now, making every allowance for the variation of tastes and of circumstances, and looking solely to what is desirable for a citizen and a man, it is impossible to refuse the claims of the department of Historical and Social study. One or two good representative historical periods might be thoroughly mastered in conjunction with the best theoretical compends of Social Philosophy.

Farther, the ideal graduate, who is to guide and not follow opinion, should be well versed in all the bearings of the Spiritual Philosophy of the time.

The subject branches out into wide regions, but not wider than you should be capable of following it. This is not a professional study merely; it is the study of a well-instructed man.

Once more. A share of attention should be bestowed early on the higher Literature of the Imagination. As, in after life, poetry and elegant composition are to be counted on as a pleasure and solace, they should be taken up at first as a study. The critical examination of styles, and of authors, which forms an admirable basis of a student's society, should be a work of study and research. The advantages will be many and lasting. To conceive the exact scope and functions of the Imagination in art, in science, in religion, and everywhere, will repay the trouble.

THE ARTS' GRADUATE IN LITERATURE.

Ever since I remember, I have been accustomed to hear of the superiority of the Arts' graduate, in various crafts, more especially as a teacher. Many of you in these days pass into another vocation—Letters, or the Press. Here too, almost everything you learn will pay you professionally. Still, I am careful not to rest the case for general education on professional grounds alone. I might show you that the highest work of all—original enquiry—needs a broad basis of liberal study; or at all events is vastly aided by that. Genius will work on even a narrow basis, but imperfect preparatory study leaves marks of imperfection in the product.

The same considerations that determine your voluntary studies, determine also the University Ideal. A University, in my view, stands or falls with its Arts' Faculty. Without debating the details, we may say that this Faculty should always be representative of the needs of our intelligence, both for the professional and for the extra-professional life; it should not be of the shop, shoppy. The University exists because the professions would stagnate without it; and still more, because it may be a means of enlarging knowledge at all points. Its watchword is Progress. We have, at last, the division of labour in teaching; outside the University, teachers too much resemble the Regent of old—having too many subjects, and too much time spent in grinding. Our teachers are exactly the reverse.

Yet, there cannot be progress without a sincere and single eye to the truth. The fatal sterility of the middle ages, and of our first and second University periods, had to do with the mistake of gagging men's mouths, and dictating all their conclusions. Things came to be so arranged that contradictory views ran side by side, like opposing electric currents; the thick wrappage of ingenious phraseology arresting the destructive discharge. There was, indeed, an elaborate and pretentious Logic, supplied by Aristotle, and amended by Bacon; what was still wanted was a taste of the Logic of Freedom.

VII.
THE ART OF STUDY.

THE ART OF STUDY.

OF hackneyed subjects, a foremost place may be assigned to the Art of Study. Allied to the theory and practice of Education generally, it has still a field of its own, although not very precisely marked out. It relates more to self-education than to instruction under masters; it supposes the voluntary choice of the individual rather than the constraint of an outward discipline. Consequently, the time for its application is when the pupil is emancipated from the prescription and control of the scholastic curriculum.

There is another idea closely associated with our notion of study—namely, learning from books. We may stretch the word, without culpable licence, to comprise the observation of facts of all kinds, but it more naturally suggests the resort to book lore for the knowledge that we are in quest of. There is a considerable propriety in restricting it to this meaning; or, at all events, in treating the art of becoming wise through reading, as different from the arts of observing facts at first hand. In short, study should not be made co-extensive with knowledge getting, but with book learning. In thus narrowing the field, we have the obvious advantage of cultivating it more carefully, and the unobvious, but very real, advantage of dealing with one homogeneous subject.

In the current phrase, "*studying under* some one," there is a more express reference to being taught by a master, as in listening to lectures. There is, however, the implication that the learner is applying his own mind to the special field, and, at the same time, is not neglecting the other sources of knowledge, such as books. The master is looked upon rather as a guide to enquiry, than as the sole fountain of the information sought.

Thus, then, the mental exercise that we now call "study" began when books began; when knowledge was reduced to language and laid out systematically in verbal compositions. A certain form of it existed in the days when language was as yet oral merely; when there might be long compositions existing only in the memory of experts, and communicable by speech alone. But study then was a very simple affair: it would consist mainly in attentive listening to recitation, so as to store up in the memory what was thus communicated. The art, if any, would attach equally to the reciter and to the listener; the duty of the one would be to accommodate his lessons in time, quantity, and mode of delivery to the retentive capacity of the other; who, in his turn, would be required to con and recapitulate what he had been told, until he made it his own, whatever it might be worth.

Even when books came into existence, an art of study would be at first very simple. The whole extent of book literature among the Jews before Christ would be soon read; and, when once read, there was nothing left but to re-read it in whole or in part, with a view of committal to memory, whether for meditative reflection, or for awakening the emotions. We see, in the Psalms of David, the emphasis attached to mental dwelling on the particulars of the Mosaic Law, as the nourishment of the feelings of devotion.

The Greek Literature about 350 B.C., when Aristotle and Demosthenes had reached manhood (being then 34), had attained a considerable mass; as one may see at a glance from Jebb's chronology attached to his Primer. There was a splendid poetical library, including all the great tragedians, with the older and the middle Comedy. There were the three great historians—Herodotus, Thucydides, and Xenophon; and the orators—Lysias, Isocrates, and Isæus; there were the precursors of Socrates in Philosophy; and, finally, the Platonic Dialogues. To overtake all these would employ several years of learned leisure; and to imbibe their substance would be a rich and varied culture, especially of the poetic and rhetorical kind. To make the most of the field, a judicious procedure would be very helpful; there was evident scope for an art of study. The fertile intellect of the Greeks produced the first systematic guides to high culture; the Rhetorical art for Oratory and Poetry, the Logical art for Reasoning, and the Eristic art for Disputation. There was nothing precisely corresponding to an Art of Study, but there were examples of the self culture of celebrated men. The most notorious of these is Demosthenes; of whom we know that, while he took special lessons in the art of oratory, he also bestowed extraordinary pains upon the general cultivation of his intellectual powers. His application to Thucydides in particular is recounted in terms of obvious mythical exaggeration; showing, nevertheless, his idea of fixing upon a special book with a view to extracting from it every particle of intellectual nourishment that it could yield: in which we have an example of the art of study as I have defined it. Then, it is said that, in his anxiety to master his author, he copied the entire work eight times, with his own hand, and had it by heart *verbatim*, so as to be able to re-write it when the manuscripts were accidentally destroyed. Both points enter into the art of study, and will come under review in the sequel.

We do not possess from the genius of Aristotle— the originator or improver of so many practical departments—an Art of Study. The omission was not supplied by any other Greek writer known to us. The oratorical art was a prominent part of education both in Greece and in Rome; and was discussed by many authors—notably by Cicero himself; but the exhaustive treatment is found in Quintilian. The very wide scope of the "Institutes of Oratory" comprises a chapter upon the orator's reading, in which the author reviews the principal Greek and Roman classics from Homer to Seneca, with remarks upon the value of each for the mental cultivation of the oratorical pupil. Something of this sort might be legitimately included in the art of study, but might also be withheld, as being provided in the critical estimates already formed respecting all writers of note.

After Quintilian, it is little use to search for an art of study, either among the later Latin classics, or among the mediæval authors generally. I proceed at once to remark upon the well-known essay of Bacon, which shows his characteristic subtlety, judiciousness, and weight; yet is too short for practical guidance. He hits the point, as I conceive it, when he identifies study with reading, and brings in, but only by way of contrast and complement, conference or conversation and composition. He endeavours to indicate the worth of book learning, as an essential addition to the actual practice of business, and the experience of life. He marks a difference between books that we are merely to dip into (books to be tasted) and such as are to be mastered; without, however, stating examples. He ventures also to settle the respective kinds of culture assignable to different departments of knowledge—history, poetry, mathematics, natural philosophy, moral philosophy, logic and rhetoric; a very useful attempt in its own way, and one that may well enough enter into a comprehensive art of study, if not provided for in the still wider theory of Education at large.

Bacon's illustrious friend, Hobbes, did not write on studies, but made a notable remark bearing on one topic connected with the art,—namely, that if he had read as much as other men, he should have remained still as ignorant as other men. This must not be interpreted too literally. Hobbes was really a great reader of the ancients, and must have studied with care some of the philosophers immediately preceding himself. Still, it indicates an important point for discussion in the art of study, in which great men have gone to opposite extremes—I mean in reference to the amount of attention to be given to previous writers, in taking up new ground.

To come down to another great name, we have Milton's ideal of Education, given in his short Tractate. Here, with many protestations of knowing things, rather than words, we find an enormous prescription of book reading, including, in fact, every known author on every one of a wide circle of subjects. This was characteristic of the man: he was a voracious reader himself, and an example to show, in opposition to Hobbes, that original genius is not necessarily quenched by great or even excessive erudition. As bearing on the art of study, especially for striplings under twenty, Milton's scheme is open to two criticisms: first, that the amount of reading on the whole is too great; second, that in subjects handled by several authors of repute, one should have been selected as the leading text-book and got up thoroughly; the others being taken in due time as enlarging or correcting the knowledge thus laid in. Think of a boy learning Rhetoric upon six authors taken together!

The transition from Milton to Locke is the inverse of that from Hobbes to Milton. Locke was also a man of few books. If he had been sent to school under Milton, as he might have been,* he would have very soon thrown up the learned drudgery prescribed for him, and would have bolted.

The practical outcome of Locke's enquiries respecting the human faculties is to be found in the little treatise named—"The Conduct of the Understanding". It is an earnest appeal in favour of devotion to the attainment of truth, and an exposure of *all* the various sources of error, moral and intellectual; more especially prejudices and bias. There are not, however, many references to book study; and such as we find are chiefly directed to the one aim of painful and laborious examination, first, of an author's meaning, and next of the goodness of his arguments. Two or three sentences will give the clue. "Those who have read of everything, are thought to understand everything too; but it is not always so. Reading furnishes the mind only with materials of knowledge; it is thinking makes what we read ours. We are of the ruminating kind, and it is not enough to cram ourselves with a great deal of collections; unless we chew them over again, they will not give us strength and nourishment." Farther: "Books and reading are looked upon to be the great helps of the understanding, and instruments of knowledge, as it must be allowed that they are; and yet I beg leave to question whether these do not prove a hindrance to many, and keep several bookish men from attaining to solid and true knowledge". Here, again, is his

* Milton had charge of pupils in 1644, when Locke was twelve.

stern way of dealing with any author:—"To fix in the mind the clear and distinct idea of the question stripped of words; and so likewise, in the train of argumentation, to take up the author's ideas, neglecting his words, observing how they connect or separate those in the question." Of this last, more afterwards.

A disciple of Locke, and a man of considerable and various powers, the non-conformist divine Isaac Watts, produced perhaps the first considerable didactic treatise on Study. I refer, of course, to his well-known work entitled "The Improvement of the Mind."; on which, he tells us, he was occupied at intervals for twenty years. It has two Parts: one on the acquisition of knowledge; the other on Communication or Teaching. The scheme is a very wide one. Observation, Reading, attending Lectures, Conversation,—are all included. To the word "Study," Watts attaches a special meaning, namely Meditation and Reflection, together with the control or regulation of all the exercises of the mind. I doubt if this meaning is well supported by usage. At all events it is not the signification that I propose to attach to the term. Observation is an art in itself: so is Conversation, whether amicable or contentious. The *proportions* that these exercises should bear to reading, would fairly claim a place in the complete Art of Study.

Watts has two short chapters on Books and Reading, containing sensible remarks. He urges the importance of thorough mastery of select authors; but assumes a power of discriminating good and bad beyond the reach of a learner, and does not show how it is to be attained. He is very much concerned all through as to the moral tone and religious orthodoxy of the books read. He also reproves hasty and ill-natured judgments upon the authors.

Watts's Essay is so pithily written, and so full of sense and propriety, that it long maintained a high position in our literature; he tells us, that it had become a text-book in the University. I do not know of any better work on the same plan. A "Student's Guide," by an American named Todd, was in vogue with us, some time ago; but anyone looking at its contents, will not be sorry that it is now forgotten. It would not, however, be correct to say that the subject has died out. If there have not been many express didactic treatises of late, there has been an innumerable host of small dissertations, in the form of addresses, speeches, incidental discussions, leading articles, sermons—all intended to guide both young and old in the path of useful study. What to read, when to read, and how to read,—have been themes of many an essay, texts of many a discourse. According as Education at large has been more and more discussed, the particular province of self-education, as here marked out, has had an ample share of attention from more or less qualified advisers.

What we have got before us, then, is, first, to define our ground, and then to appropriate and value the accumulated fruits of the labour expended on it. I have already indicated how I would narrow the subject of Study, so as to occupy a field apart, and not jumble together matters that follow distinct laws. The theory of Education in general is the theory of good Teaching: that is a field by itself, although many things in it are applicable also to self-education. To estimate the values of different acquisitions —Science, Language, and the rest, is good for all modes of culture. The laws of the understanding in general, and of the memory in particular, must be taken into account under every mode of acquiring knowledge. Yet the alteration of circumstances, when a pupil is carving out his own course, and working under his own free-will, leads to new and distinct rules of procedure. Also, that part of self-education consisting in the application to books is distinct from the other forms of mental cultivation, namely, conversing, disputing, original composition, and tutorial aid. Each of these has its own rules or methods, which I do not mean to notice except by brief allusion.

In connection with the Plan of study, it is material to ask what the individual is studying for. Each profession, each accomplishment, has its own course of education. If book reading is an essential part, then the choice of books must follow the line of the special pursuit. This is obvious; but does not do away with the consideration of the best modes of studying whatever books are suitable for the end. One man has to read in Chemistry, another in Law, another in Divinity, and so on. For each and all of these, there is a profitable and an unprofitable mode of working, and the speciality of the matter is unessèntial.

The more important differences of subject, involving differences of method, are seen in such contrasted departments as Science and Language, Thought and Style, Reality and Poetry, Generality and Particularity. In applying the mind to these various branches, and in using books as the medium of acquisition, there are considerable differences in the mode of procedure. The study of a book of Science is not on the same plan as the study of a History or a Poem. Yet even in these last, there are many circumstances in common, arising out of the constitution of our faculties and the nature of a verbal medium of communication of thought.

An art of Study in general should not presume to follow out in minute detail the education of the several professions. There should still be, for example, a distinct view of the training special in an Orator, on which the ancients bestowed so much pains; there being no corresponding course hitherto chalked out for a Philosopher as such, or even for a Poet.

Next, there is an important distinction between studies for a professional walk, and the studies of a man's leisure, with a view to gratifying a special taste, or for the higher object of independent thinking on all the higher questions belonging to a citizen and a man. Both positions has its peculiarities; and an art of study should be catholic enough to embrace them. To have the best part of the day for study, and the rest for recreation and refreshment, is one thing: and to study in by-hours, in snatches of time, and in holidays is quite another thing. In the latter case, the choice of subjects, and the extent of them, must be considerably different; while the consideration of the best modes of economizing time and strength, and of harmonizing one's life as a whole, is more pressing and more arduous. But, when the course is chalked out, the details of study must conform to the general conditions of all acquirements in knowledge through the instrumentality of books.

One, and only one, more preliminary clearing. When an instructor proceeds, as Milton in his school, or as James Mill with his son, by prescribing to each pupil a mass of books to be read, with more or less of examination as to their contents; in such a case, education from without has passed into study in our narrow sense; and the procedure for one situation is applicable to both. The two cases are equally in contrast to educating by the direct instruction of the teacher. In so far, however, as any teacher requires book study to co-operate with his own addresses, to that extent do the methods laid down for private study come into play.

Under every view, it is a momentous fact, that the man of modern times has become a book-reading animal. The acquisition of knowledge and the cultivation of the intellectual powers of the mind, form only a small part of the use of books; although the part more properly named Study. The moral tendencies are controlled; the emotions regulated; sympathy with mankind, or the opposite, generated; pleasurable excitement afforded. These other uses may be provided apart, as in our literature of amusement, or they may be given in combination with the element of knowledge, in which case they are apt to be a disturbing force, rendering uncertain our calculations as to the efficacy of particular modes of study.

The practical problem of Study is not to be approached by any high *priori* road ; in other words, by setting out from abstract principles as to the nature of the mind's receptivity and the operation of book-reading upon that receptivity. A humbler line of approach will be more likely to succeed.

There exist a number of received maxims on study, the result of many men's experience and wisdom. Our endeavour will be to collect these, arrange them in a methodical plan, so that they may give mutual aid, and supply each other's defects. We shall go a little farther, and criticise them according to the best available lights ; and, when too vague or sweeping, supply needful qualifications.

The Choice of Books, in the first instance, depends on the merits attributed to them severally by persons most conversant with the special department. In some degree, too, this choice is controlled by the consideration of the best modes of study, as will soon be apparent.

I. Our first maxim is—"Select a Text-book-in-chief". The meaning is, that when a large subject is to be overtaken by book study alone, some one work should be chosen to apply to, in the first instance, which work should be conned and mastered before any other is taken up. There being, in most subjects, a variety of good books, the thorough student will not be satisfied in the long run without consulting several, and perhaps making a study of them all; yet, it is unwise to distract the attention with more than one, while the elements are to be learnt. In Geometry, the pupil begins upon Euclid, or some other compendium, and is not allowed to deviate from the single line of his author. If he is once thoroughly at home on the main ideas and the leading propositions of Geometry, he is safe in dipping into other manuals, in comparing the differences of treatment, and in widening his knowledge by additional theorems, and by various modes of demonstration.

In principle, the maxim is generally allowed. Nevertheless, it is often departed from in practice. This happens in several ways.

One way is exemplified in Milton's Tractate, already referred to. His method of teaching any subject would appear to have been to take the received authors, and to read them one after another, probably according to date; the reading pace, and degree of concentration, being apparently equal all through. His six authors on Rhetoric were—Plato (select Dialogues, of course), Aristotle, Phalereus, Cicero, Hermogenes, Longinus. To read their several treatises through in the order named, with equal attention, would undoubtedly leave in the mind a good many thoughts on Rhetoric, but in a somewhat chaotic state. Much better would it have been to have adopted a Text-book-in-chief, the choice lying between Aristotle and Quintilian (who comes in at a prior stage of the Miltonic curriculum). The book so chosen would be read, and re-read; or rather each chapter would be gone over several times, with appropriate testing exercises and examinations. The other works might then be overtaken and compared with the principal text-book; the judgment of the pupil being so far matured, as to see what in them was already superseded, and what might be adopted as additions to his already acquired stock of ideas. Milton's views of education embraced the useful to a remarkable degree; he was no pamperer of imagination and the ornamental. His list of subjects might be said to be utility run wild:—comprising the chief parts of Mathematics, together with Engineering, Navigation, Architecture, and Fortification; Natural Philosophy; Natural History; Anatomy, and Practice of Physic; Ethics, Politics, Economics, Jurisprudence, Theology; a full course of the Orators and Poets; Logic, Rhetoric, and Poetics. He tumbles out a whole library of reading: but only in Ethics, does he indicate a leading or preferential work; the half-dozen of classical books on the subject are to be perused, "under the determinate sentence" of the scripture authorities. With all this voracity for the useful, Milton had no conception of scientific form, or method; and indeed, few of the subjects had as yet passed the stage of desultory treatment; so that the idea of casting the knowledge into some one form, under the guidance of a chosen author, would never occur to him. Better things might have been expected of James Mill, in conducting the education of his son. Yet we find his plan to have been to require an even and exhaustive perusal of nearly every book on nearly every subject, without singling out any one to impart the best known form in each case. The disadvantage of the process would be that, at first, all the writers were regarded as profitable alike. Nevertheless, in the special subjects that he knew himself, he gave his own instructions as the leading text, and his pupil's knowledge took form according to these. In some cases, accident gave a text-in-chief, as when young Mill at ten years of age, studied Thomson's Chemistry, without the distraction of any other work. If there had been half-a-dozen Chemical manuals in existence, he would probably have read them all, and fared much worse. It happens, however, that, in the more exact sciences, there is a greater sameness in the leading ideas, than in Politics, Morals, or the Human Mind; and the evil of distraction is so much smaller. Undoubtedly, the best of all ways of learning anything is to have a competent master to dole out a fixed quantity every day, just sufficient to be taken in, and no more; the pupils to apply themselves to the matter so imparted, and to do nothing else. The singleness of aim is favourable to the greatest rapidity of acquirement; and any defects are to be left out of account, until one thread of ideas is firmly set in the mind. Not unfrequently, however, and not improperly, the teacher has a text-book in aid of his oral instructions. To make this a help, and not a hindrance, demands the greatest delicacy; the sole consideration being that the pupil must be kept *in one single line of thought*, and never be required to comprehend, on the same point, conflicting or varying statements.

Even the foot-notes to a work may have to be disregarded, in the first instance. They may act like a second author, and keep up an irritating friction. There is, doubtless, a consummate power of annotation that anticipates difficulties, and clears away haze, without distracting the mind. There is also an art of bringing out relief by an accompaniment, like the two images of the stereoscope. This is most likely to arise through a living teacher or commentator, who, by his tones and emphasis, as well as by his very guarded and reserved additions, can make the meaning of the author take shape and fulness.

As the chief text-book is chosen, among other reasons, for its method and system, any defects on this head may be very suitably supplied, during the reader's progress, by notes or otherwise. When the end is clearly kept in view, we shall not go wrong as to the means: the spirit will remedy an undue bias to the letter.

The subjects that depend for their full comprehension upon a certain method and order of details, are numerous, and include the most important branches of human culture. The Sciences, in mass, are avowedly of this character: even such departments as Theology, Ethics, Rhetoric, and Criticism have their definite form ; and, until the mind of the student is fully impressed with this, all the particulars are vague and chaotic, and comparatively useless for practical application. So, any subject cast in a *polemic* form must be received and held in the connection thereby given to it. If the arguments *pro* and *con* fall out of their places in the mind of the reader, their force is missed or misconceived.

History is pre-eminently a subject for method, and, therefore, involves some such plan as is here recommended. Every narrative read otherwise than for mere amusement, as we read a novel, should leave in the mind—(1) the Chronological sequence (more or less detailed); and (2) the Causal sequence, that is, the influences at work in bringing about the events. These are best gained by application to a single work in the first place; other works being resorted to in due time.

Of the non-methodical subjects, forming an illustrative contrast, mention may be made of purely didactic treatises, where the precepts are each valuable for itself, and by itself: such as, until very recently, the works on Agriculture, and even on Medicine. A book of Domestic Receipts, consulted by index, is not a work for study.

Poems and fictitious narrations will naturally be regarded as of the un-methodical class. If there are exceptions, they consist of long poems—Epics and Dramas—whose plan is highly artistic, and must be felt in order to the full effect. Probably, however, this is the merit that the generality of readers are content to miss, especially if greater strain of attention is needed to discover it. Readers bent on enjoyment dwell on the passing page, and are not inclined to carry with them what has gone before, in order to understand what is to follow.

Very intelligent and superior men have wholly repudiated the notion of study by method. We must not lay too much stress upon these disclaimers, seeing that they are usually cited from those in advanced years, or men whose day of methodical education is passed. When Johnson said—"A man ought to read just as inclination leads him," he was not thinking of beginners, for whom he would probably have dictated a different course. Still, it is a prevailing tendency of many minds, to read all books equally, provided the interest or enjoyment of them is equal. Macaulay, Sir William Hamilton, De Quincey, as well as Johnson, and a numerous host besides, were book-gluttons, books in breeches; they imbibed information copiously, and also retained it, but as a matter of chance. The enjoyment of their life was to read; whereas, to master thoroughly a considerable field of knowledge, can never be all enjoyment. Gibbon was a book devourer, but he had a plan; he was organizing a vast work of composition. Macaulay, also, showed himself capable of realizing a scheme of composition; both his History and his Speeches have the stamp of method, even to the pitch of being valuable as models. Hamilton and De Quincey, each in his way, could form high ideals of work, and in part execute them; but their productiveness suffered from too much bookish intoxication. While readers generally mix the motive of instruction with stimulation, the class that seek instruction solely is but small; the other extreme is frequent enough.

In many subjects, the difficulties of fixing upon the proper Text-book are not inconsiderable. The mere reputation of a book may be great, and well-founded; and yet the merits may not be of the kind that fits it for the commencing student. Such conditions as the following must be taken into account. The Form or Method should be of a high order. this we shall have occasion to illustrate under the next head. It should be abreast of the time, on its own subject. It should be moderately full, without being necessarily exhaustive in detail. It is on this point that the cheap primers of the present day are mainly defective. They state general ideas, and lay down outlines; but they do not provide sufficiently expanded illustration to stamp these on the mind of the learner. A shilling primer is really a more advanced book than one on a triple scale, that should embrace the same compass of leading ideas. As a farther condition, the work chosen should not have so much of individuality as to fail in the character of representing the prevailing views. The greatest authors often err on this point; and, while a work of genius is not to be neglected, it may, for this reason, have to take the second place in the order of study. Newton's *Principia* could never be a work suited for an early stage of mathematical study. Lyell's Geology has been a landmark in the history of the subject; but it is not cast in the form for a beginner in Geology. It is, in its whole plan, argumentative; setting up and defending a special thesis in Geology; the facts being arrayed with that view. Many other great works have assumed a like form; such are Malthus on Population, Grove's Correlation of Physical Forces, Darwin's Origin of Species. Even expressly didactic works are often composed more to bring forward a peculiar view, than from the desire to develop a subject in its due proportions. Locke's Essay on the Understanding does not propose to give a methodical and exhaustive handling of the Powers of the Mind, or even of the Intellect. That was reserved for Reid.

The question as between old writers and new, would receive an easy solution upon such grounds as the foregoing, were it not for the sentiment of veneration for the old, because they are old. If an ancient writer retains a place by virtue of surpassing merits, as against all subsequent writers, his case is quite clear. In the nature of things, this must be rare: if there be an example, it is Euclid; yet his position is held only through the mutual jealousy of his modern rivals.

The only motive for commencing a study upon a very old writer is a desire to work out a subject historically; which, in some instances may be allowed, but not very often. In Politics, Ethics, and Rhetoric, the plan might have its advantages; but, with this imperative condition, that we shall follow out the development in the modern works. In proportion as a subject assumes a scientific shape, it must carefully define its terms, marshal its propositions in proper dependence, and offer strict proof of all matters of fact; now, in these respects, every known branch of knowledge has improved with the lapse of ages; so that the more recent works are necessarily the best for entering upon the study. A historical sequence may be proper to be observed; but that should be backward and not forward. The earlier stages of some subjects are absolutely worthless; as, for example, Physics, Chemistry, and most of Biology. In other subjects, as Politics and Ethics, the tentatives of such men as Plato and Aristotle have an undying value; nevertheless, the student should not begin, but end, with them.

There is an extreme form of putting our present doctrine that runs it into paradox: namely, the one-book-and-no-more maxim. Scarcely any book in existence is so all-sufficient for its purpose that a student is better occupied in re-reading it for the tenth time, than in reading some others once. Even the merits of the one book are not fully known unless we compare it with others; nor have we grasped any subject unless we are able to see it stated in various forms, without being distracted or confused. It is not a high knowledge of horsemanship that can be gained by the most thorough acquaintance with one horse.

Any truth that there is in the paradox of excluding all books but one from perusal, belongs to it as a form of the maxim we have now been considering.

There is not in existence a work corresponding to the notion of absolute self-sufficiency. Suppose we were to go over the *chef-d'œuvres* of human genius, we should not find one in the position of entire independence of all others. Take, for example, the poems of Homer; the Republic and a few other of Plato's pre-eminent Dialogues; the great speeches of Demosthenes; the Ethics and Politics of Aristotle; the poems of Dante; Shakespeare, as a whole; Bacon's Novum Organum; Newton's Principia; Locke on the Understanding; the *Méchanique Céleste* of Laplace. No one of all these could produce its effect on the mind without referring to other works, previous, contemporary, or following. The remark is not confined to works of elucidation and comment merely—as the contemporary history of Greece, or the speeches of Demosthenes—but extends to other compositions, of the very same tenor, by different, although inferior, writers. Shakespeare himself is made much more profitable by a perusal of the other Elizabethans, and by a comparison with dramatic models before and after him.

The nearest approach to a perfectly all-sufficing book is seen in scientific compilations by a conjunction of highly accomplished editors. A new edition of Quain's Anatomy, revised and brought up to date by the best anatomists, would, for the moment, probably be fully adequate to the wants of the student, and dispense with all other references whatsoever. Not that even then, it would be desirable to abstain from ever opening a different compendium; although undoubtedly there would be the very minimum of necessity for doing so. Nevertheless, literature presents few analogous instances. One of the great works of an original genius, like Aristotle, might, by profuse annotation, be made nearly sufficing; but this is another way of reading by quotation a plurality of writers; and it would be better still to peruse some of these in full, there being no need for studying them with the degree of intensity bestowed on a main work.

The example, by pre-eminence, of one self-sufficing work is the Bible. Being the sole and ultimate authority of Christian doctrine, it holds a position entirely apart; and, among Protestants at least, there is a becoming jealousy of allowing any extraneous writing to overbear its contents. Yet we are not to infer, as many have done practically, that no other work needs to be read in company with it. Granting that its genuine doctrines have been overlaid by subsequent accretions, the way to get clear of these is not to neglect the entire body of fathers, commentators, and theologians, and to give the whole attention to the scriptural text. Locke himself set an example of this attempt. He proposed, in his "Reasonableness of Christianity," to ascertain the exact meaning of the New Testament, by casting aside all the glosses of commentators and divines, and applying his own unassisted judgment to spell out its teachings. He did not disdain to use the lights of extraneous history, and the traditions of the heathen world; he only refused to be bound by any of the artificial creeds and systems devised in later ages to embody the doctrines supposed to be found in the Bible. The fallacy of his position obviously was, that he could not strip himself of his education and acquired notions, the result of the teaching of the orthodox church. He seemed unconscious of the necessity of trying to make allowance for his unavoidable prepossessions. In consequence, he simply fell into an old groove of received doctrines; and these he handled under the set purpose of simplifying the fundamentals of Christianity to the utmost. Such purpose was not the result of his Bible study, but of his wish to overcome the political difficulties of the time. He found, by keeping close to the Gospels and by making proper selections from the Epistles, that the belief in Christ as the Messiah could be shown to be the central fact of the Christian faith; that the other main doctrines followed out of this by a process of reasoning; and that, as all minds might not perform the process alike, these doctrines could not be essential to the acceptance of Christianity. He got out of the difficulty of framing a creed, as many others have done, by simply using Scripture language, without subjecting it to any very strict definition; certainly without the operation of stripping the meaning of its words, to see what it amounted to. That his short and easy method was not very successful, the history of the Deistical controversy sufficiently proves. The end in view would, in our time, be sought by an opposite course. Instead of disregarding commentators, and the successions of creed embodiments, a scholar of the present day would ascend through these to the original, and find out its meaning, after making allowance for all the tendencies that operated to give a bias to that meaning. As to putting us in the position of listening to the Bible authors at first hand, we should trust more to the erudition of a Pusey or an Ewald, than to the unassisted judgment of a Locke.

II. "What constitutes the study of a book?" Mere perusal at the average reading pace is not the way to imbibe the contents of any work of importance, especially if the subject is new and difficult.

There are various methods in use among authoritative guides. To revert to the Demosthenic traditions: we find two modes indicated—namely, repeated copying, and committing to memory *verbatim*. A third is, making abstracts in writing. A fourth may be designated the Lockian method. Let us consider the respective merits of the four.

1 Of copying a book literally through, there is this to be said, that it engages the attention upon every word, until the act of writing serves to impress the memory. But there are very important qualifications to be assigned in judging of the worth of the exercise. Observe what is the main design of the copyist. It is to produce a *replica* of an original upon paper. He cannot do this without a certain amount of attention to the original; enough at least to enable him to put down the exact words in the copy; and, by such attention, he is so far impressed with the matter, that a certain portion may remain in the

STUDY BY LITERAL COPYING.

memory. If, however, instead of the paper, he could write directly on the brain, he would be aiming straight at his object. Now, experience shows that the making of a copy of any document is compatible with a very small amount of attention to the purport. The extreme case is the copying clerk. He can literally reproduce an original, with entire forgetfulness of what it is about. If his eye takes a faithful note of the sequence of words, he may entirely neglect the meaning. In point of fact, he constantly does so. He remembers nobody's secrets; and he cannot be counted on to check blunders that make nonsense of his text. Probably no one could go on copying for eight hours a day unless the strain of attention to the originals were at a minimum. I conceive, therefore, that copying habits arising from a certain amount of experience at the vocation, would be utterly fatal to the employment of the exercise as a means of study. It may be valuable to such as have seldom used their pen except in original composition. Very probably, in school lessons, to write an exercise two or three times may be a help to the usual routine of saying off the book. I have heard experienced teachers testify to the good effects of the practice. Yet very little would turn the attention the wrong way. Even the requirement of neatness on the part of the master, or the pupil's own liking for it, would abate the desired impression. The multiplied copying set as punishment might stamp a thing on the memory through disgust; it might also engender the mechanical routine of the copyist. In short, to sit down and copy a long work is about the last thing that I should dream of, as a means of study. To copy Thucydides eight times, as the tradition respecting Demosthenes goes, would be about the same as copying Gibbon three times: and who would undertake that?

2. Committing to memory *verbatim*, or nearly so. This too belongs to the same tradition regarding Demosthenes, and is probably as inaccurate as the other. Certainly the eight copyings would not suffice for having the whole by heart. Excepting a professional rhapsodist, or some one gifted with extraordinary powers of memory that would hardly be compatible with a great understanding, nobody would think of committing Thucydides to memory. That Demosthenes should be a perfect master both of the narrated facts, and of the sagacious theorisings of Thucydides in those facts, we may take for granted. And, farther, the orations delivered by opposing speakers in the great critical debates, might very well have been committed *verbatim* by a young orator; many of them are masterpieces of oratory in every point of view. But the reason for getting them by heart does not apply to the general narrative. Even to imbibe the best qualities of the style of Thucydides would not require whole pages to be learnt *verbatim*: a much better way would readily occur to any intelligent man.

In fact, there is no case where it is profitable to load the memory with a whole book, or with large portions of a book. There are many small portions of every leading work that might be committed with advantage. Principal propositions ought to be retained to the letter. Passages, here and there, remarkable for compact force, for argumentative power, or elegant diction, might be read and re-read till they clung to the memory; but this should be the consummation of a thorough and critical estimate of their merits. To commit to memory without thinking of the meaning is a senseless act; and could not be ascribed to Demosthenes. At the stage when the young student is forming a style, he is assisted by laying up *memoriter* a number of passages of great authors; but it is never necessary to go beyond select paragraphs. Detached sentences are valuable, and strain the memory least. Entire paragraphs have a farther value in impressing good paragraph connection; but, to string a number of paragraphs together, or to learn whole chapters by memory, has nothing to recommend it in the way of mental culture.

There is a memory in *extension* that holds a long string of words and ideas together. Its value is to get readily at anything occurring in a certain train, as in a given book. It is the memory of easy reference. There is also a memory of *intension*, that takes a strong grasp of brief expressions and thoughts, and brings them out for use, on the slightest relevancy. The two modes interfere with each other's development; we cannot be great in both; while, for original force, the second is worth the most: it extracts and resets gems to tesselate our future structures; it constitutes depth as against fluency.

To commit poetical passages to memory is a valuable contribution to our stock of material for emotional resuscitation in after years. It also aids in adorning our style, even although we may not aspire to compose in poetry. But the burden of holding the connection of a long poem should be eschewed. Children can readily learn a short psalm or hymn, and can retain it in permanence; but to repeat the 119th psalm from the beginning is the mere *tour-de-force* of a strong natural memory, and a waste of power; just as much as committing an entire book of the Æneid or of Paradise Lost.

3. Making Abstracts.—This is the plan of studying that most advances our intelligent comprehension of any work of difficulty, and also impresses it on the memory in the best form. But there are many ways of doing it; and beginners, from the very fact that they are beginners, are not competent to choose the best. If a book has an obvious and methodical plan in itself, the reader can follow that plan, taking down the leading positions, selecting some of the chief examples or illustrations, giving short headings of chapters and paragraphs, and thus making a synopsis, or full table of contents. All this is useful. The memory is much better impressed through the exertion of picking, choosing, and condensing, than by copying *verbatim*; and the plan or evolution of the whole is more fully comprehended. But, if a work does not easily lend itself to a methodical abstract, the task of the beginner is much

harder. To abstract the treatises of Aristotle was fitting employment for Hobbes. The "Wealth of Nations" is not easy to abstract; but, at the present day, it would not be chosen as the Text-book-in-chief for Political Economy: as a third or fourth work to be perused at a reading pace, it would have its proper effect. The best studious exercise upon it would be to mark the agreements and disagreements with the newer authority, the weak and strong points of the exposition, and the perennial force of a certain number of the propositions and examples. Many parts could be skipped entirely as not even repaying historical study. Yet, as the work of a great and original mind, its interest is perennial.

To go back once more to the example of Thucydides. Setting aside, from intrinsic improbability, both the traditions—the copyings, and the committal to memory *verbatim*,—we can easily see what Demosthenes could find in the work, and how he could make the most of it. The narrative or story could be indelibly fixed in his memory by a few perusals, and, if need be, by a full chronology drawn up by his own hand. The speeches could be committed in whole or in part, for their arguments and language, and a minute study could be made of the turns of expression, as they seemed to be either meritorious or defective. The young orator had already studied the more finished styles of Isocrates, Lysias, Isæus, and Plato, and could make comparisons between their forms and the peculiarities of Thucydides, which belonged to an earlier age. This, however, was a discipline altogether apart, and had nothing to do with copying, committing, or abstracting. It involved one exercise more or less allied to the last, namely, *making changes upon an author according to one's best ideal at the time:* changes, if possible, for the better, but perhaps not; still requiring, however, an effort of mind, and so far favourable to culture.

Every one's first attempts at abstracting must be very bad. There is no more opportune occasion for the assistance of a tutor or intelligent monitor, than to revise an abstract. The weaknesses of a beginner are apparent at a glance; even better than by a *viva voce* interrogation. Useful abstracting comes at a late stage of study, when one or two subjects have been pretty well mastered. It is then that the pupil can best overtake more advanced works on the subjects already commenced, or can enter upon an entirely new department, in the light of previous acquisitions.

Any work that deserves thorough study deserves the labour of making an abstract; without which, indeed, the study is not thorough. It is quite possible to read so as to comprehend the drift of a book, and yet forget it entirely. The point for us to consider is —Are we likely to want any portion of it afterwards? If we can fix upon the parts most likely to be useful, we either copy or abstract these, or preserve a reference so as to turn them up when wanted. In the case of a work, containing a mass of new and valuable materials, such as we wish to incorporate with our intellectual structure, we must act the part of the beginner in a new field, and make an abstract on the most approved plan : that is, by such changes as shall at once preserve the author's ideas, and intersperse them with our own. There is an ideal balance of two opposing tendencies : one to take down the writer too literally, which fails to impress the meaning ; the other to accommodate him too much to our own language and thinking, in which case, we shall remember more, but it will be remembering ourselves and not him. He that can hit the just mean between these extremes is the perfect student.

There are easier modes of abstracting, such as serve many useful purposes, although not sufficient for the mastery of a leading Text-book, or even of a second or third in a new subject. We may pencil on the margin, or underscore, all the leading propositions, and the typical examples. In a well-composed scientific manual, the proceeding is too obvious to be impressive. Very often, however, the main points are not given in the most methodical way, but have to be searched out by carefully scanning each paragraph. This is an exercise that both instructs and impresses us ; it is the kind of change that calls our faculties into play, and gives us a better hold of an author, without superseding him.

A Table of Contents carefully examined is favourable to a comprehensive view of the whole ; and, this attained, the details are remembered in the best possible way, that is, by taking their place in the scheme. Any other form of recollection is of the desultory kind.

4. Let us next glance at Locke's method of reading, which is unique and original, like the man himself. It is given with much iteration in his Conduct of the Understanding, but comes in substance to this :

We are to fix in the mind the author's ideas, stripped of his words; to distinguish between such ideas as are pertinent to the subject, and such as are not; to keep the precise question steadily before our minds; to appreciate the bearing of the arguments; and, finally, to see what the question bottoms upon, or what are the fundamental verities or assumptions underneath.

All this is very thorough in its way; but, in the first place, it applies chiefly to argumentative works, and, in the second place, it is entirely beyond the powers of ordinary students. Such an examination of an author as Locke contemplates is not seen many times in a generation. His own controversies give but indifferent examples of it; several of Bentham's works and a few of John Mill's polemical articles also give an idea of thorough handling; but it is not so properly a studious effort, as the consummated product of a highly logical discipline, and is within the reach of only a small elect number.

Locke would have been more intelligible, if, instead of telling us to strip an author's meaning of the words, he had impressed strongly the necessity of *defining all leading terms;* and of making sure that each was always used in the same meaning. While, in order to veracious conclusions, it is necessary that every matter of fact should be truly given, it is equally necessary that the language should be free from ambiguity. If an author uses the word "law," at one time as an enactment by some authority, and at another time, as a sequence in the order of nature, he is sure to land us in fallacy and confusion, as Butler did in explaining the Divine government. The remedy is, not to perform the operation of separating the meaning entirely from the language, but to vary the language, so as to substitute terms that have no ambiguity. "Law" is equivocal; "social enactment," and "order of nature," are both unequivocal; and when one is chosen, and adhered to, the confusion is at an end.

The mere art of study is no preparation for such a task. It demands a very advanced condition of knowledge on the particular subject, as well as a logical habit of mind, however acquired; and to include it in a practical essay on the Conduct of the Understanding is to overstep the limits of the subject.

As our present head represents the very pith and marrow of the art of study, we may dwell a little longer on the process of changing the form of an author, whether by condensing, expanding, varying the expression, alte ing the order, selecting, and rejecting, —or by any other known device. Worst of all is change for the mere sake of change; it is simply better than literal copying. But, to rise above it, needs a sense of FORM already attained. According as this sense is developed, the exercise of altering or amending is more and more profitable. Consequently, there should be an express application of the mind to the attainment of form; and particular works pre-eminent for that quality should be sought out and read. "Form" is doubtless a wide word, and comprises both the logical or pervading method of a work, and the expression or dress throughout. Method by itself can be soonest acquired because it turns on a small number of points; language is a multifarious acquirement, and can hardly be forced, although it will come eventually by due application.

To show what is meant by learning Form, with a view to the more effectual study of subject-matter, I will take the example of a work on the Practice of Medicine; in which the idea is to describe Diseases *seriatim*, with their treatment or cures. At the present day, this subject possesses method or form there is a systematic classification of diseased processes and diseases; also, a regular plan of setting forth the specific marks of each disease, its diagnosis, and, finally, its remedies. There are more and less perfect models of the methodical element; while there are differences among authors in the fulness of the detailed information. There is, besides, a Logic of Medicine, representing the absolute form, in a kind of logical synopsis, by which it is more easily comprehended in the first instance: not to mention the general body of the Logic of the Inductive Sciences, of which medicine is one. Now, undoubtedly, the best work to begin with—the Text-book-in-chief—would be one where Form is in its highest perfection; the amount of matter being of less consequence. In a subject of great complication, and vast detail, the student cannot too soon get possession of the best method or form of arrangement. When a work of this character is before him, he is to read and re-read it, till the form becomes strongly apparent; he is to compare one part with another, to see how the author adheres to his own pervading method; he should, if possible, make a synopsis of the plan in itself, disentangling it from the applications, for greater clearness. The scheme of a medical work, for example, comprises the Classification of Diseases, the parting off of Diseased Processes—Fever, Inflammation, &c.— from Diseases properly so called; the modes of defining Disease; the separation of defining marks, from predications, and so on: all involved in a strict Logic of Disease. Armed with these logical or methodical preliminaries, the student next attacks one of the extended treatises on the Practice of Medicine. He is now prepared to work the process of abstracting to the utmost advantage, both for clearness of understanding, and for impressing the memory. As in such a vast subject, no one author is deemed adequate to a full exposition, and as, moreover, a great portion of the information occurs, apart from systems, in detached memoirs or monographs,—the only mode of unifying and holding together the aggregate, is to reduce all the statements to a common form and order, by help of the pre-acquired plan. The progress of study may amend the plan, as well as add to the particular information; but absolute perfection in the scheme is not so essential as strict adherence to it through all the details. To work without a plan at all, is not merely to tax the memory beyond its powers, but probably also to misconceive and jumble the facts.

To enhance the illustration of the two main heads of the Art of Study, I will so far deviate from the idea of the essay, as to take up a special branch of education, which, more than any other, has been reduced to form and rule, I mean the great accomplishment of Oratory, or the Art of Persuasion. The practical Science of Rhetoric, cultivated both by ancients and by moderns, has especially occupied itself with directions for acquiring this great engine of influencing mankind.

It was emphatically averred by the ancient teachers of the Oratorical art, that it must be grounded on a wide basis of general information. I do not here discuss the exact scope of this preparatory study, as my purpose is to narrow the illustration to what is special to the faculty of persuasion. I must even omit all those points relating to delivery or elocution, on which so much depends ; and also the consideration of how to attain readiness or fluency in spoken address, except in so far as that follows from abundant oratorical resources. We thus sink the difference between spoken oratory, and persuasion through the press.

Even as thus limited, oratory is still too wide for a pointed illustration : and, so, I propose farther to confine my references to the department of Political

Oratory; coupling with that, however, the Forensic branch—which has much in common with the other, and has given birth to some of our most splendid examples of the art of persuasion.

While declining to enter on the wide field of the general education of the orator, I may not improperly advert to the more immediate preparation for the political orator, by a familiar acquaintance with History and Political Philosophy, howsoever obtained. Then, on the other hand, the course here to be chalked out assumes a considerable proficiency in language or expression. The special education will incidentally improve both these accomplishments, but must not be relied on for creating them, or for causing a marked advance in either. The effect to be looked for is rather to give them direction for the special end.

These things premised, the line of proceeding manifestly is to study the choicest examples of the oratorical art, according to the methods already laid down, with due adaptation to the peculiarities of the case.

Now, we have not, as in a Science, two or three systematic works, one of which is to be chosen as a chief, to be followed by a reference more or less to the others. Our material is a long series of detached orations; from these we must make a selection at starting, and such selection, which may comprise ten or twenty or more, will have to be treated with the intense single-minded devotion that we hitherto limited to a single work. Repeated perusal, with a process of abstracting to be described presently, must be be stowed upon the chosen examples, before embarking, as will be necessary, upon the wide field of miscellaneous oratory.

No doubt, an oratorical education could be grounded in a general and equal study of the orators at large, taking the ancients either first or last, according to fancy. Probably the greater number of students have fallen into this apparently obvious course. Our present contention is, that it is better to make a thorough study of a proper selection of the greatest speeches, together with the most persuasive unspoken compositions. This, however, is not all. We are following the wisdom of the ancients, in insisting on the farther expedient of proceeding to the study of the great examples by the aid of an oratorical scheme. At a very early stage of Oratory in Greece, its methods began to be studied, and, in the education of the orator, these methods were made to accompany the study of exemplary speeches.

The principles of Rhetoric at large, and of the Persuasive art in particular, have been elaborated by successive stages, and are now in a tolerable state of advancement. The learner will choose the scheme that is judged best, and will endeavour to master it provisionally, before entering on the oratorical models; holding it open to amendment from time to time, as his education goes on. The scheme and the examples mutually act and re-act: the better the scheme, the more rapidly will the examples fructify; and the scheme will, in its turn, profit by the mastery of the details.

NECESSITY OF AN ORATORICAL ANALYSIS. 243

One great use of an oratorical analysis, as supplied by the teachers of Rhetoric, is to part off the different merits of a perfect oration; and to show which are to be extracted from the various exemplary orators. One man excels in forcible arguments, another in the lucid array of facts; one is impressive and impassioned, another is quiet but circumspect. Now, the benefit of studying on principle, instead of working at random, is, that we concentrate attention on each one's strong points, and disregard the rest. But it needs a preparatory analysis, in order to make the discrimination. All that the uninstructed reader or hearer of a great oration knows is, that the oration is great: this may be enough for the persons to be moved; it is insufficient for an oratorical disciple.

In the hazardous task of pursuing the illustration by naming the examples of oratory most suitable to commence with, I shall pass over living men, and choose from the past orators of our own country. Without discussing minutely the respective merits of individuals, I am safe in selecting, as in every way suitable for our purpose, Burke, Fox, Erskine, Canning, Brougham, and Macaulay. Burke's Speeches on America; Fox on the Westminster Scrutiny; Erskine on Stockdale, and on Hardy, Tooke, &c.; Canning on the Slave Trade; Brougham, Lyndhurst, and Denman in the Queen's Trial; Macaulay on the Reform Bill,—would comprise, in a moderate compass, a considerable range of oratorical excellence. I doubt if any member of the list would be more suitable for a beginning than Macaulay's Reform Speeches.

These are no mere displays of a brilliant imagination: they are known to have influenced thousands of minds otherwise averse to political change. The reader finds in them an immense repository of historical facts as well as of doctrines; but facts and doctrines, by themselves, do not make oratory. It is the use made of these, that gives us the instruction we are now in quest of. In a first or second reading, however, matter and form equally captivate the mind. It would be impossible, at that early stage, to make an abstract such as would separate the oratorical from the non-oratorical merits. Only when, by help of our scheme, we have made a critical distinction between the two kinds of excellence, are we able to arrive at an approach to a pure oratorical lesson; and, for a long time, we shall fail to make the desired isolation. We have to learn not to expect too much from any one speech: to pass over in Macaulay, what is more conspicuously shown, say in Fox, or in Erskine. If our political and historical education has made some progress, the mere thoughts and facts do not detain us; their employment for the end of persuasion is what we have to take account of.

It is impossible here to indicate, except in a very general way, the successive steps of the operation. The one summary consideration in the Rhetoric of Oratory, from which flows the entire array of details, is the regard to the dispositions and state of mind of the audience; the presenting of topics and considerations that chime in with these dispositions, and the avoiding of everything that would conflict with them.

To grasp this comprehensive view, and to follow it out in some of the chief circumstantials of persuasive address—the leading forms of argument, and the appeals to the more prominent feelings,—would soon provide a touchstone to a great oration, and lead us to distinguish the materials of oratory from the use made of them.

Take the circumstance of *negative tact;* by which is meant the careful avoidance of whatever might grate on the minds of those addressed. Forensic oratory in general, and the oratory of Parliamentary leaders in particular, will show this in perfection; and, for a first study of it, there is probably nothing to surpass the Erskine Speeches above cited. It could, however, be found in Macaulay; although, in a different proportion to the other merits.

The Macaulay Speeches have the abundance of matter, and the powers of style, that minister to oratory, although not constituting its distinctive feature. In these speeches, we may note how he guages the minds of the men of rank and property, in and out of Parliament, who constituted the opposition to Reform; how tenderly he deals with their prejudices and class interests; how he shapes and adduces his arguments so as to gain those very feelings to the side he advocates; how he brings his accumulated store of historical illustrations to his aid, under the guidance of both the positive and the negative tact of the orator; saying everything to gain, and nothing to alienate the dispositions that he has carefully measured.

After Erskine and Macaulay have yielded their first contribution to the oratorical student, he could turn with profit to Burke, who has the materials of oratory in the same high order as Macaulay, but who in the employment of them so often miscarries—sometimes partially, at other times wholly. It then becomes an exercise to distinguish his successes from his failures; to resolve these into their elementary merits and defects, according to the oratorical scheme. The close study of one or two orations is still the preferable course; and the most profitable transition from the Burke sample is to the selected speech or speeches of some other orator as Canning or Brougham. All the time, the pupil must be enlarging and improving his analytic scheme, which is the means of keeping his mind to the point in hand, amid the distraction of the orator's gorgeous material.

The subsequent stages of oratorical study are much plainer than the commencement. A time comes when the pupil will roam freely over the great field of oratory, modern and ancient, knowing more and more exactly what to appropriate and what to neglect. He will be quite aware of the necessity of rivalling the great masters in resources of knowledge on the one hand, and of style on the other; but he will look for these elsewhere, as well as in the professed orators.

Moreover, as the persuasive art is exemplified in men that have never been public speakers, the oratorical pupil will make a selection from the most influential of this class. He will find, for example, in the argumentative treatises of Johnson, in the Letters of

Junius, in the writings of Godwin, in Sydney Smith, in Bentham, in Cobbett, in Robert Hall, in Fonblanque, in J. S. Mill, in Whately, and a host besides, the exemplification of oratorical merits, together with materials that are of value. It is understood, however, that the search for materials and the acquisition of oratorical form, are not made to advantage on the same lines, and, for this and other reasons, should not go together.

The extreme test of the principle of concentration as against equal application, is the acquirement of Style, or the extending of our resources of diction and expression in all its particulars. Being a matter of endless minute details, we may feel ourselves at a loss to compass it by the intensive study of a narrow and select example. Still, with due allowance for the speciality of the case, the principle will still be found applicable. We should, however, carry along with us, the maxim exemplified under oratory, of separating in our study, as far as may be, the style from the matter. We begin by choosing a treatise of some great master. We may then operate either (1) by simple reading and re-reading, or (2) by committing portions to memory *verbatim*, or (3), best of all, by making some changes according to an already acquired ideal of good composition. This too shows the great importance of attaining as early as possible some regulating principles of goodness of style: the action and re-action of these, on the most exemplary authors, constitute our progress in the art, and, in the quickest way, store the memory with the resources of good expression.

III. The head just now finished includes really by far the greatest portion of the economy of study. There are various other devices of importance in their way, but much less liable to error in practice. Of these, a leading place may be assigned to the best modes of Distributing the Attention in reading. Such questions as the following present themselves for consideration to the earnest student. How many distinct studies can be carried on together? What interval should be allowed in passing from one to another? How much time should be given to the art of reading, and how much to subsequent meditating or ruminating on what has been read? These points are all susceptible of being determined, within moderate limits of error. As to the first, the remark was made by Quintilian, that, in youth, we can most easily pass from one study to another. The reason of this, however, is, that youth does not take very seriously to any study. When a special study becomes engrossing, the alternatives must rather be recreative than acquisitive; not much progress being made in what is slighted, or left over to the exhaustion caused by attention to the favourite topic. A more precise answer can be made to the second and third queries, namely, as to an interval for recall and meditation, after putting down a book, and before turning the attention into other channels. There is a very clear principle of economy here. We should save as far as possible the fatigue of the reading process, or make a given amount of attention to the printed page yield the greatest impression on the memory. This is done by the exercise of recalling without the book; an advantage that we do not possess in listening to a lecture, until the whole is finished, when we have too much to recall. To hurry from book to book is to gain stimulation at the cost of acquisition.

I have alluded to the case of an engrossing subject, which starves all accompanying studies. There are but two ways of obviating the evil, if it be an evil; which it indeed becomes, when the alternative demands also are legitimate. The one is peremptorily to limit the time given to it daily, so as to rescue some portion of the strength for other topics. The other is to intermit it wholly for a certain period, and let other subjects have their swing. In advancing life, and when our studious leisure is only what is left from professional occupation, two different studies can hardly go on together. The alternative of a single study needs to be purely recreative.

One other point may be noted under this head. In the application to a book of importance and difficulty, there are two ways of going to work : to move on slowly, and master as we go ; or to move on quickly to the end, and begin again. There is most to be said for the first method, although distinguished men have worked upon the other. The freshness of the matter is taken off by a single reading ; the re-reading is so much flatter in point of interest. Moreover, there is a great satisfaction in making our footing sure at each step, as well as in finishing the task when the first perusal is completed. We cannot well dispense with re-reading, but it need not extend to the whole; marked passages should show where the comprehension and mastery are still lagging.

IV. Another topic is Desultory Reading. This is the whole of the reading of the unstudious mass; it is but a part of the reading of the true student. It may mean, for one thing, jumping from book to book, perhaps reading no one through, except for pure amusement. It may also include the reading of periodicals, where no one subject is treated at any length. As a general rule, such reading does not give us new foundations, or constitute the point of departure of a fresh department of knowledge; yet the amount of labour and thought bestowed upon articles in periodicals, may render them efficacious in adding to a previous stock of materials, or in correcting imperfect views. The truth is, that to the studious man, the desultory is not desultory. The only difference with him is that he has two *attitudes* that he may assume—the severe and the easy-going; the one is most associated with systematic works on leading subjects; the other with short essays, periodicals, newspapers, and conversation. In this last attitude, which is reserved for hours of relaxation, he skips matters of difficulty, and absorbs scattered and interesting particulars without expressly aiming at the solution of problems or the discussion of abstract principles. There is no reason why an essay in a periodical, a pamphlet, or a speech in Parliament, may not take a first place in anyone's education. All the labour and resource that go to form a work of magnitude may be concentrated in any one of these. Still, they are presented in the form that we are accustomed to associate with our desultory work, and our times of relaxation; and so, they seldom produce in the minds of readers the effect that they are capable of producing. The thorough student will not fail to extract materials from one and all of them, but even he will scarcely choose from such sources the text for the commencement of a new study.

The desultory is not a bad way of increasing our resources of expression. Although there be a systematic and a best mode of acquiring language, there is also an inferior, yet not ineffective mode; namely, reading copiously whatever authors have at once a good style and a sustaining interest. Hence, for this purpose, shifting from book to book, taking up short and light compositions, may be of considerable value; anything is better than not reading at all, or than reading compositions inferior in point of style. The desultory man will not be without a certain flow of language as well as a command of ideas; notwithstanding which, he will never be confounded with the studious man.

V. A fifth point is the proportion of book-reading to Observation of the facts at first hand. From want of opportunity, or from disinclination, many persons have all their information on certain subjects cast in the bookish mould, and do not fully conceive the particular facts as these strike the mind in their own character. A reader of History, with no experience of affairs, is likely to have imperfect bookish notions; just as a man of affairs, not a reader, is subject to narrowness of another kind. It was remarked by Sir G. Cornewall Lewis, that the German historians of the Athenian Democracy write like men that never had any actual experience of popular assemblies. A lawyer must be equally versed in principles and in cases as heard in court: this is a type of knowledge generally. In the Natural History Sciences, observation and reading go hand in hand from the first. In the science of the Human Mind, there are general doctrines, contrived to embrace the world of mental phenomena: the student may have to begin with these, and work upon them exclusively for a time, but, in the end, phenomena must be independently viewed by him in their naked character, as exhibited directly in his own mind, and inferentially in the minds of those that fall under his observation. Book knowledge of Disease has to be coupled with bed-side knowledge; neither will take the place of the other.

VI. I began by limiting the meaning of study to the reading of books, and have reviewed the various points in the economy of this process. The other means of attaining, enlarging, deepening our knowledge, namely, Observation of facts, Conversation, Disputation, Composition, have each an art of its own—especially Disputation, which has long been reduced to rule. Observation also admits of specific directions, but, in stating the necessity of combining observation with book theories and descriptions, I have assumed the knowledge of how to observe.

Of all the adjuncts of study, none is so familiar, so available, and, on the whole, so helpful, as Conversation. The authors of Guides to Students, as Isaac Watts, give elaborate rules for carrying on conversation, a good many of them being more moral than intellectual; but an art of conversation would be very difficult to formulate; it would take quite as long an essay as I have devoted to study, and even then would not follow half of the windings of the subject. The only notice of it that my plan requires, is such as I have already bestowed upon Observation: namely, to point out the advantage of combining a certain amount of reading with conversation; a thing that almost everybody does according to their opportunities. To rehearse what we have read to some willing and sympathizing listener, is the best way of impressing the memory and of clearing up difficulties to the understanding. It brings in the social stimulus, which ranks so high among human motives. It is a wholesome change of attitude; relieving the fatigue of book-study, while adding to its fruitfulness. Even beginners in study are mutually helpful, by exchanging the results of their several book acquirements; while it is possible to raise conversation to the rank of a high art, both for intellectual improvement and for mutual delectation. I cannot say that the ideal is often realized; since two or more must combine to conversation, and it is not often that the mutual action and re-action is perfectly adjusted for the highest effect.

The last great adjunct of study is original Composition, which also would need to be formulated distinct from the theory of book-study. Viewed in the same way as we have viewed the other collateral exercises, one can pronounce it too an invaluable adjunct to book-reading, as well as an end in itself; it is a variation of effort that diverts the mental strain, and re-acts powerfully upon the extraction of nutriment from books. Besides the pride of achievement, it evokes the social stimulus with the highest effect; our compositions being usually intended for some listeners. But, when to begin the work of original composition, as distinct from the written exercises upon books, in the way of abstracting, amending, and the rest; what forms it should assume at the outset, and by what steps it should gradually ascend to the culminating effects of the art,—would all admit of expansion and discussion as an altogether separate theme. Enough to remark here, that a course of book-reading without attempts at original composition is as faulty an extreme, as to begin and carry on writing upon a stinted basis of reading. The thorough student, as concerned in my present essay, carrying on book-study in the manner I have sketched, will almost infallibly end, at the proper time, in a self-thinker, and a self-originator. An adequate familiarity with the great writers of the past both checks presumptuous or hasty efforts of reproduction, and encourages modest attempts of our own as we feel ourselves becoming gradually invigorated through the combined influence of all the various modes of well-directed study.

VIII.

RELIGIOUS TESTS AND SUBSCRIPTIONS.

RELIGIOUS TESTS AND SUBSCRIPTIONS.

EVERY man has an interest in arriving at truth for himself. However useful it may be to mislead other people, however sweet to look down from a height on the erring throng beneath, it is neither useful nor sweet to be ourselves at sea without a compass. We may not care to walk by the light we have, but we do not choose to exchange it for darkness.

This reflection is most obvious with reference to the order of Nature. Our life depends on adapting means to ends; which supposes that we know cause and effect in the world around us. A long story is cut short by the adage, "Knowledge is power"; otherwise rendered, "Truth is bliss".

The bearing of truth is free from all doubt when the problem is, how to gain certain ends—how to be fed, how to get from one place to another, how to cure disease. A new case is presented by the choice of ends. The tyrannical French minister, when appealed to by a starving peasantry in the terms, "We must live," replied, "I do not see the necessity". There was here no question of true and false, no problem for science to solve. It was a question of ends, and could not be reargued. The only possible retort was to ask, " What does your Excellency consider a necessity?" If the reply were, "That I and my King may rule France and be happy," then might the starving wretches find some aid from a political scientist who could show that, in the order of nature, ruler and people must stand or fall together. So, it is no question of true or false in the order of nature, whether I shall adopt, as the end of life, my own gratification purely, the good of others purely, or part of both. In like manner the Benthamite, who propounds happiness as the general end of human society, cannot prove this, as Newton could prove that gravity follows the inverse square of the distance; nor can his position be impugned in the way that Newton impugned the vortices of Descartes, by showing that they were at variance with fact.

There is a third case. Assertions are made out of the sphere of the sensible world, and beyond the reach of verification by the methods of science There is a region of the supersensible or supernatural where cause and effect may be affirmed and human interests involved, but where we cannot supply the same evidence or the same confutation as in sublunary knowledge. That all human beings shall have an existence after death is matter of truth or falsehood, but the evidence is of a kind that would not be adduced for proving that a caterpillar becomes a butterfly or that a seed turns to a plant. The reasoning employed, no doubt, makes references to facts of the order of nature; but it is circuitous and analogical, and is admitted merely because better cannot be had.

The peculiarity of this last class of affirmations is that they give great room for the indulgence of our likings. So little being fixed with any precision, we can shape our beliefs to please ourselves. Even as regards the sensible world, we can sometimes accommodate our views to what we wish, as when we assume that our favourite foods and stimulants are wholesome; but such license soon meets with checks in the physical sphere, while there are no such checks in the realms of the superphysical.

Now, in all these three departments of opinion, the interest of mankind lies in obtaining the best views that can possibly be obtained. As regards the first and third—the region of true and false, one in the sensible, the other in the supersensible world—we are clearly interested in getting the truth. As regards the second—the region of ends—if there be one class of ends preferable to another, we should find out that class.

The only doubt that can arise anywhere is, whether in the third case—the case of the supernatural,—truth is of the same consequence to us. Such a doubt, however, begs the whole question at issue. If the truth be of no consequence here, it is because we shall never be landed in any reality corresponding to what is declared: that the nature of the future life is purely imaginary and not to be converted into fact; in other words, that there is no future life; that there is merely a land of dreams and fiction, which can never be proved true and never proved false. It would then be a projection of thought from the present life, and would cease with that life. All that people could claim in the matter would be the liberty of imagination; and this being so, we are not to be committed to any one form. In short, we are to picture what we please in a world that cannot be made out to exist. The point is not, to be true or false; it is, to be well or ill imagined.

What, then, is to be the criterion of proper or improper imagination? On what grounds are we to make our preference between the different schemes of the supersensible world? Is each one of us to be free to imagine for ourselves, or are we to submit to the dictation of others? These questions lead up to another. How far are the interests of the present life concerned in the form given to our conceptions of a future life?

It would seem to be an unanswerable assumption that, in all the three situations above supposed, we should do the very best that the case admits of. In the order of nature we should get, as far as possible, the truth and the whole truth; in the choice of ends for this life we should embrace the best ends; in the shaping of another life we should be free to follow out whatever may be the course suitable to the operation.

The means for arriving at truth in the order of nature is an active search according to certain well-known methods. It farther involves the negative condition of perfect freedom to canvass, to controvert, or to refute, every received doctrine or opinion. There is no use in going after new facts, or in rising to new generalities, if we are not to be allowed to displace errors. This is now conceded, except at the points of contact of the natural and the supernatural. In spite of the wide separation of the two worlds—the world of fact and the world of imagination,—we cannot conceive the second except in terms of the first; and if the shaping of the supernatural acquires fixity and consecration, the natural facts made use of in the fabric acquire a corresponding fixity, even although the rendering is found to be inaccurate. The prevailing conception of a future life needs a view of the separate and independent subsistence of the mental powers of man, very difficult to reconcile with present knowledge.

The growth of intolerance is quite explicable, but the explanation is not necessarily a justification. Although every division of the human family must have passed through many social phases, and must therefore have experienced revolutionary shocks, yet the rule of man's existence has been a rigorous fixity of institutions, with a hatred of change. Innovations, when not the effect of conquest, would be made under the pressure of some great crisis, or some tremendous difficulty that could not otherwise be met. The idea of individuals being allowed, in quiet times, to propose alterations in government, in religion, in morals, or even in the common arts of life, was thought of only to be stamped out. There was a step in advance of the ancient and habitual order of things, when an innovating citizen was permitted to make his proposal to the assembled tribe, with a rope about his neck, to be drawn tight if he failed to convince his audience. This might make men think twice before advancing new views, but it was not an entire suppression of them.

The first introduction of the great religions of the world would in each case afford an interesting study of the difficulties of change and of the modes of surmounting these difficulties. There must always have concurred at least two things,—general uneasiness or discontent from some cause or other; and the moral or intellectual ascendency of some one man, whose views, although original, were yet of a kind to be finally accepted by the people. These conditions are equally shown in political changes, and are historically illustrated in many notable instances. It is enough to cite the Greek legislation of Lycurgus and of Solon.

Such changes are the exceptions in human affairs; they occur only at great intervals. In the ordinary course of societies, the governing powers not merely adhere to what is established, but forbid under severe penalties the very suggestion of change. The chronic misery of the race is compatible with unreasoning acquiescence in a state of things once established, incipient reformers are at once immolated *pour encourager les autres*. It is the aim of governments to make themselves superfluously strong; they take precautions against unfavourable ideas no less than against open revolt. In this, they are seconded by the general community, which would make things too hot even for a reforming king.

It is said by the evolution or historical school of politicians, that this was all as it should be. The free permission to question the existing institutions, political and religious, would have been incompatible with stability. In early society more especially, religion and morality were a part of civil government; a dissenter in religion was the same thing as a rebel in politics; the distinction between the civil and the religious could not yet be drawn.

Without saying whether this was the case or not—for I should not like to commit myself to the position, "Whatever was, was right" at the time—I trust we are now far on the way to being agreed that the civil and the religious are no longer to be identified; that the State, as a state, is not concerned to uphold any one form of religious belief. Modern civilized communities are believed capable of existing without an official religion; the citizens being free to form themselves into self-governed religious bodies, as various as the prevailing modes of religious belief. It may be long ere this goal be fully reached; but even the upholders of the present state religions admit that, supposing these were not in existence, nobody would now propose to institute them.

The foregoing remarks may appear somewhat desultory, as well as too brief for the extent of the theme. They must be accepted, however, as an introduction to a more limited topic, which presupposes in some measure the general principle of toleration by the state of all forms of religious opinion.

Whether with or without established religions, perfect freedom of dissent is now demanded, and, with some hankering reservations, pretty generally conceded. Individuals are allowed to congregate into religious societies, on the most various and opposite creeds.

So far good. Yet there remains a difficulty. Long before the age of toleration, when each state had an established religion, the people in general formed their habits of religious observance in connection with the State Church—its doctrines, its ritual, its buildings, and its sacred places. When disruption took place, the separatists formed themselves into societies on the original model, merely dropping the matters of disagreement. Fixity of creed and of ritual was still enacted; the only remedy for dissatisfaction on either subject was to swarm afresh, and set up a new variety of doctrine or of ritual, to which a rigid adherence was still expected as a condition of membership.

By this costly and troublesome process, Churches have been multiplied according to the changes of view among sections of the community. A certain energy of conviction has always been necessary to such a result. Equally great changes of opinion occur among members of the older Church communities, without inducing them to break with these; so that nominal membership ceases to be a mark of real adhesion to the articles of belief.

These few commonplaces are meant to introduce the enquiry—now a pressing one—whether, and how far, fixed creeds are desirable or expedient in religious bodies generally; no difference being made between state Churches and voluntary Churches. This is the question of Subscription to Articles by the clergy.

Let us now review the evils attendant on subscription, and next consider the objections to its removal.

In the first place, the process of restraining discussion by penal tests is inherently untenable, absurd, and fallacious.

In support of this strong assertion, we have only to repeat, that every man has an interest in getting at the truth, and consequently in whatever promotes that end. We live by the truth; error is death. To stand between a man and the attainment of truth, is to inflict an injury of incalculable amount. The circumstances wherein the prohibition of truth is desirable, must be extraordinary and altogether exceptional. The few may have a self-interest in withholding truth from the many; neither the few nor the many have an interest in its being withheld from themselves. Each one of us has the most direct concern in knowing on what plan this universe is constituted, what are its exact arrangements and laws. Whether for the present life, or for any other life, we must steer our course by our knowledge, and that knowledge needs to be true. Obstruction to the truth recoils upon the obstructors. To flee to the refuge of lies is not the greatest happiness of anybody.

It has been maintained that there are illusions so beneficial as to be preferable to truth. Occasionally, in private life, we practise little deceptions upon individuals when the truth would cause some great temporary mischief. This case need not be discussed. The important instance is in reference to religious belief. A benevolent Deity and a future life are so cheering and consoling, it is said, that they should be secured against challenge or criticism; they ought not to be weakened by discussion. This, of course, assumes that these doctrines are unable to maintain themselves against opponents, that, with all their intrinsic charm (which nobody can be indifferent to), they would give way under a free handling. Such a confession is fatal. Men will go on cherishing pleasing illusions, but not such as need to be *protected* in order to exist. According to Plato, the belief in the goodness of the Deity was of so great importance that it was to be maintained by state penalties— about the worst way of making the belief efficacious for its end. What should we think of an Act passed to imprison whoever disputed the goodness of King Alfred, the Man of Ross, or Howard?

Granting that certain illusions are highly beneficial, it does not follow that they are to be exempted from criticism. Their effect depends on the prestige of their truth. That is, they must have reasons on their side. But a doctrine is not supported by reasons, unless the objections are stated and answered; not sham objections, but the real difficulties of an enquiring mind. If the statement of such difficulties is forcibly suppressed, the rational foundations will sooner or later be sapped.

If illusions are themselves good, freedom of thought

will give us the best. Why should we protect inferior illusions against the discovery of the superior? The unfettered march of the intellect may improve the quality of our illusions as illusions, while also strengthening their foundations. If religion be a good thing, the best religion is the best thing; and we cannot be sure of having the best, if men are forbidden to make a search.

Supposing, then, truth is desirable, the means to the end are desirable. Now one of the means is perfect liberty to call in question every opinion whatsoever. This is not all that is necessary; it is not even the principal condition of the discovery of new truth. It is, however, an indispensable adjunct, a negative condition. While laborious search for facts, care in comparing them, genius in detecting deep identities, are the highways to knowledge,—the permission to promulgate new doctrines and to counter-argue the old is equally essential. Men cannot be expected to go through the toil of making discoveries at the hazard of persecution. If a few have done so, it is their glory and everybody else's shame.

That the torch of truth should be shaken till it shine, is generally admitted. Still, exceptions are made; otherwise the present argument would be superfluous. On certain subjects there is a demand for protection against innovating views. The implication is that, in these subjects, truth is better arrived at by delegating the search to a few, and treating their judgment as final. I need not ask where we should have been, if this mode of arriving at truth had been followed universally. The monopoly of enquiry claimed for the higher subjects, if set up in the lower, would be treated as the empire of darkness.

Second. The subscription to articles, and the enforcement of a creed by penalties, are nugatory for their own purpose; they fail to secure uniformity of belief.

This is shown in various ways. For instance, to inculcate adhesion to a set of articles, is merely to ensure that none shall use words that formally deny one or other of the doctrines prescribed. It does not say, that the subscriber shall teach the whole round of doctrines, in their due order and proportion. A preacher may at pleasure omit from his pulpit discourses any single doctrine; so that, in so far as his ministrations are concerned, to the hearers such doctrine is non-existent; without being denied, it is ignored. Against omission, a prosecution for heresy would not hold. In this way, the clergy have always had a certain amount of liberty, and have freely used it. In so doing, they have altered the whole character of the prescribed creed, without being technically heterodox. Everyone of us has listened to preachers of this description. Some ignore the Trinity, some the Atonement; many nowadays, without denying future punishment, never mention hell to ears polite. If the rigorous exclusion of a leading doctrine should excite misgivings, a very slight, formal, and passing admission may be made, while the stress of exhortation is thrown upon quite different points.

To attain a conviction for heresy, involving deprivation of office, the forms of justice must be respected. It is only under peculiar circumstances, that the ecclesiastical authority can be content with saying, "I do not like thee, Dr. Fell, or Dr. Smith, and I depose thee accordingly". A regular trial, with proof of specific contradiction of specific articles, allowing the accused the full benefit of his explanations, must be the rule in every corporation that respects justice. In the Church of England, a man cannot be deprived unless he contradict the articles clearly and consistently; the smallest incoherence on his part, the slightest vacillation in the rigour of his denial, is enough to save him. We may easily imagine, therefore, how widely a clergyman may stray from the fair, ordinary, current rendering of the doctrines of the Church, without danger. The whole essence of Christianity may be perverted under a few cunning precautions and by observing a few verbal formalities.

It has been pointed out, many times over, that the legally imposed creeds were the creatures of accident and circumstances at the time of their enactment, and are wholly unsuitable to the conservation of the more permanent and essential articles of the Christian faith. The amount of heresy, as against the more truly representative doctrines, that may pass through their meshes is very great.

This weakness is aggravated by another—the want of any provision for amending the creed from time to time. If it were desirable to adopt measures for maintaining uniformity of opinions among the clergy, the creed should be excised, or added to, according to the needs of every age. That this is not done, shows that the machinery of tests is altogether abnormal; it is not within the type of regular legislation. That any given creed should be regarded as out of keeping, as both redundant and defective, and yet that the ecclesiastical authority should shrink from applying a remedy to its most obvious defects, proves that the system itself is bad. All healthy legislation lends itself to perpetual improvement; that the enactments of articles of belief cannot be reconsidered, is a sign of rottenness.

A third objection to tests is, that mere dogmatic uniformity, if it were more complete than any tests can make it, is at best but a part of the religious character. It does nothing to secure or promote fervour, feeling, the emotional element in religion. It is by moral heat, far more than by its mould of doctrine, that religion influences mankind. There is no means of censuring preachers for coldness or languid indifference · or rather, there is another and more legitimate means than penal prosecutions, namely, expressed dissatisfaction and the preference of those that excel in the quality. A warm, glowing manner, an unctuous delivery, commands hearers and conducts to popularity and importance. The men of cold and unfeeling natures may get into office, but they are lightly esteemed. They are not had up to a public trial and deposed, but they are treated, and spoken of, in such a way as to discourage men of their type from becoming preachers, and to encourage the other sort. There are many qualifications that go to forming a good preacher; the holding of the creed of the body is only one. Yet, with the exception of gross immorality or abandonment of duty, correctness of creed is the only one that is subjected to the extreme penalty of loss of office; the others are secured by different means. Is it too much to infer that, without the extreme penalty, a reasonable conformity to the prevailing creed might also be secured?

The importance of the element of feeling has been most perceived in times when the religious current was strongest. At these times, its expression would not be hemmed in by rigorous formulas. The first communication of religious doctrines has always partaken of a broad and free rendering; apparent discrepancies were disregarded. To reduce all the utterances of the prophets and the apostles to definite forms and rigid dogmas, was to misconceive the situation. We may well suppose that the New Testament writers would have refused to subscribe the Athanasian Creed or the Westminster Confession not because these were in flat contradiction to Scripture, but because the way of embodying the religious verities in these documents would be repugnant to their ideas of form in such matters. The creed-builders may have been never so anxious to give exact equivalents of the original authorities; yet their fine distinctions and subtle logic would have, in all probability, been ranked by Paul and Peter among the latter-day perversions of the faith. The very composition of a creed would have been as distasteful to the first century, as it is incongruous to the nineteenth.

The evil operation of religious tests, and of the accompanying intolerance of the public mind as shown towards any form of dissent from the stereotyped orthodoxy, admits of a very wide handling. It is of course the problem of religious liberty. Some parts of the argument need to be reproduced here, to help us in replying to the objections against an unconditional abolition of compulsory creeds.

In conversing, many years ago, with the late Jules Mohl, the great Oriental scholar, professor of Persian in the College de France, I was much struck with his account of the nature of his duties as an expounder of the modern Persian authors. These authors, for example the poet Sadi, were in creed adherents of the ancient Persian fire-worship, notwithstanding the Mohammedan conquest of their country. They were, of course, forbidden to avow that creed directly; and in consequence, they had recourse to a form of composition by *doubles entendres*, veiling the ancient creed under Mohammedan forms. Mohl's business, as their expounder, was to strip off the disguise and show the true bearings of the writers, under their show of conformity to the established opinions.

This is a typical illustration of what has happened in Europe for more than two thousand years. The first recorded martyr to free speculation in philosophy was Anaxagoras in Greece. Mulcted in the sum of five talents, and expelled from Athens, he was considered fortunate in being allowed to retire to Lampsacus and end his days there. His fate, however, was soon eclipsed by the execution of Socrates,—an event whereby the Athenian burghers were enabled to bias the expression of free opinions from that time to this. The first person to feel the shock was Plato. That he was affected by it, to the extent of suppressing his views on the higher questions, we can infer with the greatest probability.

Aristotle was equally cowed. A little before his death, the chief priest of Eleusis, following the Socratic precedent, entered an indictment against him for impiety. This indictment was supported by citations of certain heretical doctrines from his published writings; on which Grote makes the significant remark, that his pæan in honour of his friend Hermeias would be more offensive to the feelings of an ordinary Athenian citizen than any philosophical dogma extracted from the *cautious prose compositions* of Aristotle. That is to say, the execution of Socrates was always before his eyes; he had to pare his expressions so as not to give offence to Athenian orthodoxy. We can never know the full bearings of such a disturbing force. The editors of Aristotle complain of the corruptness of his text; a far worse corruptness lies behind. In Greece, Socrates alone had the courage of his opinions. While his views as to a future life, for example, are plain and frank, the real opinion of Aristotle on the question is an insoluble problem. Now, considering the enormous sway of Aristotle in modern Europe,—how desirable was it that his real sentiments had reached us unperverted by the Athenian burgher and the hemlock!

It would be too adventurous to continue the illustration in detail through the Christian ages. It is well known that the later schoolmen strove to represent reason as against authority, but wrote under the curb of the Papal power; hence their aims can only be divined. A modern instance or two will be still more effective.

It can at last be clearly seen what was the motive of Carlyle's perplexing style of composition. We now know what his opinions were, when he began to write, and that to express them then would have been fatal to his success; yet he was not a man to indulge in rank hypocrisy. He, accordingly, adopted a studied and ambiguous phraseology, which for long imposed upon the religious public, who put their own interpretation upon his mystical utterances, and gave him the benefit of any doubts. In the "Life of Sterling" he threw off the mask, but still was not taken at his word. Had there been a perfect tolerance of all opinions he would have begun as he ended; and his strain of composition, while still mystical and high-flown, would never have been identified with our national orthodoxy.

I have grave doubts as to whether we possess Macaulay's real opinions on religion. His way of dealing with the subject is so like the hedging of an unbeliever that, without some good assurance to the contrary, I must include him also among the imitators of Aristotle's "caution". Some future critic will devote himself, like Professor Mohl, to expounding his ambiguous utterances.

When Sir Charles Lyell brought out his "Antiquity

of Man" he too was cautious. Knowing the dangers of his footing, he abstained from giving an estimate of the extension of time required by his evidences of human remains. Society in London, however, would not put up with that reticence, and he had to disclose at dinner parties what he had withheld from the public —namely, that, in his opinion, the duration of man could not be less than fifty thousand years.

These few instances must suffice to represent a long history of compelled reticence on the part of the men best qualified to instruct mankind. The question now is—What has been gained by it? What did the condemnation of Socrates do for the Athenian public? What did the chief priest of Eleusis hope to attain by indicting Aristotle? Unless we can show, as is no doubt attempted, that the set of opinions that happen to be consecrated at any one time, whether right or wrong, were essential to the existence of society,—then the attempt to improve upon them was truly meritorious, instead of being censurable. If the good of society as a whole is not plainly implicated, there remains only the interest of the place-holders under the existing system, as opposed to the interest of the mass of the people, who are, one and all, concerned in knowing the truth.

Again contracting the discussion to the narrow limits of the title of the essay, I must urge the special injury done to mankind by disfranchising the whole clerical class; that is to say, by depriving their authority of its proper weight in matters of faith. It is an incontrovertible rule of evidence, that the authority of an interested party is devoid of worth. Reasons are good in themselves, whoever utters them; but in trusting to authority, apart from reason, we need a disinterested authority. This the clergy at present are not, except on the points left undecided by the articles. If a man has five thousand a year, conditional on his holding certain views, his holding those views says nothing in their favour. For a much less bribe, plenty of men can be got to maintain any opinions whatsoever. When to this is added that, for certain other views, the holders are subjected to loss —it may be to fine, imprisonment, or death,—the value of men's adhesion to the favoured creed, as mere authority, is simply *nil*.

Truth, honesty, outspokenness, are not so well established as virtues, that we can afford to subject them to discouragement. The contrary course would be more for the general good in every way. When the law is intolerant in principle, men will be hypocrites from policy You cannot train children to speak the truth if, from whatever cause, they have an interest in deception. A repressive discipline induces a coarse outward submission, but cannot reach the inward parts: it only engenders hatred, and substitutes for open revolt an insidious secret retaliation. Those only that come under the generous nurture of freedom can be counted on for hearty and willing devotion. If we would reap the higher virtues, we must sow on the soil of liberty. Encourage a man to say whatever he thinks, and you make the most of him; for difficult questions, where the mind needs all its powers, there should be no burdensome 'caution' in giving out the results.

The imposing of subscription has its defenders, and these have to be fairly met. First, however, let us advert to the reasons why relaxation is more pressing now than formerly.

It is known that, among dissentients from the leading dogmas of the prevailing creed of Christendom, are to be included some of the most authoritative names of the last three centuries; our present formulas would not have been subscribed by Bacon, Newton, Locke, Kant; unless from mere pliancy and for the sake of quiet, like Hobbes. If they had been in clerical orders, and had freely avowed their opinions as we know them, they would have been liable to deposition. Yet the difficulties that these men might feel were far less than those that now beset the profession of our prevailing creeds. The advances of knowledge on all the subjects that come into contact with the various articles, as received by the orthodox Churches, may not, indeed, compel the relinquishment of those articles, but will force the holders to change front, to re-shape them in different forms. To such necessary modification, the creeds are a fatal obstacle. On a few points, such as the Creation in six days, these have been found elastic. The doctrine that death came by the fall has been explained away as spiritual death. This process cannot go much further, without too much paltering with obvious meanings. The recently-proclaimed doctrine of the Antiquity of Man comes into apparent conflict with man's creation and fall, as set forth in Genesis, on which are suspended the most vital doctrines of our creed. A reconciliation may be possible, but not without a very extensive modification of the scheme of the Atonement. It is not necessary to press Darwin's doctrine of Evolution; the deficiency of positive proof for that hypothesis may always be pleaded, as against the havoc it would make with the more distinctive points of Christian doctrine. But the existence of man on the earth, at the very lowest statement, must be carried back twenty thousand years; this is not hypothesis, but fact. The record of the creation and the fall of man will probably have to be subjected to a process of allegorising, but with inevitable loss. Now, whoever refuses a matter of fact counts on being severely handled; it is a different thing to refuse an allegory.

The modern doctrine named the "struggle for existence" is the old difficulty, known as "the origin of evil," presented in a new shape. It is rendered more formidable, as a stumbling-block to the benevolence of the Author of nature, by making what was considered exceptional the rule. It gathers up into one comprehensive statement the scattered occasions of misery, and reveals a system whereby the few thrive at the expense of the many. The apologist for Divine goodness has thus an aggravation of his load, and needs to be freed from all unnecessary trammels in the shaping of his creed.

It has not escaped attention, that the honours paid

to the illustrious Darwin, are an admission that our received Christianity is open to revision. In consequence of a few conciliatory phrases, Darwin has been credited with theism; nevertheless he has ridden rough-shod over all that is characteristic in our established creeds. Can the creeds come scathless out of the ordeal?

It is passing from the greater to the less, to dwell upon the increasing difficulties connected with the Inspiration of the Bible. The Church-of-Englander luckily escapes making shipwreck here; the legal interpretation of the formularies saves him. Yet to mankind, generally, it seems necessary that a superior weight should attach to a revealed book; and the other Churches cling to some form of inspiration, notwithstanding the growing difficulties attending it. Here too there must be more freedom given to the men that would extricate the situation. At all events, the doctrine should be made an open question. Even Cardinal Newman suggests doubts as to its being an imperative portion of the creed.

The attacks made on all sides against the Miraculous element in religion will force on a change of front. When an eminent popular writer and sincere friend of the Church of England surrenders miracles without the slightest compunction, it needs not the elaborate argumentation of "Supernatural Religion" to show that some new treatment of the question is called for. But may it not be impossible to put the new wine into the sworn bottles?

Like most great innovations, the proposal to liberate the clergy from all restraint as to the opinions that they may promulgate, necessarily encounters opposition. We are, therefore, bound to consider the reasons on the other side.

These reasons may be quoted in mass. As regards Established Churches in particular, it is said there is a State compact or understanding with the clergy that they should teach certain doctrines and no other; that if tests were abolished, there would be no security against the most extreme opinions; men eating the bread of a Reformed Church might inculcate Romanism instead of Protestantism; the pulpits might give forth Deism or Agnosticism. No sect could hope to maintain its principles, if the clergy might preach any doctrine that pleased themselves. More especially would it be monstrous and unjust, to allow the rich benefices of our highly endowed Church of England to be enjoyed by men whose hearts are in some quite different form of religion, or no religion, and who would occupy themselves in drawing men away from the faith.

On certain assumptions, these arguments have great force. Clearly a man ought not to take pay for doing one thing and do something quite different. When a body of religionists come together upon certain tenets, it would be a *reductio ad absurdum* for any of its ministers to be occupied in denying and controverting these tenets.

All this supposes, however, that men will not be made to conform by any means short of prosecution and deprivation; that the suspending of a severe penalty over men's heads is in itself a harmless device; and that religious systems are now stereotyped to our satisfaction, so that to deviate from them is mere wantonness and love of singularity. Such are the assumptions that we feel called upon to challenge.

The plea that the Church has engaged itself to the State to teach certain tenets, in return for its emoluments and privileges, has lost its point in our time. 'L'état, c'est moi.' The Church and the State are composed of the same persons. Gibbon's famous *mot* has collapsed. The religions of the Roman world,' he says, 'were all considered by the people as equally true, by the philosopher as equally false, and by the magistrate as equally useful.' The people are now their own magistrates, and the true and the useful must contrive to unite upon the same thing. If the Church feels subscription and fixity of creed a burden, it has only to turn its members to account in their capacity of citizens of the State to relieve itself. If it silently ignores the creed, it is still responsible mainly to itself.

The more serious objection is the possible abuse of the freedom of the clergy to utter opinions at variance with the prevailing creed. This position needs a careful scrutiny.

In the first place, the argument supposes a condition of things that has now ceased. When creeds were accepted in their literality by the bodies professing them, when the state of general opinion contained nothing hostile, and suggested no difficulties,—for any one member of a body to turn traitor may have well seemed mere perversity, temper, love of singularity, or anything but a wish to get at truth. The offence assumed the character of a moral obliquity, and discipline can never be relaxed for immorality proper.

All the circumstances are now changed. The ministers and members of religious communities no longer cherish the same set of doctrines with only immaterial varieties; they no longer accept their articles in the sense of the original framers. The body at large has contracted the immoral taint; the whole head is sick; any remaining soundness is not with the acquiescent mass, but with the out-spoken individuals. In such a state of things, ordinary rules are inapplicable. There is a sort of paralysis of authority, an uncertainty whether to punish or to wink at flagrant heresy. To say in such a case that the relaxation of the creed is not a thing to be proposed, is to confess, like Livy on the condition of Rome, that we can endure neither our vices nor their remedies.

Too much has at all times been made of individual divergences from the established creed. The influence of a solitary preacher smitten with the love of heretical peculiarity has been grossly overrated. The assumption is, that his own flock will, as a matter of course, follow their shepherd; that is to say, the adhesion of individual congregations to the creed of the Church depends upon its being faithfully reproduced by their regular minister. Such is not by any means the fact; the creed of the members of a Church is not at the mercy of any passing influence. It has been engrained by a plurality of influences; one man did not make it, and one man cannot unmake it. Moreover, allowance should be made for the spirit of opposition found in Church members, as well as in other people.

It may be said that persons ought not to be subjected to the annoyance of hearing attacks upon their hereditary tenets, in which they expect to be more and more confirmed by their spiritual teacher. This is of course, in itself, an evil. We are not to expect ordinary men to recognise the necessity of listening to the arguments against their views, in order to hold these all the stronger. If this height were generally reached, every Church would invite, as a part of its constituted machinery, a representative of all the heresies afloat; a certain number of its ministers should be the avowed champions of the views most opposed to its own—*advocati diaboli*, so to speak. There would then be nothing irregular in the retention of converts from its own number to these other doctrines. It would be, however, altogether improper to found any argument on the supposition of such a state of matters.

It is an incident of every institution made up of a large collection of officials, that some one or more are always below the standard of efficiency, whence those that depend on their services must suffer inconvenience. A great amount of dulness in preaching has always to be tolerated; so also might an occasional deviation from orthodoxy; the more so, that the severity of the discipline for heresy has a good deal to do with the dulness.

If heretical tendencies have shown themselves in a Church communion, either they are absurd, unmeaning, irrelevant—perhaps a reversion to some defunct opinion,—or they are the suggestion of new knowledge in theology, or outside of it. In the first case, they will die a natural death, unless prosecution gives them importance; in the other case, they are to be candidly examined, to be met by argument rather than by deposition. An individual heretic can always be neglected; if he is enthusiastic and able, he may have a temporary following, especially when the community has sunk into torpor. If two or three in a hundred adopt erroneous opinions, it is nothing; if thirty or forty in a hundred have been led astray, the matter hangs dubious, and discretion is advisable. When a majority is gained, the fulness of the time has arrived; the heresy has triumphed.

However strong may be the theoretical reasons for the abolition of the penal sanctions to orthodoxy, they do not dispense with the confirmation of experience; and I must next refer to the more prominent examples of Churches constituted on the principle of freedom to the clergy.

The most remarkable and telling instance is that furnished by the English Presbyterian Church, with its coadjutor in Ireland. The history of this Church is not unfamiliar to us; the great lawsuit relating to Lady Hewley's charity gave notoriety to the changes of opinion that had come over it in the course of a century. But whoever is earnest on the question as to the expediency of tests should study the history thoroughly, as being in every way most instructive. The leading facts, as concerns the present argument, are mainly these:—

First, the great decision at the Salters' Hall conference, on the 10th of March, 1719, when, by a majority of 73 to 69, it was resolved to exact no test from the clergy as a condition of their being ordained ministers of the body. The point more immediately at issue was the Trinity, on which opinions had been already divided; but the decision was general. The principle of the right of private judgment admitted of no exceptions.

Second. Long before this decision, the minds of the ministers had been ripening to the conviction, that creeds and subscriptions could do no good, and often did harm. Indeed, the terms employed by some of them are everything that we now desire. For example, Joseph Hunter, on the eve of the decision, wrote thus: "We have always thought that such human declarations of faith were far from being eligible on their own account, since they tend to narrow the foundations of Christianity and to restrain that latitude of expression in which our great Legislator has seen fit to deliver His Will to us".

Third. Most remarkable is it to witness the consequences of this great act of emancipation. A hundred and sixty-five years have elapsed—a sufficient time for judging of the experiment. The Presbyterian body at the time were made up partly of Arians, partly of Trinitarians, who held each other in mutual tolerance; the ministers freely exchanging pulpits. No bad consequence followed. We do not hear of individual ministers going to extravagant lengths in either direction. A large body gravitated, in the course of time, to the modern Unitarian position; but, considering the start, the stride was not great. In such a century as the eighteenth, there might well have been greater modifications of the creeds than actually occurred. Evidently, in the absence of any compulsory adherence to settled articles, there was an abundant tendency to conservatism. Commencing with Baxter, Howe, and Calamy, we find, in the course of the century, such names as Lardner, Price, Priestley, Belsham, Kippis, James Lindsay, Lant Carpenter—men of liberal and enlightened views on all political questions, and earnest in their good works. These men's testimony to what is truth in religion, is of more value to us than the opinions of the creed-bound clergy. Reason is still reason, but the weight of authority is with the free enquirers.

Fourth. The history of the Presbyterians answers a question that may be properly asked of the creed-abolitionist; namely, What bond is left to hold a religious community together? The bond, in their case, simply was voluntary adhesion and custom. A religious community may hold together, like a political party, with only a vague tacit understanding. When a body is once formed, it has an outward cohesion, which is quite enough for maintaining it in the absence of explosive materials. The established

Churches could retain their historical continuity under any modification of the articles. By the present system, they have been habituated to take their creed as their legal definition; for that they could substitute their history and framework.

Various modes have been suggested for making the transition from the present system.

One way is, to fall back upon the Bible as a test. This is the same as no test at all. A man could not call himself a Christian minister, if he did not accept the Bible in some sense; and it would be obviously impracticable to frame a libel, and conduct a process for heresy, on an appeal to the Old and New Testaments at large. The Bible may be the first source of the Christian faith, but other confluent streams have entered into its development; and we must accept the consequences of a fact that we cannot deny. However much religion may have to be broadened and liberalised, the operation cannot consist in reverting to the literal phraseology of the Bible.

A second method is, to prune away the portions of the creed that are no longer tenable. It could not have been intended by the original framers of the creeds, that they should remain untouched for centuries. With many Churches, there was a clear understanding that the formulas should be revised at brief intervals. The non-established Churches show a disposition to resume this power. The United Presbyterian Church of Scotland has had the courage to make a beginning; still, relief will not in this way be given to minorities, and small changes do not correspond to the demands of new situations.

A more effectual mode is to discourage and suspend prosecutions for heresy. The practice of heresy-hunting might be allowed to fall into disuse. Instead of deposing heretics, the orthodox champions should simply refute them.

In the Church of England, in particular, a change of the law may be necessary to give the desired relaxation. The judges before whom heretics are tried are very exacting in the matter of evidence, but they cannot stop a prosecution made in regular form. The Church of Scotland has more latitude in this respect, and has already given indications of entering on the path leading to desuetude.*

* See, at the end, p. 319, Notes and References on the history and practice of Subscription and Penal Tests.

IX.

PROCEDURE OF DELIBERATIVE BODIES.

THE PROCEDURE OF DELIBERATIVE BODIES.[1]

THAT great institution of political liberty, the Deliberative Assembly, seems to be on the eve of breaking down. I do not speak merely of the highest assembly in the country, but of the numerous smaller bodies as well, from many of which a cry of distress may be heard. The one evil in all is the intolerable length of the debates. Business has increased, local representative bodies have a larger membership than formerly, and, notwithstanding the assistance rendered by committees, the meetings are protracted beyond bounds.

In this difficulty, attention naturally fastens, in the first instance, on the fact that the larger part of the speaking is entirely useless; neither informing nor convincing any of the hearers, and yet occupying the time allotted for the despatch of business. How to eliminate and suppress this ineffectual oratory would appear to be the point to consider. But as Inspiration itself did not reveal a mode of separating in advance the tares from the wheat, so there is not now any patent process for insuring that, in the debates of

[1] *Contemporary Review*, November, 1880.

corporate bodies, the good speaking, and only the good speaking, shall be allowed.

Partial solutions of the difficulty are not wanting. The inventors of corporate government—the Greeks, were necessarily the inventors of the forms of debate, and they introduced the timing of the speakers. To this is added, occasionally, the selection of the speakers, a practice that could be systematically worked, if nothing else would do. Both methods have their obvious disadvantages. The arbitrary selection of speakers, even by the most impartial Committee of Selection, would, according to our present notions, seem to infringe upon a natural right, the right of each member of a body to deliver an opinion, and give the reasons for it. It would seem like reviving the censorship of the press, to allow only a select number to be heard on all occasions.

May not something be done to circumvent this vast problem? May there not be a greater extension given to maxims and forms of procedure already in existence?

First, then, we recognize in various ways the propriety of obviating hurried and unpremeditated decisions. Giving previous notice of motions has that end in view; although, perhaps, this is more commonly regarded simply as a protection to absentees. Advantage is necessarily taken of the foreknowledge of the business to prepare for the debates. It is a farther help, that the subject has been already discussed somewhere or other by a committee of the body, or by the agency of the public press. Very often an assembly is merely called upon to decide upon the adoption of a proposal that has been long canvassed out of doors. The task of the speakers is then easy—we might almost say no speaking should be required: but this is to anticipate.

In legislation by Parliament, the forms allow repetition of the debates at least three times in both Houses. This is rather a cumbrous and costly remedy for the disadvantage, in debate, of having to reply to a speaker who has just sat down. In principle, no one ought to be called to answer an argumentative speech on the spur of the moment. The generality of speakers are utterly unfit for the task, and accordingly do it ill. A few men, by long training, acquire the power of casting their thoughts into speaking train, so as to make a good appearance in extempore reply; yet even these would do still better if they had a little time. The adjournment of a debate, and the reopening of a question at successive stages, furnish the real opportunities for effective reply. In a debate begun and ended at one sitting, the speaking takes very little of the form of an exhaustive review, by each speaker, of the speeches that went before.

It is always reckoned a thing of course to take the vote as soon as the debate is closed. There are some historical occasions when a speech on one side has been so extraordinarily impressive that an adjournment has been moved to let the fervour subside; but it is usually not thought desirable to let a day elapse between the final reply and the division. This is a matter of necessity in the case of the smaller corporations, which have to dispose of all current business at one sitting; but when a body meets for a succession of days, it would seem to be in accordance with sound principle not to take the vote on the same day as the debate.

These few remarks upon one important element of procedure are meant to clear the way for a somewhat searching examination of the principles that govern the entire system of oral debate. It is this practice that I propose to put upon its trial. The grounds of the practice I take to be the following:—

1. That each member of a deliberative body shall be provided with a complete statement of the facts and reasons in favour of a proposed measure, and also an equally complete account of whatever can be said against it. And this is a requirement I would concede to the fullest extent. No decision should be asked upon a question until the reasonings *pro* and *con* are brought fairly within the reach of every one; to which I would add—in circumstances that give due time for consideration of the whole case.

2. The second ground is that this ample provision of arguments, for and against, should be made by oral delivery. Whatever opportunities members may have previously enjoyed for mastering a question, these are all discounted when the assembly is called to pronounce its decision. The proposer of the resolution invariably summarizes, if he is able, all that is to be said for his proposal; his arguments are enforced and

supplemented by other speakers on his side; while the opposition endeavours to be equally exhaustive. In short, though one were to come to the meeting with a mind entirely blank, yet such a one, having ordinary faculties of judging, would in the end be completely informed, and prepared for an intelligent vote.

Now, I am fully disposed to acquiesce in this second assumption likewise, but with a qualification that is of considerable moment, as we shall see presently.

3. The third and last assumption is as follows:— Not only is the question in all its bearings supposed to be adequately set forth in the speeches constituting the debate, but, in point of fact, the mass of the members, or a very important section or proportion of them, rely upon this source, make full use of it, and are equipped for their decision by means of it; so much so, that if it were withdrawn none of the other methods as at present plied, or as they might be plied, would give the due preparation for an intelligent vote; whence must ensue a degradation in the quality of the decisions.

It is this assumption that I am now to challenge, in the greatest instance of all, as completely belied by the facts. But, indeed, the case is so notoriously the opposite, that the statement of it will be unavoidably made up of the stalest commonplaces; and the novelty will lie wholly in the inference.

The ordinary attendance in the House of Commons could be best described by a member or a regular official. An outsider can represent it only by the current reports. My purpose does not require great accuracy ; it is enough, that only a very small fraction of the body makes up the average audience. If an official were posted to record the fluctuating numbers at intervals of five minutes, the attendance might be recorded and presented in a curve like the fluctuations of the barometer ; but this would be misleading as to the proportion of effective listeners—those that sat out entire debates, or at all events the leading speeches of the debates, or whose intelligence was mainly fed from the speaking in each instance. The number of this class is next to impossible to get at ; but it will be allowed on all hands to be very small.

Perhaps, in such an inquiry, most can be made of indirect evidences. If members are to be qualified for an intelligent decision in chief part by listening to the speeches, why is not the House made large enough to accommodate them all at once ? It would appear strange, on the spoken-debate theory of enlightenment, that more than one-third should be permanently excluded by want of space. One might naturally suppose that, in this fact, there was a breach of privilege of the most portentous kind. That it is so rarely alluded to as a grievance, even although amounting to the exclusion of a large number of the members from some of the grandest displays of eloquence and the most exciting State communications, is a proof that attendance in the House is not looked upon as a high privilege, or as the *sine quâ non* of political schooling.

If it were necessary to listen to the debates in order

to know how to vote, the messages of the whips would take a different form. The members on each side would be warned of the time of commencement of each debate, that they might hear the comprehensive statement of the opener, and remain at least through the chief speech in reply. They might not attend all through the inferior and desultory speaking, but they would be ready to pop in when an able debater was on his legs, and they would hear the leaders wind up at the close. Such, however, is not the theory acted on by the whips. They are satisfied if they can procure attendance at the division, and look upon the many hours spent in the debate as an insignificant accessory, which could be disregarded at pleasure. It would take the genius of a satirist to treat the whipping-up machinery as it might well deserve to be treated. We are here concerned with a graver view of it—namely, to inquire whether the institution of oral debate may not be transformed and contracted in dimensions, to the great relief of our legislative machinery.

Of course, no one is ignorant of the fact that the great body of members of Parliament refrain altogether from weighing individually the opposing arguments in the several questions, and trust implicitly to their leaders. This, however, is merely another nail in the coffin of the debating system. The theory of independent and intelligent consideration, by each member, of every measure that comes up, is the one most favourable to the present plan, while, even on that theory, its efficiency breaks down under a critical handling.

It is time now to turn to what will have come into the mind of every reader of the last few paragraphs—the reporting of the speeches. Here, I admit, there is a real and indispensable service to legislation. My contention is, that in it we possess what is alone valuable; and, if we could secure this, in its present efficiency, with only a very small minimum of oral delivery, we should be as well off as we are now. The apparent self-contradiction of the proposal to report speeches without speaking, is not hard to resolve.

To come at once, then, to the mode of arriving at the printed debates, I shall proceed by a succession of steps, each one efficient in itself, without necessitating a farther. The first and easiest device, and one that would be felt of advantage in all bodies whatsoever, would be for the mover of a resolution to give in, along with the terms of his resolution, his reasons—in fact, what he intends as his speech, to be printed and distributed to each member previous to the meeting. Two important ends are at once gained—the time of a speech is saved, and the members are in possession beforehand of the precise arguments to be used. The debate is in this way advanced an important step without any speaking; opponents can prepare for, instead of having to improvise their reply, and every one is at the outset a good way towards a final judgment.

As this single device could be adopted alone, I will try and meet the objections to it, if I am only fortunate enough to light on any. My experience of public bodies suggests but very few; and I think the strongest is the reluctance to take the requisite trouble. Most men think beforehand what they are to say in introducing a resolution to a public body, but do not consider it necessary to write down their speech at full. Then, again, there is a peculiar satisfaction in holding the attention of a meeting for a certain time, great in proportion to the success of the effort. But, on the other hand, many persons do write their speeches, and many are not so much at ease in speaking but that they would dispense with it willingly. The conclusive answer on the whole is—the greater good of the commonwealth. Such objections as these are not of a kind to weigh down the manifest advantages, at all events, in the case of corporations full of business and pressed for time.

I believe that a debate so introduced would be shortened by more than the time gained by cutting off the speech of the mover. The greater preparation of everyone's mind at the commencement would make people satisfied with a less amount of speaking, and what there was would be more to the purpose.

We can best understand the effects of such an innovation by referring to the familiar experience of having to decide on the Report of Committee, which has been previously circulated among the members. This is usually the most summary act of a deliberative body; partly owing, no doubt, to the fact that the concurrence of a certain proportion is already gained; while the *pros* and *cons* have been sifted by a regular conference and debate. Yet we all feel that we are in a much better position by having had before us in print, for some time previous, the materials necessary to a conclusion. At a later stage, I will consider the modes of raising the quality and status of the introductory speech to something of the nature of a Committee's Report.[1]

The second step is to impose upon the mover of every amendment the same obligation to hand in his speech, in writing, along with the terms of the amendment. Many public bodies do not require notice of amendments. It would be in all cases a great improvement to insist upon such notice, and of course a still greater improvement to require the reasons to be given in also, that they might be circulated as above. The debate is now two steps in advance without a moment's loss of time to the constituted meeting; while what remains is likely to be much more rapidly gone through.

The movers of resolutions and of amendments should, as a matter of course, have the right of reply; a portion of the oral system that would, I presume, survive all the advances towards printing direct.

There remains, however, one farther move, in itself as defensible, and as much fraught with advantage as the two others. The resolution and the amendments being in the hands of the members of a body, together with the speeches in support of each, any member might be at liberty to send in, also for circulation in print, whatever remarks would constitute his speech

---

[1] I have often thought that the practice of circulating, with a motion, the proposer's reasons, would, on many occasions, be worthy of being voluntarily adopted.

in the debate, thereby making a still greater saving of the time of the body. This would, no doubt, be felt as the greatest innovation of all, being tantamount to the extinction of oral debate; there being then nothing left but the replies of the movers. We need not, however, go the length of compulsion; while a certain number would choose to print at once, the others could still, if they chose, abide by the old plan of oral address. One can easily surmise that these last would need to justify their choice by conspicuous merit; an assembly, having in print so many speeches already, would not be in a mood to listen to others of indifferent quality.

Such a wholesale transfer of living speech to the silent perusal of the printed page, if seriously proposed in any assembly, would lead to a vehement defence of the power of spoken oratory. We should be told of the miraculous sway of the human voice, of the way that Whitfield entranced Hume and emptied Franklin's purse; while, most certainly, neither of these two would ever have perused one of his printed sermons. And, if the reply were that Whitfield was not a legislator, we should be met by the speeches of Wilberforce and Canning and Brougham upon slavery, where the thrill of the living voice accelerated the conviction of the audience. In speaking of the Homeric Assembly, Mr. Gladstone remarks, in answer to Grote's argument to prove it a political nullity, that the speakers were repeatedly cheered, and that the cheering of an audience contributes to the decision.

Now, I am not insensible to the power of speech, nor to the multitudinous waves of human feeling aroused in the encounters of oratory before a large assembly. Apart from this excitement, it would often be difficult to get people to go through the drudgery of public meetings. Any plan that would abolish entirely the dramatic element of legislation would have small chance of being adopted. It is only when the painful side of debate comes into predominance, that we willingly forego some of its pleasures: the intolerable weariness, the close air, the late nights, must be counted along with the occasional thrills of delirious excitement. But as far as regards our great legislative bodies, it will be easy to show that there would still exist, in other forms, an ample scope for living oratory to make up for the deadness that would fall upon the chief assembly.

A friend of mine once went to Roebuck to ask his attention to some point coming up in the House of Commons, and offered him a paper to read. Roebuck said, "I will not read, but I will hear". This well illustrates one of the favourable aspects of speech. People with time on their hands prefer being instructed by the living voice; the exertion is less, and the enlivening tones of a speaker impart an extraneous interest, to which we have to add the sympathy of the surrounding multitude. The early stages of instruction must be conducted *vivâ voce*; it is a late acquirement to be able to extract information from a printed page. Yet circumstances arise when the advantage of the printed page predominates. The more frequent experience in approaching public men is to be told, that they will not listen but will read. An hour's address can be read in ten minutes: it is not impossible, therefore, to master a Parliamentary debate in one-tenth of the time occupied in the delivery.

A passing remark is enough to point out the revolution that would take place in Parliamentary reporting, and in the diffusion of political instruction through the press, by the system of printing the speeches direct. The full importance of this result will be more apparent in a little. There has been much talk of late about the desirability of a more perfect system of reporting, with a view to the preservation of the debates. Yet it may be very much doubted, whether the House of Commons would ever incur the expense of making up for the defects of newspaper reporting, by providing short-hand writers to take down every word, with a view to printing in full.

Before completing the survey of possible improvements in deliberative procedure, I propose to extend the employment of another device already in use, but scarcely more than a form; I mean the requiring of a seconder before a proposal can be debated. The signification of this must be, that in order to obtain the judgment of an assembly on any proposal, the mover must have the concurrence of one other member; a most reasonable condition surely. What I would urge farther in the same direction is that, instead of demanding one person in addition to the mover, as necessary in all cases, there should be a varying number according to the number of the assembly. In a copartnery of three or four, to demand a seconder to a motion would be absurd; in a body of six or eight it is scarcely admissible. I have known bodies of ten and twelve, where motions could be discussed without a seconder; but even with these, there would be a manifest propriety in compelling a member to convince at least one other person privately before putting the body to the trouble of a discussion. If, however, we should begin the practice of seconding with ten, is one seconder enough for twenty, fifty, a hundred, or six hundred? Ought there not to be a scale of steady increase in the numbers whose opinions have been gained beforehand? Let us say three or four for an assembly of five-and-twenty, six for fifty, ten or fifteen for a hundred, forty for six hundred. It is permissible, no doubt, to bring before a public body resolutions that there is no immediate chance of carrying; what is termed "ventilating" an opinion is a recognized usage, and is not to be prohibited. But when business multiplies, and time is precious, a certain check should be put upon the ventilating of views that have as yet not got beyond one or two individuals; the process of conversion by out-of-door agency should have made some progress in order to justify an appeal to the body in the regular course of business. That the House of Commons should ever be occupied by a debate, where the movers could not command more than four or five votes, is apparently out of all reason. The power of the individual is unduly exalted at the expense of the collective body. There are plenty of other opportunities of gaining adherents to any proposal that has something to be said for it; and these should be plied up to the point of securing a certain minimum of concurrence, before the ear of the House can be commanded. With a body of six hundred and fifty, the number of previously obtained adherents would not be extravagantly high, if it were fixed at forty. Yet considering that the current business, in large assemblies, is carried on by perhaps one-third or one-fourth of the whole, and that the quorum in the House of Commons is such as to make it possible for twenty-one votes to carry a decision of the House, there would be an inconsistency in requiring more than twenty names to back every bill and every resolution and amendment that claimed to be discussed. Now I can hardly imagine restriction upon the liberty of individual members more defensible than this. If it were impossible to find any other access to the minds of individual members than by speeches in the House, or if all other modes of conversion to new views were difficult and inefficient in comparison, then we should say that the time of the House must be taxed for the ventilating process. Nothing of the kind, however, can be maintained. Moreover, although the House may be obliged to listen to a speech for a proposal that has merely half a dozen of known supporters, yet, whenever this is understood to be the case, scarcely any one will be at the trouble of counter-arguing it, and the question really makes no way, the mover is looked upon as a bore, and the House is impatient for the extinguisher of a division. The securing of twenty names would cost nothing to the Government, or to any of the parties or sections that make up the House: an individual standing alone should be made to work privately, until he has secured his backing of nineteen more names, and the exercise would be most wholesome as a preparation for convincing a majority of the House.

If I might be allowed to assume such an extension of the device of seconding motions, I could make a much stronger case for the beneficial consequences of the operation of printing speeches without delivery. The House would never be moved by an individual standing alone; every proposal would be from the first a collective judgment, and the reasons given in along with it, although composed by one, would be revised and considered by the supporters collectively. Members would put forth their strength in one weighty statement to start with; no pains would be spared to make the argument of the nominal mover exhaustive and forcible. So with the amendment, there would be more put into the chief statement, and less left to the succeeding speakers, than at present. And, although the mover of the resolution and the mover of the amendment would each have a reply, little would be left to detain the House, unless when some great interests were at stake.

Of course the preparation of the case in favour of each measure would be entrusted to the best hands; in Government business, it would be to some official in the department, or some one engaged by the chief in shaping the measure itself. The statement so prepared would have the value of a carefully drawn-up report, and nothing short of this should ever be submitted to Parliament in the procuring of new enactments. In like manner, the opponents and critics could employ any one they pleased to assist them in their compositions. A member's speech need not be in any sense his own; if he borrows, or uses another hand, it is likely to be some one wiser than himself, and the public gets the benefit of the difference.

I may now go back for a little upon the details of the scheme of direct printing, with the view of pressing some of its advantages a little farther, as well as of considering objections. I must remark more particularly upon the permission, accorded to the members generally, to send in their speeches to be circulated with the proceedings. This I regard as not the least essential step in an effective reform of the debating system. It is the only possible plan of giving free scope to individuals without wasting the time of the assembly. There need be no limit to the printing of speeches; the number may be unnecessarily great, and the length sometimes excessive, but the abuse may be left to the corrective of neglect. The only material disadvantage attending the plan of sending in speeches in writing, without delivery, is that the speakers would have before them only the statements-in-chief of the movers of motion and amendment. They could not comment upon one another, as in the oral debate. Not but this might not be practicable, by keeping the question open for a certain length of time, and circulating every morning the speeches given in the day previously; but the cumbrousness of such an operation would not have enough to recommend it. The chief speakers might be expected to present a sufficiently broad point for criticism; while the greater number are well content, if allowed to give their own views and arguments without reference to those of others. And not to mention that, in Parliament, all questions of principle may be debated several times over, it is rare that any measure comes up without such an amount of previous discussion out of doors as fully to bring out the points for attack and defence. Moreover, the oral debate, as usually conducted, contains little of the reality of effective rejoinder by each successive speaker to the one preceding.

The combined plan of printing speeches, and of requiring twenty backers to every proposal, while tolerable perhaps in the introduction of bills, and in resolutions of great moment, will seem to stand self-condemned in passing the bills through Committee, clause by clause. That every amendment, however trivial, should have to go through such a roundabout course, may well appear ridiculous in the extreme. To this I would say, in the first place, that the exposing of every clause of every measure of importance to the criticism of a large assembly, has long been regarded as the weak point of the Parliamentary system. It is thirty years since I heard the remark that a Code would never get through the House of Commons; so many people thinking themselves qualified to cavil at its details. In Mill's "Representative Government," there is a suggestion to the effect, that Parliament should be assisted in passing great measures by consultative commissions, who would have the preparation of the details; and that the House should not make alterations in the clauses, but recommit the whole with some expression of disapproval that would guide the commission in re-casting the measure.

It must be self-evident that only a small body can work advantageously in adjusting the details of a measure, including the verbal expressions. If this work is set before an assembly of two hundred, it is only by the reticence of one hundred and ninety that progress can be made. Amendments to the clauses of a bill may come under two heads: those of principle, where the force of parties expends itself; and those of wording or expression, for clearing away ambiguities or misconstruction. For the one class, all the machinery that I have described is fully applicable. To mature and present an amendment of principle, there should be a concurrence of the same number as is needed to move or oppose a second reading; there should be the same giving in of reasons, and the same unrestricted speech (in print) of individual members, culminating in replies by the movers. If this had to be done on all occasions, there would be much greater concentration of force upon special points, and the work of Committee would get on faster As to the second class of amendments, I do not think that these are suitable for an open discussion. They should rather be given as suggestions privately to the promoter of the measure. But, be the matter small or great, I contend that nothing should bring about a vote in the House of Commons that has not already acquired a proper minimum of support.

I am very far from presuming to remodel the entire procedure of the House of Commons. What I have said applies only to the one branch, not the least important, of the passing of bills. There are other departments that might, or might not, be subjected to the printing system, coupled with the twentyfold backing; for example, the very large subject of Supply, on which there is a vast expenditure of debating. The demand for twenty names to every amendment would extinguish a very considerable amount of these discussions.

There is a department of the business of the House that has lately assumed alarming proportions—the putting of questions to Ministers upon every conceivable topic. I would here apply, without hesitation, the printing direct and the plural backing, and sweep away the practice entirely from the public proceedings of the House. No single member unsupported should have the power of trotting out a Minister at will. I do not say that so large a number of backers should be required in this case, but I would humbly suggest that the concurrence of ten members should be required even to put a public question. The leader of the Opposition, in himself a host, would not be encumbered with such a formality, but everyone else would have to procure ten signatures to an interrogative: the question would be sent in, and answered; while question and answer would simply appear in the printed proceedings of the House, and not occupy a single moment of the legislative time. This is a provision that would stand to be argued on its own merits, everything else remaining as it is. The loss would be purely in the dramatic interest attaching to the deliberations.

The all but total extinction of oral debate by the revolutionary sweep of two simple devices, would be far from destroying the power of speech in other ways. The influence exerted by conversation on the small scale, and by oratory on the great, would still be exercised. While the conferences in private society, and the addresses at public meetings, would continue, and perhaps be increased in importance, there would be a much greater activity of sectional discussion, than at present; in fact, the sectional deliberations, preparatory to motions in the House, would become an organized institution. A certain number of rooms would be set aside for the use of the different sections; and the meetings would rise into public importance, and have their record in the public press. The speaking that now protracts the sittings of the House would be transferred to these, even the highest oratory would not disdain to shine where the reward of publicity would still be reaped. As no man would be allowed to engage the attention of the House without a following, it would be in the sections, in addition to private society and the press, that new opinions would have to be ventilated, and the first converts gained.

Among the innovations that are justified by the principle of avoiding at all points hurried decisions, there is nothing that would appear more defensible than to give an interval between the close of a debate and the taking of the vote. I apprehend that the chief and only reason why this has never been thought of is, that most bodies have to finish a mass of current business at one sitting. In assemblies that meet day after day, the votes on all concluded debates could be postponed till next day; giving a deliberate interval in private that might improve, and could not deteriorate, the chances of a good decision. Let us imagine that, in the House of Commons, for example, the first hour at each meeting should be occupied with the divisions growing out of the previous day's debates. The consequences would be enormous, but would any of them be bad? The hollowness of the oral debate as a means of persuasion would doubtless receive a blasting exposure; many would come up to vote, few would remain to listen to speeches. The greater number of those that cared to know what was said, would rest satisfied with the reports in the morning papers.

We need to take account of the fact that even greater moderation in the length of speeches would not entirely overcome the real difficulty—the quantity of business thrown upon our legislative bodies.

Doubtless, if there were less talk upon burning questions there would be more attention given to unobtrusive matters at present neglected. The mere quantity of work is too great for an assembly to do well. If this amount cannot be lessened—and I do not see how it can be—there are still the six competing vehicles at old Temple Bar. The single legislative rail is crowded, and the only device equal to the occasion is to remove some of the traffic to other rails. Let a large part of the speaking be got rid of, or else be transferred to some different arena.

I regard as unassailable Lord Sherbrooke's position that every deliberative body must possess the entire control of its own procedure, even to the point of saying how much speaking it will allow on each topic. The rough-and-ready method of coughing down a superfluous speaker is perfectly constitutional, because absolutely necessary. If a more refined method of curtailing debates could be devised, without bringing in other evils, it should be welcomed. The forcible shutting of anyone's mouth will always tend to irritate, and it is impossible by any plan to prevent a minority from clogging the wheels of business. The freedom of print seems to me one good safety-valve for incontinent speech-makers; it allows them an equal privilege with their fellows, and yet does not waste legislative time.

I remember hearing, some time ago, that our Chancellor of the Exchequer was induced, on the suggestion of the *Times*, to put into print and circulate to the House beforehand the figures and tables connected with his financial statement. I could not help remarking, why might the Chancellor not circulate, in the same fashion, the whole statement, down to the point of the declaration of the new taxes? It would save the House at least an hour and a half, while not a third of that time would be required to read the printed statement. I believe the first thing that would occur to anyone hearing this suggestion would be—" so the Chancellor might, but the same reason would apply to the movers of bills, and to all other business as well ".

Our English Parliamentary system having been matured by centuries of experience, has become a model for other countries just entering upon representative government. But the imitation, if too literal, will not be found to work. Our system supposes a large gentry, staying half the year in London for pure pleasure, to which we may add the rich men of business resident there. A sufficient number of these classes can at any time be got to make up the House of Commons ; and, the majority being composed of such, the ways of the House are regulated accordingly. Daily constant attendance, when necessary, and readiness to respond to the whip at short notice, are assumed as costing nothing. But in other countries, the case is not the same. In the Italian Chamber I found professors of the University of Turin, who still kept up their class-work, and made journeys to Rome at intervals of a week or two, on the emergence of important business. Even the payment of members is not enough to bring people away from their homes, and break up their avocations, for several months every year. The forms of procedure, as familiar to us, do not fit under such circumstances. The system of printed speeches, with division days at two or three weeks' interval, might be found serviceable. But, at all events, the entire arrangements of public deliberation need to be revised on much broader grounds than we have been accustomed to ; and it is in this view, more than with any hope of bringing about immediate changes, that I have ventured to propound the foregoing suggestions.

Since the foregoing paper was written, opinions have been expressed favourable to the use of printing as a means of shortening the debates in the House of Commons. Among the most notable of the authorities that have declared their views, we may count Lord Derby and Lord Sherbrooke. Both advocate the printing of the answers by ministers to the daily string of questions addressed to them. Lord Derby goes a step farther. He would have everyone introducing a bill to prepare a statement of his reasons, to be circulated among members at the public expense. Even this small beginning would be fruitful of important consequences ; the greatest being the inevitable extension of the system.

I am not aware that my suggestion as to requiring

a plurality of members to back every bill and every proposal, has gained any degree of support. It was urged that, if the power were taken away from single members to move in any case whatever, the few that are accustomed to find themselves alone, would form into a group to back each other. I do not hesitate to say that the supposition is contrary to all experience. Crotcheteers have this in common with the insane, that they can seldom agree in any conjoined action. Even in the very large body constituting our House of Commons, it is not infrequent for motions to be made without obtaining a seconder. The requirement of even five concurring members would put an extinguisher upon a number of propositions that have at present to be entertained.

The last session (1883) has opened the eyes of many to the absurdity of allowing a single member to block a bill. When it is considered that, in an assembly of six hundred, there is probably at least one man, like Fergus O'Conner, verging on insanity, and out of the reach of all the common motives,—we may well wonder that a deliberative body should so put itself at the mercy of individuals. Surely the rule, for stopping bills at half-past twelve, might have been accompanied with the requirement of a seconder, which would have saved many in the course of the recent sessions. It is the gross abuse of this power that is forcing upon reluctant minds the first advance to plural backing, and there is now a demand for five or six to unite in placing a block against a measure.

It occurred to Mr. Gladstone, during the autumn

session of 1882, to take down the statistics of attendance in the House for several days running. His figures were detailed to the House, in one of his speeches, and were exactly what we were prepared for. They completely "pounded and pulverised" the notion, that listening to the debates is the way that members have their minds made up for giving their votes.

The recent parliamentary recess has witnessed an unusual development in the out-of-door discussion of burning questions. In addition to a full allowance of vacation oratory, and the unremitted current of the newspaper press, the monthlies have given forth a number of reasoned articles by cabinet ministers and by men of ministerial rank in the opposition. The whole tendency of our time is, to supersede parliamentary discussion by more direct appeals to the mind of the public.

To stop entirely the oral discussion of business in Parliament would have some inconveniences; but the want of adequate consideration of such measures as possessed the smallest interest with any class, would not be one of them.

Notes and References in connection with Essay VIII., on Subscription.

It may be useful here to supply a few memoranda as to the history and present practice of Subscription to Articles.

In the *Quarterly Review*, No. 117, the following observations are made respecting the first imposition of Tests after the English Reformation:—

"Before the Reformation no subscription was required from the body of the clergy, as none was necessary. The bishops at their consecration took an oath of obedience to the King, in which, besides promising subjection in matters temporal, they 'utterly renounced and clearly forsook all such clauses, words, sentences, and grants, which they had or should have of the Pope's Holiness, that in any wise were hurtful or prejudicial to His Highness or His Estate Royal'; whilst to the Pope they bound themselves by oath to keep the rules of the Holy Fathers, the decrees, ordinances, sentences, dispositions, reservations, provisions, and commandments Apostolic, and, to their powers, to cause them to be kept by others. And, as their command over their clergy was complete, and they could at once remove any who violated the established rule of opinion, no additional obligation or engagement from men under such strict discipline was requisite. The statement, therefore (by Dean Stanley), that 'the Roman Catholic clergy, and the clergy of the Eastern Church, neither formerly, nor now, were bound by any definite forms of subscription; and that the unity of the Church is preserved there as the unity of the State is preserved everywhere, not by preliminary promises or oaths, but by the general laws of discipline and order'; though true to the letter, is really wholly untrue in its application to the argument concerning subscriptions. For it is to the total absence of liberty, and to the severity of 'the general laws of discipline and order,' and not to a liberty greater than our own, that this absence of subscription is due.

"In point of fact, the requirement of subscription from the clergy was coeval with the upgrowth of liberty of opinion; while the circumstances of the English Reformation of religion made it essential to the success and the safety of that great movement. It was essential to its success; for as it was accomplished mainly by a numerical minority, both of the clergy and laity of the land, there could be no other guarantee of its maintenance than the assurance that its doctrines would be honestly taught, and its ritual observed by the whole body of the conforming clergy.

"Thus the *Reformation subscriptions aimed at the prevention of covert Popery*, a danger to which the Reforming laity felt that they were exposed by the strong wishes of a majority of their own class; by the undissembled bias of many of the parochial clergy; and by the secret bias of some even of the bishops; whilst the diminution of their absolute control over the clergy lessened the power of enforcing the new opinions when the bishop was sincerely attached to them."

The entire article is of value both for its historical information as to the history of Tests in the English Church, and for its mode of advocating the retention of subscription to the Articles, as at present enforced.

The Report of the Royal Commission of 1864, on Subscription in the English Church, supplied a complete account of all the changes in subscription from the Reformation downwards. Reference may also be made to Stoughton's "History of Religion in England," for the incidents in greater detail.

Perhaps the most remarkable defence of Liberty, as against the prevailing view in the English Church, is Dean Milman's speech before the Clerical Subscription Commission, of which he was a member. It is printed in *Fraser's Magazine*, March, 1865, and is included in the criticism of the *Quarierly Review* article, already quoted.

The Dean's Resolution submitted to the Commission was as follows :—

"Conformity to the Liturgy of the Church of England being the best and the surest attainable security for 'the declared agreement of the Clergy with the doctrines of the Church'; with many the daily, with all the weekly public reading of the services of the Church of England (containing, as they do, the ancient creeds of the Church Catholic), and the constant use of the Sacramental offices and other formularies in the Book of Common Prayer, being a solemn and reiterated pledge of their belief in those doctrines, the Subscription to the thirty-nine Articles is unnecessary. Such Subscription adds no further guarantee for the clergyman's faithfulness to the doctrines of the Church ; while the peculiar form and controversial tone in which the Articles were compiled is the cause of much perplexity, embarrassment, and difficulty, especially to the younger clergy and to those about to enter into Holy Orders."

Much doubt was entertained, whether this motion came within the terms of the Commission. It was not pressed by the Dean.

I give the following quotation from the speech :—

. . . "And if I venture to question the expediency, the wisdom, I will say the righteousness of retaining subscription to the thirty-nine Articles as obligatory on all clergymen, I do so, not from any difficulty in reconciling with my own conscience what, during my life, I have done more than once, but from the deep and deliberate conviction that such subscription is altogether unnecessary as a safe guard for the essential doctrines of Christianity, which are more safely and fully protected by other means. It never has been, is not, and never will be a solid security for its professed object, the reconciling or removing religious differences, which it tends rather to create and keep alive; is embarrassing to many men who might be of the most valuable service in the ministry of the Church; is objectionable as concentrating and enforcing the attention of the youngest clergy on questions, some abstruse, some antiquated, and in themselves at once so minute and comprehensive as to harass less instructed and profound thinkers, to perplex and tax the sagacity of the most able lawyers and the most learned divines. . . .

"One of my chief objections to subscription to the thirty-nine Articles as a perpetual test of English Churchmanship is that they are throughout controversial, and speak, as of necessity they must speak, the controversial language of their day; they cannot, therefore, in my opinion, be fully, clearly, and distinctly understood without a careful study and a very wide knowledge of the disputes and opinions of those times, a calm yet deep examination of their meaning, objects, limitations, which cannot be expected from young theological students, from men fresh from their academical pursuits. I venture to add, indeed to argue, that their true bearing and interpretation seems to me to have escaped some of our most eminent judges from want of that full study and perfect knowledge; and I must say that, in these laborious and practical days, it may be questioned whether this study of controversies, many of them bygone, will be so useful, so profitable, as entire devotion to the plainer and simpler duties of the clergyman.

"Their immense range, too, the infinite questions into which they branch out (it has been said, I know not how truly, that five hundred questions may be raised upon them), is a further objection to their maintenance as a preliminary and indispensable requirement before the young man is admitted to Holy Orders. On the whole I stand, without hesitation, to my proposition, that the doctrines of the English Church are not only more simply, but more fully, assuredly, more winningly, taught in our Liturgy and our Formularies than in our Articles."

The very elaborate work of Mr. Taylor Innes, entitled the "Law of Creeds," is exhaustive for Scotland; including both the Established Church and the various sects of Protestant Dissenters. It also incidentally takes notice of some of the more critical decisions on heresy cases in the English Church. Mr. Innes properly points out, that the abolition of Subscription is compatible with compulsory adherence to Articles. The relaxation of the forms of Subscription in the English Church, by the Act of 1865, gave a certain amount of relief to the consciences of the clergy, but left them as much exposed as ever to suits for heresy.

For the usages of the Reformed Churches, on the Continent, and in America, a mass of valuable information has been furnished in the Report of the Second General Council of the Presbyterian Alliance, convened at Philadelphia, September, 1880. At the previous meeting of the Council, held at Edinburgh, July, 1877, a Committee was appointed to Report on the Creeds and Subscriptions in use among the various bodies forming the Alliance. It is unnecessary to refer to the answers given in to the Committee's Queries, from Great Britain and Ireland, except to complete the history of the Presbyterian Church of England, so long distinguished for the abeyance of clerical subscription.

It was in 1755, that the Presbytery of Newcastle made a movement towards disclaiming the Arian, Socinian and other heresies, but without proposing a Confession. In 1784, the same Presbytery adopted a Formula accepting the Westminster Confession; in 1802, however, subscription to the Formula was rescinded. Through Scottish influence, the return to the Westminster Confession was gradually brought about in the early part of the century. That Confession was formally adopted by the Presbytery of Newcastle in 1824; and since 1836, all the ministers of the body have been required to accept it in the most unqualified manner.

The Calvinistic Methodists of Wales drew up, in 1823, a Confession consisting of forty-four articles, agreeing substantially with the Westminster Confession. Subscription is not required: but the clergy, prior to ordination, make a statement of their doctrinal views, which amounts to nearly the same thing. Like the Roman Catholic Church, the Methodists depend upon discipline rather than upon Subscription.

The Congregational Churches take up almost the same attitude towards their clergy. There is no subscription; but any great deviation from the prevailing views of the body leads to forfeiture of the position of brotherhood, and possibly also to severance from the charge of a congregation. Still, the absence of a binding and penal test is favourable to freedom, from the present tendency of men's minds in that direction.

As regards the Presbyterian Church in the United States of America, we find that the first Presbytery was constituted in 1705. No formal statement of doctrine was considered necessary till the lapse of about a quarter of a century, when the spread of Arianism in England urged the Synod of Philadelphia to pass what was called the "Adopting Act" in 1729, by which they hoped to exclude from American churches British ministers tainted with Arian views. They agreed "that all the ministers of this Synod, or that shall hereafter be admitted into this Synod, shall declare their agreement in and approbation of the Confession of Faith, with the Larger and Shorter Catechisms of the Assembly of Divines at Westminster, as being, in all the essential and necessary articles, good forms of sound words and systems of Christian doctrine," "and we do also adopt the said confession and the catechisms as the Confession of our Faith".

The formula subscribed by ministers at their ordination is, however, less stringent than that in use in the Churches of Scotland.

Turning next to the Continent we may refer, first, to the French Protestant Church, now consisting of two divisions —(1) The Reformed Church united to the State, and (2) The Union of the Evangelical Churches.

The Gallic Confession, styled "La Rochelle," the joint work of Calvin and Chaudien, was adopted as the doctrinal standard of the Reformed French Churches in their first national synod, which met at Paris in May, 1559, and was revised and confirmed by the seventh synod, which assembled at La Rochelle under the presidency of Theodore Beza in 1571. It is composed of forty articles, which reproduce faithfully the Calvinistic doctrine. But it is not accepted as infallible; the final authority, in the light of which successive synods may reform it, is the Bible.

"The reformed doctrine, as sanctioned by the Confession of La Rochelle, was, in its essential features, recognised and professed by all Protestant France; and, notwithstanding its sufferings and internal dissensions, the Church during the first quarter of the 17th century held its own course and remained faithful to itself. A consistory, that of Caen, had, even as late as 1840, restored in the churches of its jurisdiction the Confession of La Rochelle in its full vigour. Little by little, however, under the influence of the naturalistic philosophy of the 18th century, the negative criticism of Germany, and above all the religious indifference which followed the repose which the Church was enjoying after two centuries of persecution, the Confession of Faith as well as the discipline fell into disuse. It was never really abrogated. . . . However, it is a practical fact that the partisans of one of the two sections which to-day divide the Reformed Church of France, not only do not consider themselves bound by the Confession of La Rochelle, but, tending more and more towards Rationalism, and seeing in Protestantism only the religion of free thought, have come to reject the great miracles of the gospel, and to demand for their pastors, in the bosom of the Church, unlimited freedom in teaching. While on the one hand the sovereignty of the Holy Scriptures is claimed, on the other is held the rule of individual conscience."

The majority of the official synod which met at Paris in September, 1848, refused to put an end to the doctrinal disorder in the Church by establishing in the Church a clear and positive law of faith. The minority, regarding the adverse vote as an official sufferance of indifference on doctrinal matters, separated themselves from their brethren, and founded the " Union of the Evangelical Churches of France ".

In 1872, " in the face of attacks directly aimed, in the bosom of the Church, at the unity of her doctrine," the thirtieth general synod, assembled at Paris, drew up, not a complete Confession of Faith, but a declaration determining the doctrinal limits of the Church, and proclaiming " the sovereign authority of the Holy Scriptures with regard to belief, and salvation through faith in Jesus Christ, the only begotten Son of God, who died for our sins and rose again for our justification ".*

Down to 1824, new pastors indicated their adherence to the Confession of Faith by signature. In 1824, however, signature was replaced by a solemn promise. "Since that time different formulas have been used at the will of the pastors performing the ordination, without any one of them having the sanction of a synod, and without the manner of adherence having been expressly stipulated."

"Since the Synod of 1872, in ordinations over which pastors attached to the Synodal Church have presided, candidates are required to conform formally, in the presence of the congregation, to the declaration of faith adopted by the Synod. Article 2, of the complete law, declares : 'Every candidate for holy orders must, before receiving ordination, affirm that he adheres to the faith of the Church as stated by the general synod '."

Theological professors were sometimes appointed without conditions. Still they were not permitted to teach doctrines in glaring contradiction to the general belief of the Churches. For example, in 1812, M. Gasc, professor of theology at Montauban, attacked in his lectures the doctrine of the Trinity, whereupon several consistories required him either to retract his opinions or to resign his post. M. Gasc retracted his opinions.

"The Evangelical Churches of France, composed of members who have made an explicit and individual profession of faith, and who recognise in religious matters no other authority than that of Jesus Christ, the only and sovereign head of the Church," accept the Old and New

---

* The debates in this Synod were conducted with the highest ability on both sides. Guizot took a part on the side of orthodoxy. The published Report will be found abstracted in the *British Quarterly*, No. CXIV.

Testaments as directly inspired by God and so constituting the only and infallible rule of faith and life.

The Churches of Switzerland have the pre-eminence in the relaxation or disuse of Tests. The following is a summary of their practice :—

The Reformed Church of the Canton of Vaud.

According to the ecclesiastical law of May 19, 1863 (slightly modified by a decree of December 2, 1874), the *National Church* of the Canton of Vaud " desires chiefly that its members should lead a Christian life," and " admits no other rule of instruction than the Word of God contained in the Holy Scriptures ". Every candidate for the ministry is required by the ecclesiastical law of December 14, 1839, to " swear that he will discharge conscientiously the duties which the National Reformed Evangelical Church imposes upon its ministers, and that he will preach the Word of God in its purity and integrity as it is contained in the Holy Scriptures ". " When accusation is brought against any minister on the ground of doctrine, the proceedings are distinctly marked ; but in reality it is simply required that 'the jurymen give a conscientious verdict'."

The *Free Evangelical Church* of the Canton of Vaud requires that candidates for the ministry be examined as to their religious life, their calling to the ministry, their doctrine and their ecclesiastical principles by a committee of the synodical commission, with pastors and elders. After examination the candidate must " declare his cordial adhesion to the doctrines and institutions of the Free Church". This pledge is verbal.

Independent Evangelical Church of Neuchatel.

The ancient Reformed Church of Neuchatel never put

forth any special Confession of Faith. The assembly of Pastors, the governing body of the Church, down to 1848, accepted the Holy Scriptures, the forms used in baptism and the communion, and the Apostles' Creed as fully adequate to express the faith of the Church. The Synod, who took over the government of the Church in 1848, maintained the same position, refusing in 1857 to sanction an abridged Confession.

On May 20, 1873, the Grand Council of the Republic and Canton of Neuchatel passed a new law regulating the relation of Church and State. Article 12 says: "Liberty of conscience in matters of religion is inviolable; it may neither be fettered by regulations, vows, or promises, by disciplinary penalties, by formulas or a creed, nor by any measures whatsoever".

Hence resulted the separation of those that formed the Independent Evangelical Church of Neuchatel, which, in 1874, adopted a Confession "acknowledging as the only source and rule of its faith the Old and New Testaments, and proclaiming the great truths of salvation contained in the Apostles' Creed". The ministers, on ordination, take an oath to advance the honour and glory of God above all things; to maintain his word at the risk of life, body, and property; to be in unity with the brethren in the doctrines of religion and in the holy ministry; and to avoid all sectarianism and schism in the Church.

National Protestant Church of Geneva.

During the 16th century, from 1536 onwards, the National Protestant Church of Geneva was in constant turmoil through the insistence on, and the opposition to, the doctrines laid down by Calvin in his Confession of Faith and System of Ecclesiastical Ordinances. The 17th century is marked by the conflicts of Calvinism and Arminianism. After numerous variations, the oath of consecration was, in June 1725, changed back to the form provided by the Ecclesiastical Ordinance of 1576 : "You swear to hold the doctrine of the holy prophets and apostles, as it is contained in the books of the Old and New Testaments, of which doctrine our Catechism is a summary". This oath remained in force for nearly a century, till 1806. "It was asserted in the discussion (in the Assembly) that no one should be forced to follow entirely Calvin's Catechism. It is further expected that the candidates for the ministry should be requested not to discuss in the pulpit any striking or useless matter which might tend to disturb the peace. At this time, the Confession of Faith of the 17th century was abolished to return to that of the 16th century, interpreting the latter with much freedom. The Lower Council ratified this decision, but ordered the Assembly to keep the most absolute silence upon this subject, especially in the presence of strangers." In 1788, the Assembly adopted a new Catechism, containing numerous points of divergence from the orthodox Catechism of Calvin, which it superseded with the sanction of the Lower Council. In 1806, the new formula of consecration threw out the Catechism; it ran thus— "You promise to teach divine truth as it is contained in the books of the Old and New Testaments, of which we have an abridgment in the Apostles' Creed". In 1810, after long deliberation, there was published a revision in the latitudinarian and utilitarian sense of the Larger Catechism. In the same year, the Apostles' Creed was thrown out of the pledge of the ministers, which now read thus : "You promise . . . to preach, in its purity, the gospel of our Lord Jesus Christ, to recognise as the only infallible rule of faith and conduct the word of God, as it is contained in the sacred books of the Old and New Testaments". Presently, however, in 1813, a religious revival led to dangerous discussions, and the ministers were bound "to abstain from all sectarian spirit, to avoid all that would create any schism and break the union of the Church"—an addition suppressed towards 1850; and in 1817, they were required to pledge themselves to abstain from discussing four points in particular—the manner of the union of the divine and human nature in the person of Jesus Christ; original sin; the manner in which grace operates, or saving grace; and predestination; and, if led to utter their thoughts on any one of these subjects, they were "to do so without too much positiveness, to avoid expressions foreign to the Holy Scriptures, and to use, as much as possible, the terms which they employ". In 1847, the organisation of the Protestant worship was set forth in a special law, and in 1849, the Consistory called in accordance with this, adopted an organic rule for the Church. According to Article 74, the functionaries of the Church may be subjected to discipline "in case of teaching, preaching, or publicly professing any doctrine that may bring scandal upon the Church". Various modifications followed. In 1874 (April 26), Article 123 was made to declare that "each pastor teaches and preaches freely on his own responsibility, and no restraint can be put upon this liberty either by the Confession of Faith or by the liturgic formulas". In the end of the same year, however (Oct. 3), the State Council promulgated a new organic law, "in virtue of which a pastor can either be suspended or dismissed by the Consistory or by the Council of State for dogmatic motives". In 1875, the pastor obtained the right to use in his religious teaching any catechetical manual he preferred, provided he informed the Consistory of his choice. The use of the *liturgical prayers*, published by the Consistory, became optional. The pastors were now required merely to declare before God that "they will teach and preach conscientiously, according to their lights and faith the Christian truth contained in our holy books". The *liturgical collection*, published by the Consistory in 1875, contains two series of formulas, expressed in a dogmatic sense on the one hand, and in a liberal sense on the other. The Apostles' Creed is optional.

Free Evangelical Church of Geneva.

The Free Evangelical Church of Geneva demands only a formal adherence to its Profession of Faith from the elders (including the ministers) and the deacons. "Some of these officers have even been permitted to hold certain reserves on such or such article."

Germanic Switzerland.

Pastor Bernard of Berne, having enumerated the symbolical writings of Germanic Switzerland, says: "For centuries the pastors were obliged to sign them, although it is true that the Second Confession of Helvetic Faith was alone recognised as the general rule imposed upon pastors. The signing of the Formula Consensus was exacted only temporarily (being discarded about 1720). It has been only from the beginning of this century that, under the influence of rationalism, pastors have been required to preach the Gospel merely according to the *principles* of the Helvetic Confession. To-day we find all confession of faith abolished in our Germanic Swiss Churches. Pastors preach what pleases them. Chosen by the parishes, they owe to them solely an avowal of their doctrines."

The Hungarian Reformed Church has a singular history, in respect of Creeds. The Report of the Council goes very minutely into the detail of eleven confessions held successively by that church. Of these, there survive two—the

Helvetic Confession and the Catechism of Heidelberg, by which ministers and office-bearers are still bound.

Next as to Germany. As the several states have their separate ecclesiastical usages, the same rule does not apply everywhere. For an extreme case of absence of toleration, we may refer to the Grand Duchy of Mecklenburg. Lutheranism is the established religion; and the Duchy is the stronghold of mediæval conservatism both in politics and in religion. The removal of Baumgarten from the University of Rostock is an example in point; and the decree is so characteristic and illustrative that it deserves to be given at length.

"We have to our sincere regret been given to understand that, in your writings published in and since the year 1854, you have advanced doctrines and principles that are in the most important points at variance with the doctrines and principles of the symbolic books of our Evangelical-Lutheran Church and of our rules of Church Discipline, to such an extent as to amount to an attempt to shake to the very foundation the basis whereon these doctrines and principles and our church rest. In order to reach more exact certainty on these things, we have assembled our Consistory to consider this matter, and from them we have received the annexed opinion, by which the above-mentioned view has been fully confirmed.

"Whereas, then, it is required by our Church Ordinances of 1552 and 1602 (1650) that the Christian doctrine shall be taught 'pure and unchanged, as it is contained in Holy Writ, the general symbols of the Christian Church, in Dr. Luther's Catechism and Confession, and in the Augsburg Confession of 1530, and that, if an academical teacher fall away from these, he shall be proceeded against; whereas, further, in Articles II. to IV. of the Reversals of 1621, the sovereigns gave the States the assurance that in the University of Rostock there should be neither appointed nor tolerated any other teachers but such as should be attached to the Augsburg Confession and the Lutheran religion; the establishment of the University of Rostock on the pure doctrine of the Christian symbols and of the Augsburg Confession has been repeated in § 4 of the Regulations upon the relations of the town of Rostock to the State University of 1827, and once again in § 1 of the Statutes of the University of 1837; no less do the statutes of the Theological Faculty of Rostock of 1564, and the later Regulation as to this Faculty of 1791, bind the members of the Faculty to expound the writings of the Prophets and the Apostles in the sense laid down in the general Christian symbols, in the Augsburg Confession, the Smalkald Articles, and the writings of Dr. Luther; your appointment of 31st August, 1850, referred you to the Statutes of the University and of the Theological Faculty, and also directed you to comport yourself in accordance with the rule and line of the revealed word of God, the unchanged Augsburg Confession, the *formula concordiæ*, and all the other symbolic books received in our (lands) country, as well as with the Mecklenburg Church Ordinances relating to these, without any innovation; you also on your induction on the 19th of Oct., 1850, bound yourself by oath to the duties contained in your appointment and to the Statutes of the University and of the Theological Faculty;

"We can the shorter time entrust you with the vocation of an academic teacher of the Evangelical-Lutheran Theology as you have united with your backslidings in theological doctrine at the same time political doctrines of the most delicate kind, deduced relatively from those; and we will, therefore—after hearing of our High Consistory, and after the foregoing resolution of our ministry according to § 10, Lit. H. of the Ordinance of 4th April, 1853, relating to the organisation of the Ministers—hereby remove you from the office, hitherto filled by you, of an ordinary Professor of Theology in our State University of Rostock."

In Prussia, the Clergy, and especially the University Professors of Theology, enjoy more liberty than in Mecklenburg; but they are not wholly secure from the attempts of the Church Courts to enforce discipline against heretical teaching. The following are recent cases.

1. The St. Jacobi Gemeinde (parish) in Berlin, belonging, as is the rule in Prussia, to the "Unirte Kirche"—a fusion of the Lutheran and the Reformed Churches—in 1877, chose, as its pastor, Lic. Horzbach. The Consistory of Brandenburg, within whose jurisdiction Berlin lies, refused to admit him on account of his heterodox views. By the ecclesiastical law, a pastor translated from one consistory to another, has to be approved of by the one he enters; which gives an opportunity of exercising a disciplinary power, not beyond what is possessed by the consistory where he has once been admitted, but more opportunely and conveniently brought into play. St. Jacobi parish, having apparently a taste for advanced views, next chose a Dr. Schramm; but he too was rejected on the same grounds. The third selection fell on Pastor Werner (Guben); this was confirmed by the Consistory, but was quashed by the "Oberkirchenrath," or supreme ecclesiastical authority of the country, located in Berlin. The parish was now considered to have forfeited its right of election; and a pastor was chosen for it by the Oberkirchenrath. Happily his views were not too strict for the congregation, and peace was restored. In all the three instances, the rejection took place on the complaint of a small orthodox minority in the parish.

2. Rev. Lühr, pastor at Eckenforda, in the Prussian Province of Schleswig-Holstein, was accused of heresy, and deprived by the Provincial Consistory of Kiel in December, 1881. Pastor Lühr appealed to the Berlin Oberkirchenrath, who reversed the sentence, and let him off with a reproof for the use of incautious language.

There have been two still more notorious heresy hunts: one, the case of Dr. Sydow in Berlin; the other, Pastor Kalthoff, who was ultimately deposed, and is now minister of an independent congregation in Berlin.

Both the central ecclesiastical authority and the provincial consistories, being nominated by the Government, reflect the religious tendencies of the Emperor and his Ministers for the time being. At present, these are probably behind the country at large in point of liberality.

Next to Switzerland, Holland is most distinguished for advanced views as to the remission of Tests, and the liberty of the clergy. A very complete account of the history and present position of the Dutch sects is given in a pamphlet, entitled "The Ecclesiastical Institutions of Holland, by Philip H. Wicksteed, M.A. (Williams & Norgate)".

It is pretty well known that in doctrinal views the majority in the Dutch Church is Calvinist; while a minority forms the "Modern School," a school partaking of the rationalism of our century in matters of faith. The battle of the Confessions began in 1842, and is not yet finished. In this year an attempt was made to revive the binding authority of the old confessions. The General Synod in that and the following years successfully resisted the movement. In 1854, a new formula of subscription applicable to candidates for the ministry was introduced, less stringent and more liberal than the old one. The orthodoxy party endeavoured to make it more stringent, the liberals proposed to make it still less so. In 1874, a majority of the General Synod passed the following declaration:

"The doctrine contained in the Netherland Confession, the Heidelberg Catechism, and the Canons of the Synod of Dort, forms the historical foundation of the Reformed Church of the Netherlands.

"Inasmuch as this doctrine is not confessed with sufficient unanimity by the community, there can, under the existing circumstances, be no possibility of 'maintaining the doctrine' in the ecclesiastical sense. The community, building on the principles of the Church, as manifested in her origin and development, continues to confess her Christian faith, and thereby to form the expression which may in course of time once more become the adequate and unanimous Confession of the Church.

"Meantime, care for the interests of the Christian Church in general and the Reformed in particular, quickening of Christian religion and morality, increase of religious knowledge, preservation of order and unity, and furtherance of love for King and Fatherland—are ever the main object of all to whom any ecclesiastical office is entrusted, and no one can be rejected as a member or a teacher who, complying with all other requirements, declares himself to be convinced in his own conscience that in compliance with the above-named principles, he may belong to the Reformed Church of the Netherlands."

---

* Mr. Wicksteed makes the following curious remark:—"I am often asked whether the 'Moderns' are Unitarians. The question is rather startling. It is as if one were asked whether the majority of English astronomers had ceased to uphold the Ptolemaic system yet. The best answer I can give is a reference to the chapter on 'God' in a popular work by Dr. Matthes which has run through four editions. In this chapter there is not a word about the Trinity, but at the close occurs this footnote: 'On the antiquated doctrine of the *Trinity*, see the fourteenth note at the end of the book,'—where, accordingly, the doctrine is expounded and its confusions pointed out rather with the calm interest of the antiquarian than the eagerness of the controversialist."

This declaration, however, did not pass the Provincial Church Courts, which possess the right of veto; and the law therefore remained as it was. But, in 1881, a new proposal for altering the formula of subscription passed the General Synod. Next year, it was definitely approved, and is now the law of the church. According to it, licentiates to the Ministry, on being admitted by the Provincial Church Courts, are made to promise that they will labour in the Ministry according to their vocation with zeal and faithfulness; that they will further with all their power the interests of the kingdom of God, and, so far as consistent therewith, the interests of the Dutch Reformed Church, and give obedience to the regulations of that Church.

There is, however, both in orthodox and in semi-orthodox circles, a wide-spread dissatisfaction with this amount of latitude, and fears are entertained for its continuance.